Table of Contents

W9-CCD-593

Introduction

SOLDIERS, HUNTERS, AND fishermen go through roughly the same evolution. Soldiers who have never seen combat believe in their hearts that they, and they alone, will be spared. But the longer they spend in combat, the more they change their minds about the odds. Hunters and fishermen go through roughly the same process. The greenhorns see nature as benevolent. They are the ones who head into the mountains in the sunshine, in their shirtsleeves, and when the snow comes and the temperature drops 50 degrees in a matter of hours, their error is brought home to them. They are the ones who think a trout stream the very picture of serenity . . . until a stone turns underfoot, and their waders and then their lungs fill with water, and it occurs to them in their last instant that nature is not benevolent but indifferent.

This is what old hunters and fishermen know: That Ma Nature and her creatures are not malicious or hostile, but simply uncaring of whether you live or die. Indeed, that is how they got to be old hunters and fishermen. I think of a hard-case Montana guide I used to hunt with. We built a fire one excruciatingly cold day, and were warming ourselves by it, looking out on a landscape where a man without a fire would not last a day. "I love this country," he muttered, "but it scares the hell out of me."

The basis of this book is the fact that the outdoors can be pretty damned dangerous. In token of this statement, here are some of the things I know about:

I knew an African professional hunter who was killed by an elephant.

I know two African professional hunters who were mauled by leopards.

I know of the son and son-in-law of a friend who were hunting bear along Alaska's coast. Their boat vanished. No trace of it—or them—was ever found.

I knew a hunter and his guide whose plane crashed into a mountaintop in the fog. Wolves ate their remains.

I know of a Midwestern grouse hunter who went into the woods with an old dog and a young dog. Only the young dog came out of the woods.

I know a hunter who was swept off an Alaska mountain by a boulder. It mangled his foot beyond use. He had a cell phone, and there was a Fed Ex plane overhead that picked up his call for help and saved his life.

I know of an African professional hunter who was driving his Land Rover through a patch of woodland. A piece of an iron-hard mopane tree punched through the floor of the vehicle and punctured his femoral artery. He bled to death where he sat.

I knew a bowhunter whose horse bucked him into the air as he was riding back from an elk hunt. An arrow broke loose from his bow quiver and stabbed him in the groin as he hit the ground. He bled to death on the trail.

I know of a Montana hunter who fell out of his saddle. His foot hooked in a stirrup, and his horse walked the 12 miles back to the ranch, dragging him slowly to death.

And that's just the stuff I know about.

Whether we like to admit it or not, this element of danger is a good part of the attraction of the outdoors. Contemplating one's end courtesy of cancer, or heart attack, or automobile accident is simply depressing. But mixing it up with an elephant or a brown bear or a Cape buffalo or a shark is so exotic that death recedes into the background and the excitement remains.

This kind of gut-freezing stuff is also a lot of fun to read about because you're not the guy who had to go through it. I've spoken with people who have had leopards shot off them, and they tell me that being chewed on is not even remotely enjoyable. I've read about hunting buffalo, and I've tracked a wounded buffalo, and I can promise you that I liked reading about it more. (We found the critter dead, to my unspeakable relief.) So, enjoy, and note one thing: All the people who contributed to this book came out of their scrapes alive. A lot of men don't. You will never read their stories.

David E. Petzal
Executive Editor, FIELD & STREAM

THE WORLD OF

Incredible Outdoor Adventures

SINCE 1895

FIELD & STREAM

THE SOUL OF THE AMERICAN OUTDOORS

CREATIVE PUBLISHING international

MINNETONKA, MINNESOTA

414
$5−

Field & Stream
The World of Incredible Outdoor Adventures

Introduction by David E. Petzal, Executive Editor, Field & Stream

President/CEO: David D. Murphy
Vice President/Editorial: Patricia K. Jacobsen
Vice President/Retail Sales & Marketing: Richard M. Miller

Executive Editor, Outdoor Group: Don Oster
Project Leader and Article Editor: David R. Maas
Managing Editor: Denise Bornhausen
Associate Creative Director: Brad Springer
Photo Researcher: Angie Spann
Copy Editor: Janice Cauley
Mac Production: Joe Fahey
Photographers: Rex Irmen, Jamey Mauk
Publishing Production Manager: Stasia Dorn

Special thanks to: Jason E. Klein, President, Field & Stream; Duncan Barnes,
Slaton White and the staff of Field & Stream magazine

Contributing Photographers: *Stephen J. Krasemann*, Polebridge, MT © Stephen J.
Krasemann: p. 151; *Tom & Pat Leeson*, Vancouver, WA © Tom & Pat Leeson: pp. 146-
147; *John G. Shedd Aquarium*, Chicago, IL © John G. Shedd Aquarium: p. 79 all;
Tom Stack & Associates, Key Largo, FL © *David M. Dennis*/Tom Stack & Associates:
p. 152, © *Thomas Kitchin*/Tom Stack & Associates: p. 143, © *Larry Tackett*/Tom Stack
& Associates: p. 148; *Garrett VeneKlasen/InterAngler*, Angel Fire, NM © Garrett
VeneKlasen: pp. 72 all, 73, 78.

Printed on American paper by: World Color

10 9 8 7 6 5 4 3 2

Library of Congress Cataloging–in–Publication Data

The world of incredible outdoor adventures.
     p. cm. – – (Field & stream)
    ISBN 0–86573–092–X (hc.) . – – ISBN 0–86573–093–8 (softcover)
    1. Hunting. 2. Fishing. 3. Adventure and adventures.
I. Creative Publishing International. II. Series.
SK35.W8925 1999
799– –dc21   98–54429

There is fishing, and then there is fishing. Snoozing on a
bank with a cane pole is as tranquil an activity as you can find, but
if you venture out onto big water, that is something else entirely.
The sea—or any sizable lake—can go from millpond to maelstrom
in minutes, and there you are at the mercy of forces whose fury most
of us cannot even begin to comprehend.

Or you can decide to take on that most ancient and successful
of predators, the shark. You are out of your element, but it is right at
home, and so perfectly adapted that it has not changed since the
dinosaurs breathed. Most sharks are harmless, but there are some
that are not, and these are the most popular with anglers. They are
called "requiem" sharks. The dictionary defines requiem as
"…a Mass for the souls of the dead." It's not a coincidence.

SINCE 1895

FIELD & STREAM

THE SOUL OF THE AMERICAN OUTDOORS

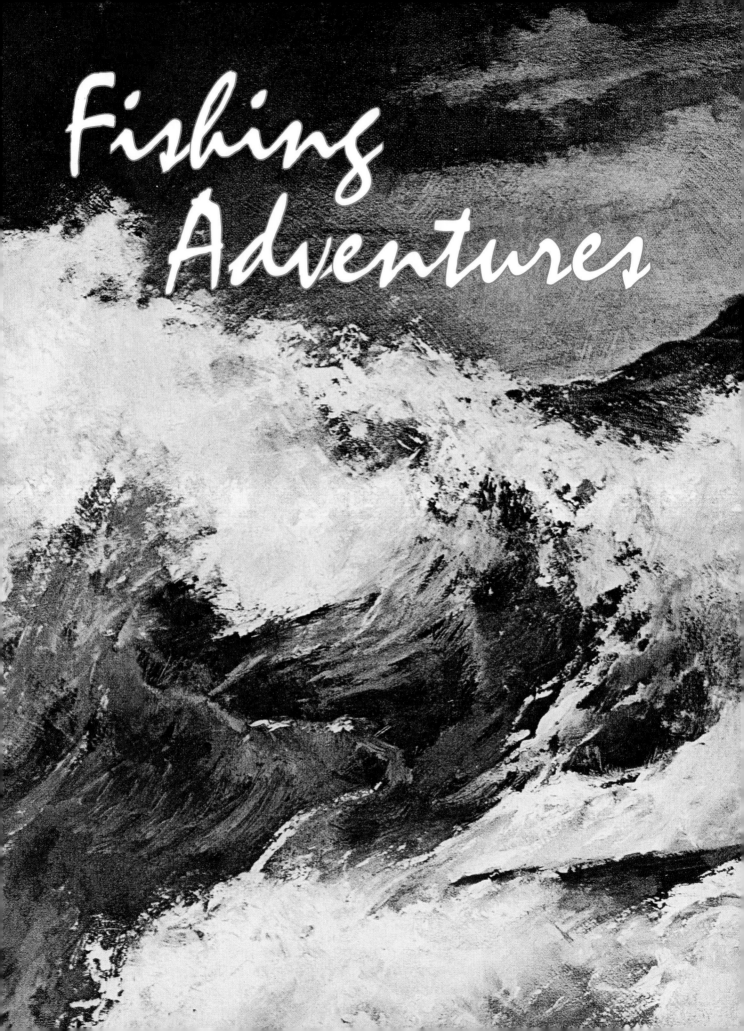

IT WAS TO BE THE MATE'S LAST DAY ON EARTH, BUT HE HAD NO WAY OF KNOWING HIS DEATH WOULD RESULT IN AN ACTION-PACKED FISHING TRIP.

By Thomas William Helm III

WAKE *of the* KILLER

AS A GENERAL RULE, the chance of tracking down and killing one particular shark is almost out of the question. Most of them are nomadic sea rovers, and what proves to be an ideal feeding ground at dawn may by noon be populated by nothing more than a scattered school of chopas. Because of the one infallible rule that a shark is always hungry, he is almost sure to stay on the move in his never-ending search for food and more food.

The habits and actions of sharks, however, were of little concern to the big Jamaican negro as he nosed his battered little sailing craft through the break in the treacherous coral reef that shut off a tiny bay on the low jungle coast of Honduras. In the sheltered waters behind that reef a coastwise lugger lay on the bottom, and her cargo, which consisted of boxes of trade goods, was well worth the trouble to salvage.

The ship had gone down in a gale a few months earlier after the skipper inadvisedly attempted to cross the dangerous reef. The mainmast had been snapped by the high wind, and the small crew was poorly trained. The crossing would have been risky even in ideal weather. The attempt was made, however, and just as the skipper was within yards of reaching safe water a swell went down and settled the fast-moving ship on a jagged finger of razor-sharp coral.

It was only a matter of minutes before the gutted ship keeled over and went down on the inshore side of the reef. The skipper and two deck-hands were drowned. But the big Jamaican who had been the mate and two other crew members somehow made their way to the beach. Now they were returning to take back from the sea that which was rightfully theirs.

Finding the location of the ship was no task for a seaman such as the mate, for his life had been spent almost wholly on the decks of ships and his mind and eyes were trained to carefully record details. Now back in the same waters he stood upright and pointed to a spot where they would drop the anchor. Down it went for five fathoms through the clear green water. It landed in a cloud of roiled sand. The mate was satisfied. Allowing for the swing of the tide, they would still be clear of the reef, yet near enough to work on the cargo of the sunken ship beneath them.

Unlike big-time salvage operations, there were few preliminaries to go through before the job actually began. No pumps to be started and no air hose to be inspected. In fact, no diving gear at all. Simply take off the straw hat and jump overboard, swim down to the wreck and start prying off the hatch covers. Each of the three men could stay beneath the water for nearly three minutes of working time, and perhaps longer if absolutely necessary. A lot can be accomplished by a skilled skin-diver in two or three minutes under water.

Two at a time they went down and fastened a line on a hatch cover. Back on the surface, they joined forces and yanked the cover off. After a few moments of rest, they went back for the next chore. An hour or so of this, and suddenly one of the men who was on deck at the time sighted a tall gray fin knifing its insidious way along over the smooth surface of the bay—

straight as an arrow toward the spot where the salvage operations were being carried on.

Grabbing a steering sweep, the man pounded savagely on the water and shouted cries of warning to his companions. The shouts were heard by the sea birds resting on exposed portions of the reef, but the pounding on the water was transmitted down through the depths to the men and they quickly swam to the surface.

Shading their eyes against the glare of late morning sun, the three divers watched the approach of the huge shark. It came in close to their ship and circled slowly, as if on an inspection tour. For a while it lolled contentedly near the surface; then, with almost imperceptible motion, the huge creature nosed over and slid down toward the torn hulk of the dead ship on the bottom.

Like a giant watch-dog it settled down near the sand and waited. There was a water-box on deck, and through the glass bottom the men took turns studying the thing that had interrupted their work. Later, when the novelty had worn off, they chunked at it with scraps of iron and broken shells on deck. But there was no response from the great shark.

They noticed a long, ragged scar just forward of the dorsal fin that ran down the left side, and wondered what had caused it. Maybe the shark had been harpooned years before and had pulled free. Again, it may have been hit by the blubber lance from a whaling vessel. Still again, the long white scar might have been inflicted by some fight with another creature of the sea. Whatever caused the scar was of little importance at the moment.

"I shall drive him away," the mate declared suddenly. "He is a devil which has been sent to guard the stores of the sunken ship!"

As the tall black man spoke he drew the long double-edged knife from the sheath on the belt around his waist and dived over into the shimmering green water. Slowly at first, then with a sudden burst of speed the mate lanced down toward the resting shark. The two men on deck could see the sunlight glint off the knife blade clenched between their comrade's lips.

As the man descended deeper the shark turned lazily around and planed upward for a dozen yards. His tall tail swept to and fro a couple of times. The men on deck, with their faces crowded into the water-box, could see the two underseas creatures hesitate for a moment and face one another.

They saw the man reach up with his right hand and take the knife from his mouth. A lopsided silver bubble came wabbling to the surface. Somewhere off toward the palm-fringed shore a pair of frigate birds squawked at each other in raucus voices. The man released his grip on the piece of rigging he had been clinging to and waved his arms at the shark. The huge fish backed off a foot or two and watched the strange black invader of his watery domain.

In one sudden rush the man darted under the shark. The men on the surface saw their comrade swivel expertly so that he passed beneath the shark. They saw the big fish jerk convulsively and then drive ahead. A tiny trail of gray smoke spurted from a hole somewhere along his white belly. The man turned and made another pass at the creature. But something suddenly went wrong! The shark swerved and the blade of the knife missed its mark completely.

Instead of darting away from the thing that had injured him, the shark only circled around above the man. Again the mate grabbed onto a jut of rigging from the sunken ship and emitted two more air bubbles from his straining lungs while he watched the bleeding shark above him. Perhaps he was wondering if he had not played the part of a fool to think he could kill the big shark with a weapon so small as a mere knife. He knew he must make his way to the surface, for even a skilled West Indian skin-diver can remain under for only so long. And he was still a very long way from the surface.

Slowly he stroked upward, keeping a wary

eye on the shark. The man was half-way to the surface, and the shark acted as if he were going to let him pass. But it was only an act! With a sudden burst of speed the shark swept toward the man, hitting him with his nose and knocking him around at a crazy angle down there in the water. A great volume of air wabbled to the surface as the man fought to regain control of himself.

In horrified awe at the spectacle they were watching, the two men in the boat clutched the sides of their water-box and saw their leader spiral downward again in an effort to escape the jaws of the enraged shark. A school of frightened shiners skittered into the arena, hard pressed by a hungry jack. The sight of the disturbance shot them off at a sharp oblique, and the jack gave up the chase and went the other way as fast as his forked tail would drive him. Time had suddenly run out now, and the big black man dropped his knife and clawed blindly at the water around him.

Later, when the two men were telling about it, they shuddered as they related how the giant shark swept in and slapped his powerful jaws shut around the man's body. An eruption of blood turned the water gray, and in a matter of seconds the great shark had swallowed the negro. The horrified men hauled up the anchor and headed back up the coast. They told how, after returning to Porto Cortez, they had both become very drunk and stayed in that condition for a very long time, or at least until their limited supply of money ran out and no more rum could be purchased on credit.

⟢⟤⟣

MY FRIEND ED BOOTH and I listened to the story about the huge killer shark and asked questions about the bay behind the reef and about the type of trade goods that had been carried on the lugger. Both of us discounted the chance that the huge shark would still be in the bay, or that we could hope to catch him even if he might still be there. Still the two men assured us that the cargo on the lugger would be well worth salvaging, and if the shark just happened to be there we might have a chance of catching him. Added to this, they both agreed to sign on our small schooner

as deck hands for a certain percentage of the material recovered.

Our business was trading in the Caribbean, but trading has its slack season, as do most other businesses, and we were currently in the midst of a dead slump. There seemed to be nothing better to do at the time; so we decided to sign the two men on, and set sail on this will-o'-the-wisp adventure in a tiny bay that neither of us had previously bothered to investigate.

A rain squall was just roaring in from the southwest when we sighted the opening to the bay. With the story of the wrecked lugger still fresh in our minds, we stood well off from the reef while the elements did their savage best to strip the sea from the bottom. Through the glasses I studied the violent upheaval taking place as one monstrous comber after another bore down and exploded on the ragged surface of the reef. It seemed inconceivable that anyone could have been so hard driven as to attempt passage through that boiling cauldron. Darkness settled prematurely over the area, and for better than two hours we watched the progress of the storm through lightning-laced clouds. During the early part of the evening the storm passed and the weather steadied down to ideal conditions.

When we finished breakfast, dawn was little more than a thin gray ribbon looping along the eastern horizon. It had been our decision that the best thing to do would be to leave the ship anchored out from the reef and make at least the first trip through the reef in the two small skiffs we carried on deck. In this way we could look the situation over, study the channel, and stand a better chance of getting through later with the ship. Besides, I was anxious to make a crack at fishing for the killer shark if by chance he still happened to be in the bay.

Since we planned to spend almost the entire day, we loaded the boats well. For tackle I took along a 12/0 reel loaded with some new 54-thread line I had just received from the States. My rod was an old standby with a 23-ounce tip. Not much for looks, but I had caught fish with it from one side of the Caribbean to the other, and I knew it could be depended on if I should latch onto a sizeable shark.

"I'll stop him for you," Ed grinned, patting the stock of his .30-06 rifle as he eased it down in the skiff beside him.

By the time the first slanting rays of pale morning sunlight were in the sky we were picking our way across the reef. The swells were slow and easy. Through the glassy surface I looked down on the little mountain range of coral which so effectively blocked the entrance to the bay. Varicolored fish of all sizes and descriptions literally swarmed beneath our skiffs. Now and then I spotted sharks, but for the most part they were small inoffensive types that wobbled along beside us for a moment or so to see what we looked like, then swerved off to get on with the business of eating.

Once, I glanced over to Ed's boat and saw him slipping a shell into his rifle. For a moment he hesitated, the gun almost to his shoulder, then relaxed and extracted the shell.

"What's after you over there?" I called.

"He's gone now," Ed laughed. "But I was just about to put a hole through a big hammerhead."

Suddenly we were over the reef, and from water that a moment before had been only a few feet deep we were now riding over several fathoms of sparkling clear water. José, the squat brown man in the boat with me, feathered his oars and called across to his companion in the boat with Ed. For a moment or so they debated the exact direction of the sunken ship. They argued with each other about landfalls and reckoning points until they finally managed to recall where they had dropped anchor a short while before. Slowly the two men brought their memory into focus and pointed to some invisible spot which they both finally agreed upon.

The lugger was just about where the two men had said it was. When we reached the spot, they started again to tell us in excited voices just how and where their comrade had been killed by the great killer shark. The ship was down almost in the shadow of the huge reef, and its graying hulk lay still and foreboding, etched there against the white sand of the bottom. Carefully I scanned the area for sight of the big shark, or for any shark. But there were none to be seen.

Tying a chunk of lead to a split mullet, I

tossed it over the side and watched it spiral down. Almost before it touched the bottom, half a dozen snappers left their hiding places in the torn hull of the ship and scrambled out to take possession of the tidbit. Again and again we repeated the performance. Fish seemed to materialize from everywhere to join in the free feast.

"We may not find any sharks," Ed mused. "But one thing is certain: we'll be able to get all the eating fish we want as long as we stay here."

While my friend was speaking I noticed a sudden change in the action of the feeding fish. For a second or two they all seemed to hesitate. Then they began scattering out in different directions. I guess all four of us saw the shark at the same time. It was a huge man-eater shark! He was moving unhurriedly along the bottom, looking for all the world like some sinister submarine.

Hastily I skewered a mullet with the heavy shark hook on my line and lowered it down in the path of the underseas giant. There was a dry feeling in the back of my throat and the palms of my hands were wet with perspiration as I stripped the line off the big reel. When the bait was several feet from the bottom, I stopped it and waited. None of us spoke as the shark approached. But there was a tenseness to the atmosphere such as that which occurs immediately after the gong sounds for the first round of a prize fight.

With nonchalant carelessness the big fish ambled up to the mullet, almost touched it with the end of his pointed nose, then turned and slid beneath an overhanging part of the lugger's hull.

"Not interested!" Ed said in an explosive sigh.

Once or twice during the next hour we caught sight of his gray bulk beneath his shelter. Just as we were about to leave the spot for our trip to shore the big devil suddenly left his hiding place and surged toward the surface. The four of us swung around in an effort to see where he was going. As we turned we caught sight of two small porpoises that had crossed the reef and were now heading out toward the middle of the bay.

The two seagoing mammals must have

spotted the killer at the same instant. Together they turned on a burst of speed. But one of them had already been singled out. The surface boiled white for a few seconds. I caught sight of the big gray tail as the shark somersaulted over in a surface dive. A moment later, several hundred yards farther out, the shark again came to the top, but this time he was swimming slowly, with his tall gray dorsal fin slicing the surface.

Again we waited, and after a while the shark returned to the sunken ship and settled down to rest beneath the hull. The morning was growing late, and there obviously was no need for us to remain over the sunken ship any longer with the intentions of catching that shark with the simple bait we had aboard. He was after bigger game, and we would have to use different tactics if we wanted to entertain any hopes of sinking a hook into his ugly jaws. One thing was certain: none of us had the slightest desire to begin diving operations until that big killer was out of the way.

For the next two days we tried every trick we knew to make him take the hook. In the meantime we managed to maneuver the schooner through a break in the reef, and in the evenings we sat on deck and watched for signs of the great killer. Now and then, during that time, we saw him take some big fish that swam too near. On the third day, late in the afternoon, he came up beside the schooner and spent several minutes circling around. We shot at him several times, but always he stayed just below the effective range of the bullets.

Ed and José went ashore early on the fourth morning, and when they returned Ed tossed the carcass of a small wild pig on deck. "Here's something for your shark. See if he likes pork," he said.

To catch that shark had by now become an obsession with all four of us. The idea of using the small pig for bait seemed to hold new prospects, and once again José and I loaded one of the skiffs with fishing gear and rowed the short distance over to the sunken ship. There was a light wind blowing, and the tiny waves kicked up over the reef made it necessary for us to use a water-box to see below the surface.

There was little trouble in locating the shark. In the time we had been there we had learned just about what his habits were. And there was no doubt in our minds that this was the same shark which had killed the mate sometime before. On numerous occasions we had seen the long scar on his back. There was little question that he would hesitate to attack any of us had we attempted to swim around his hangout.

Perhaps some months before, shortly after the ship had wrecked, he came into the bay and found the sunken ship. It afforded him a safe place to rest unnoticed, yet he was always ready to spot anything in the way of food as his victims crossed the top of the reef.

In order to make the bait more bloody, and what I hoped to be more appetizing, I hacked off a section of the pig. One foreleg and part of the side was tied to the heavy braided cable leader and partway down the shank of the big hook. While José held the boat in position I let the ragged chunk of meat down toward the spot where I thought I could distinguish the gray body of the shark. This time I let it touch the bottom. Immediately a few scavenger fish set about the task of picking at it. Then the shark slid out from under his shelter and moved over toward the bait.

I am not sure just what I expected when the killer did decide to accept my offering. Maybe I fancied it would happen in a sudden rush, or perhaps I expected him to attempt to yank the rod and reel out of my grasp. But I do know that the strike, if it could be called a strike, was nothing like I had expected. The shark simply eased up to the hunk of fresh pork and drew it into his mouth. As he turned I could tell by the way the line was pulling off that he was swallowing the meat, hook and all.

Flipping off the free-spool lever, I forced myself to wait until I was sure the hook would snag somewhere deep down inside his gullet. Then I lifted my head up from the water-box and gave one mighty heft on the rod. The line suddenly grew taut and I yelled at the top of my voice. "I've got him!"

There was an answer from the schooner, and out of the corner of my eye I could see Ed and Henry scrambling about as they loaded equipment in the second skiff. José didn't utter a word, but he was skillfully backing the skiff away from the sunken wreck below us. Still the shark was showing no signs of alarm and making no attempt to battle the hook that stuck in his throat. Just a slow pull that carried the line off my reel at a steady pace. When about a third of the backing had been stripped off the reel, I gave him slack for a few yards, then horsed back on the rod for the second time.

Then it happened! The second jerk must have convinced the giant fish that something was decidedly wrong with the tidbit of pork he had swallowed. There was a sudden jolt so powerful that it all but wrenched the rod from my hands. The next instant he was driving out toward the middle of the bay. I continued to tighten down on the star drag until the force was lifting me up from my seat.

Ed was shoving his boat away from the side of the schooner now, and I yelled for him to stay clear of my path. José was fighting the oars in an effort to stem the rush of the shark, which was actually pulling us along behind him. Then, as quickly as it had begun, the tension relaxed and I sat there pumping in yard after yard of slack line.

"He's turning around!" José sputtered, still pulling on the oars in fast, short strokes. "Maybe he's going back to the ship."

But José was wrong. The shark was driving toward the surface, and in a second he churned into view out in front of us. The sharp, ugly head jutted out of the water like a huge log suddenly released from the bottom. Then he was off again in a wild rush.

Racing along in the wake of the killer, I struggled to maintain a sitting position. Line was stripping off my reel so fast that I fancied I could smell burning oil as the drag burned against the revolving spool. Sweat was now streaming down my face. There was no fast whipping and jerking of the rod, but what was of more concern to me at the moment was the terrific strain I was exerting on the rod against the hard-pulling fish. There was nothing to do but give up more line. I watched it go out until the spool was more than half empty.

Something had to be done, and I yelled for José to row faster. At the same time I sat down on the drag and fought back with the rod. I realized that urging the man in the boat with me to row faster was a waste of time, since the shark already was pulling us faster than the boat could have possibly been propelled with oars.

"Take your oars out and stick one of them over the stern like a sweep!" I called over my shoulder. "See if you can turn the boat enough to slow him down!"

José quickly followed my instructions, and the trick worked. He held the sweep over to one side until boiling foam was lacing over the gunwale near the bow; then he'd swing the sweep around the other way, and we would go swishing off in the other direction at a rapid clip until the strain became too great, then back the other way.

Seeming to grow tired of this free transportation, the shark suddenly came to a standstill. We watched him rise to the surface and loll motionless a couple of hundred yards out from us. It was the first breathing spell I had gotten since the battle began, and I relaxed as much as possible, flexing first one arm and then the other.

Looking back in the direction of the schooner, I could see Ed and Henry both pulling hard at the oars in an effort to get closer to us. The sun was high in the sky by now, and the heat from it was beating down on us unmercifully. I looked at José and tried to manage a smile, which he returned with a sick grin. Both of us knew we had bitten off a bigger hunk than we had expected to chew.

"Now he is starting again," José said, pointing over toward the tall gray fin.

I looked and, sure enough, there was again motion to it. But the shark was heading straight toward the boat! There was nothing to do but keep pumping in the line as fast as I could turn the reel crank. If he ever piled up a few yards of slack in that line and then tangled it around himself the show was sure to be over. His sandpaper hide would cut the line as quickly as the blade of a sharp knife.

Suddenly the shark put on an extra burst of speed. His head was surging along near the surface, and through the churn I could see his open tooth-filled mouth. I shouted a quick warning to José, and a second later the giant struck the side of the skiff. The blow was not a solid one, but even then the force all but shook us out. I heard one of the planks crack, and I tried to imagine how much damage might have been done to the boat.

Ed was closing in now, and I could see him crouching in the bow of his skiff. Again the tug of war began, and this time we were headed back toward the reef. Ed yelled instructions to Henry and they swung around in a direction that would meet the path the shark was now taking. I saw my friend rise up to a full standing position and draw a harpoon back.

"Don't, Ed!" I yelled.

But the harpoon hurtled down. The bronze point of the harpoon found its mark, and a geyser of water erupted as the shark rolled over in an effort to find the thing that had stung him. The big fish struck the boat and Ed toppled over. I saw him claw at the gunwale, and in almost as little time as it took him to fall over he was scrambling back into the now questionable safety of the skiff.

Ed had not stopped to consider the forthcoming danger of the two boats being towed by the same source of power when he threw the harpoon. The shark was off on another run now with harpoon line streaming out of the bow of Ed's boat. I yelled to Henry and José to hold their steering oars over the stern in opposite directions to prevent the two boats from coming together.

"I'm going to shoot him if he comes to the surface again!" Ed shouted across to me. I nodded my head vigorously and secretly hoped the big killer would speed up his next surface trip. We were getting dangerously near the reef, and with the tide out as far as it now was I didn't relish the idea of trying to go over it. The obvious results were all too evident. The shark would pick his way through while we ripped into the first spine of coral that jutted too near the surface.

Just before he reached the obstruction, however, the shark seemed to change his mind, and once again he bobbed to the surface. Ed was waiting for him, and even before his boat

lost headway my friend stood up and fired. The first bullet may have come close, but it was certainly not a hit. Again the .30-06 cracked, and this one did a job. The great killer literally bounced into the air. Again Ed hit him. After this the shark went down, but he was far from dead. Twice we worked him back to the surface and near enough for Ed to send a third bullet into his hide. On and on the struggle continued. Then the shark began to show definite signs of weakening.

When we were able to draw him up alongside the boats, Ed put the finishing touches on the killer by sending five more bullets into him. He had been hooked in the throat for almost three hours, a harpoon had been driven into his back, and a total of eight .30-06 bullets pumped in him. Still there was enough life left in that creature to make him dangerous even after we had gotten him back to the schooner and attached a hoist line around his tail.

We were a tired bunch after the fight with that great killer shark was done, and we spent the rest of the day lounging around the deck. When we actually got around to putting the tape on him, he measured nearly fifteen feet. For a while I was a little disappointed in his actual measurement. Because he had looked as big as a whale while I was fighting him, I was sure he would go well over twenty feet. But that's the way it is with fish. I guess every fisherman is inclined to expand the length of his catch until he's brought face to face with the tape.

The important thing was that we had caught a shark we were certain had killed a man. The scar, obviously the result of an old and very severe wound, unmistakably branded him as the killer.

On the following morning we broke out the diving gear and began the salvage work. Suffice to say the rewards were at least enough to pay the expenses of the trip. I'm going back down there and try my luck around that old barnacle-crusted hulk again some day. Chances are another killer will have taken up residence there and be hungry for a pork shoulder.

—February, 1951

HERE IS THE FIRST-HAND ACCOUNT OF FOUR
WALLEYE FISHERMEN WHO RODE OUT A HURRICANE
THAT SWEPT THE LAKE OF THE WOODS.

By Paul I. Wellman

THE DAY THE LAKE WENT MAD

JOE McKEEVER, shock-haired and sardonic, looked us over as we started from camp. "I wrote you that the ice broke up late. But you hardheads would come anyway. Serves you right. You won't get anything."

It was the morning of June 7, 1954—admittedly early for Ontario's lake country—and we were going out for walleyes in the teeth of McKeever's ridicule. But we were used to his ridicule, and returned it in kind. "As soon as we show your guides where the fishing places are we'll get 'em," said Doc.

"We ought to charge McKeever a fee for educating his guides every summer," jeered Moore.

"Yeh," agreed Gyp. "We always have to feed his camp. He ought to be paying us, instead of the other way around."

McKeever gave us his customary glance of derision. "If I let you four go out alone beyond that portage, we'd never find you again," he said witheringly, "and that's such a good idea I've just got a notion to do it."

Now, this was a gratuitous slur, since we are all old hands at the Lake of the Woods and its smaller sister, Shoal Lake. But we took no offense, any more than he took offense at our gibes. Though a stranger might have imagined us bitter enemies if he had overheard our bickering, actually the five of us are close friends.

McKeever, whose camp is situated at Portage Bay, on the narrow peninsula between Lake of the Woods and Shoal Lake, knows everything about fish and game and people, and is the kind of human porcupine that invents a special new insult for each of his favorite guests every morning. In fact, that is the one way you have of knowing how you progress in his esteem. As long as he speaks to you with studied politeness you are just one of the transients at camp. But if some morning he greets you with a barbed blackguardism, you know that you're in—the camp boss has admitted you to his acknowledgedly restricted circle of intimates.

"What's the radio weather forecast?" I asked.

It is not in McKeever to give an answer directly or without a few barbs. "Blizzards, tornadoes, hurricanes," he jeered. "What difference does it make to you? You're not going to catch any fish."

"We'll make you eat those words—and the fish we catch," retorted Moore.

But Aileen, Joe's wife, a slim, pretty and sunny Irish lass, was on the path. "Winnipeg says 15-mile winds and scattered showers," she called, smiling.

We thanked her and started across the short portage over the peninsula to Shoal Lake, where our two boats and motors awaited. It was a good forecast. Nobody minds a healthy chop on the water or a little rain. The fish bite better rather than worse for it. Yet none of us knew, least of all McKeever, that he was much closer to the truth than either Aileen or the Winnipeg radio weather man.

⋆—⊨◆⊨—⋆

LEADING THE WAY across the portage—and fighting mosquitoes furiously, as usual—went Moore. His full name is Clayton C. Moore, and he is a humorous, slow-talking Kentuckian who owns the Golden Maxim thoroughbred racing stables at Louisville, has one of the honored boxes at Churchill Downs, and makes fishing his life avocation. He was followed by his boat partner, Gyp Blair, also of Louisville, a genial, smiling man who runs a sporting goods business, is celebrated for being able to snore in four parts at once—bass, tenor, alto and coloratura soprano—and has never had an enemy in the world.

My boat partner was Dr. J. Robert Tolle, a wiry, sunburned cowman with a trim mustache and bowlegs, who had calmly chucked a lucrative medical practice to enjoy life running a cattle ranch in the Siskiyou Mountains of Oregon, with hunting and fishing on the side. As for myself, I am slightly more than rotund, on the wrong side of fifty, and make a living by writing at my home in Los Angeles. The four of us travel more than 13,000 man-miles each year just to spend two weeks together in the magical Canadian lake country. And we fish, by preference, for walleyes.

Now, we are aware that some fishermen look with contempt upon the walleye as a sporting fish, although why we don't know. The walleye is a noble fish, a soul-satisfying fish when he comes into the boat, and, if he has size, with enough fight to satisfy any honest angler, and unsurpassed in the pan.

That morning we had decided to fish the

extreme northwest part of Shoal Lake, a dozen miles from camp, since in that area streams enter from which the walleyes might be returning after spawning. As we raced across the water Doc, who was in the prow of our boat, leaned back to me. "Feel the warm and cold air?" he asked.

I nodded. It was as if we passed through alternate bands of heated and chilled atmosphere, something I had not before experienced. Had we known it, that was an augury of the awesome thing to come.

Beyond Cash Island, with its rocky promontories and pine-clad slopes, we began to troll. I should say here that our remarks to McKeever about "educating" his guides were persiflage. We had two of the best. Our guide, who ran the boat while Doc and I trolled, was Ken Penasse, and performing a similar service for Moore and Blair was Jimmie Mandamin—full-blooded Ojibwa Indians both, expert boatmen and woodsmen who knew the lake intimately.

Penasse throttled down the new 10-horse motor, which my wife had given me for a Christmas present, to a sweet, purring steadiness through the water—the slow lure is best for walleyes, the fast one for northerns and muskellunge. Our lines went out. Suddenly Doc let out a yell—a cowboy whoop, shrill and joyful, which meant fish. Net in hand, Penasse stood up in the boat, looking down into the clear water as Doc fought his fish. "Walleye!" he announced.

A few dashes by the well-hooked fish, the net dipped, and up came the beautiful, gleaming thing and into the boat. Doc stood up and yowled his sheer delight for Moore and Gyp to hear. We saw their lines come in and their boat turn toward the reef we were fishing, for walleyes run in schools and the first strike might mean more.

I will not describe the fishing that followed. It was gorgeous. We caught beautiful fish after beautiful fish. Each time we chortled at how we would confound McKeever when we displayed our catch that night. About ten o'clock there was big excitement in the other boat, and a huge fish, hooked by Moore, was netted. A little later Gyp got its mate. Then, just before noon, after a furious battle, Doc landed a mighty fish.

We landed on an island for lunch and looked over the catch. Already we had taken almost our limits, many in the 6- and 7-pound class. Those three big ones weighed more than 10 pounds apiece by my fish scales—lordly fish with dark backs and beautiful golden sides, worth rejoicing over.

We did rejoice as we ate lunch—bacon, sliced onions, baked beans, coffee, bread and butter and wonderful slabs of golden-brown fried fish—and listened to Moore tell one of his inimitable stories. Yet I remember an odd thing about that luncheon camp. Usually on the lake the air is full of bird sounds—the veery spiraling his beautiful song, loons laughing across the water, song sparrows and warblers spattering out brilliant arias, wild cries from gulls. But this noon the birds were strangely silent.

Penasse glanced anxiously at the horizon. "Might blow," he said. It did not look it. The sky was almost cloudless.

— ❧❦❧ —

OUR BOATS RETURNED to the reef to get the few fish to complete our limits; but whereas before lunch the walleyes bit viciously, not a strike did we get after lunch. It was as if the whole show had ended with a silent noonday signal. Penasse shook his head. Now clouds began scudding across the sky. In an hour businesslike waves were building up. Still no strikes.

"We better get out of here," Penasse said suddenly and seriously.

Doc and I began to reel in, and in that instant I got the heavy strike I had been awaiting.

"Good boy!" yelled Doc, who always roots for his fishing partner.

The fish hung back like a bulldog, shaking his head and arching my rod, but not breaking water. I felt the boat begin to pitch crazily. Moore and Gyp were under full speed for the lee of a distant island. Penasse, sitting erect at our tiller, was gazing out toward the open lake, every attitude indicating impatience to get going.

I glanced back, and what I saw made my heart jump. The day had grown suddenly dark and a squall was sweeping toward us. I could see the approaching ominous white line of foam under the blast of the wind with the rain black behind it.

No time now to play my fish. We were right under a sheer cliff of jagged rock up which breaking waves already dashed madly as if to climb it, and the squall was bearing down on us with racehorse speed. Desperately I horsed in my fish, actually hoping that line or leader would break. Still Penasse held the boat against the incoming waves by increasing the motor speed. I brought the fish to the side and heaved it in by main force. Awkward, but necessary. The squall was upon us.

To my surprise, the fish was not a walleye. It was a northern, and not even a very large one. Somehow it had snared itself with the leader after being hooked, which accounted for its hard pull and its actions so resembling a deep-fighting walleye. As the pike, thrashing and spattering, hit the bottom of the boat the squall struck us with a screaming wind. Frothing white, the churning waves roared as if to engulf us.

Suddenly we were lifted on the crest of a huge billow and carried backward. The blinding spate of rain almost obscured the deadly rock-toothed cliff and the furious smother of water and foam at its base, but I peered in fascination through the lacing downpour at the disaster toward which we were being hurled. Not thirty feet from the cliff the boat seemed to catch itself, held its own, gradually fought its way across the back of the wave and into the trough beyond. Another wave flung buckets of water into the boat, but we gained headway and clawed off the rocks.

On the shore, dimmed by level sheets of rain, trees heaved and bent in the gale. I saw a 40-foot jack-pine snap off short. Then another, and another. Spray beat stingingly in our faces. But Penasse, with wonderful boatmanship, evaded one racing comber after another and ran behind a small cape that offered shelter in its lee. There we caught our breath and donned rain garments. The squall roared past, and briefly the sun shone, though waves still hurled angrily on the shore.

"We better go," Penasse warned.

We were on the windward shore, but we could not stay where we were if the storm grew worse. If we were to run for shelter, it must be between squalls. Even as he spoke the sky darkened again with heavier clouds, and the three quarters of a mile of billowing lake between us and the little archipelago of pine-clad islands which was our first safety looked menacing.

It became infinitely more so. We were hardly half-way across when the air filled with the rush of a mighty wind. So viciously did it strike that spray hitting my cheek felt like the slap of a hand. Instantly the waves rose ragingly. It was worse than I had imagined or, I believe, than Penasse had imagined.

"Ho, ho, ho!" I heard him say. It is one of his few expressions, and can mean amusement, or satisfaction, or awareness of a crisis, or even awe.

I saw what he meant. So great already were the waves that our 14-foot boat, when in the troughs between them, seemed cut off from the world, hedged in by mountainous waters. But now a series of fearsomely gigantic combers was roaring toward us.

We rose on the first, cutting the crest cleanly with the thrust of the motor but getting some spray over the side, and slid down its foaming hill of water to the trough. The second broke on our bow, hurling water blindingly over us, but again we coasted dizzily over into the trough beyond.

The third sea was the greatest. We did not rise rapidly enough and the angle of the boat was not right for it. I saw the wave tower over us, white-fanged and malignant, and the sharp nose of the boat seemed about to plunge into it midway below its crest. I said to myself that it would breach us from stem to stern; an aluminum boat, filled to the gunwales by such a wave while carrying three men, a motor and other heavy gear, would founder instantly.

In the moment before the wave broke over us, though I accepted the imminence of death, for no swimmer could live in such a storm, I found I was not particularly frightened. I

glanced at Doc on the thwart ahead, his hawk face turned in profile to me. It was intensely alert and watchful. But I do not believe it is in him to be afraid. He was only profoundly interested.

Then Penasse, that genius in boat handling, made his move. He met the crest of the wave not head on, but at a last-minute angle. So cunningly timed and aimed was the angle that it did a hairline thing. Somehow, at the last possible second, it offered the bulge of the side to the final toppling crest, yet did not turn sufficiently broadside to be overwhelmed, either by the billow or by the now-unbelievable wind that screamed over us.

We shipped water—barrels of it, it seemed. But somehow we staggered over the crest without foundering, and while Doc and I bailed madly Penasse brought the boat into the lee of the island toward which we had been fighting our way. Moore, Gyp and Mandamin were already there, bailing also, their rubber coats gleaming wet. They, too, had experienced a very rough time, but, being ahead of us, had missed the worst of the second squall.

"Good job," I said to Penasse.

He gave a wintry grin.

The wind, already far beyond gale force, did not decrease this time as it had done before. Instead it now rose to a still mightier thrumming sound—hurricane fury. Trees began to crack like matchsticks on the island behind which we huddled for shelter. Three tall poplars snapped off and fell into the water quite close to us as we stared at the white waves roaring past on each side of our small island.

"Look at that!" cried Moore suddenly.

I glanced up and saw the hurricane wind take forty feet of the top right out of a 60-foot pine on the ridge above. Although weighing tons, it did not fall, but sailed through the air like a tumbleweed, right toward us. For an instant the great trunk with its threshing branches seemed to loom over us. Then with a foaming crash it plunged into our little cove, right beside our boats.

We looked at each other. Clearly we could not stay where we were. Trees continued to split and crash, and the only safe place on that island was the bare, exposed windward side. After beaching and securing our boats we struggled up to the crest, leaning against the wind at impossible angles and clawing for every foot of the way.

About us trees toppled deafeningly, a confusion of imminent danger. One great birch almost got Moore and Gyp, but the Kentuckians, cool and alert even in this immense hurly-burly, watched it, and stepped aside just in time.

A particularly fierce blast caught Doc and hurled him several feet to the ground. Doc is an athletic man, weighing 168 pounds, and no light breeze could fell him. He scrambled up unhurt, and a moment later we reached the exposed cliff that overhung the churning lake on the windward. There we lay flat, hugging the earth, forced by the impossibility of finding any shelter to gaze out at the incredible spectacle of this, the fiercest storm the lake ever experienced.

Sometimes rain beat upon us, driven level and sharp as sleet. And once the sun shone pallidly and fitfully through a momentary break in the clouds. That produced another sensation. The sun, gleaming on the madness of wind-driven spindrift, created in it a huge, misshapen spectrum of colors, adding with its ghastly travesty of the serene beauty of the true rainbow the last touch of crazed ferocity to the scene. Breakers, wind and crashing trees made a tumult so vast that we had to shout when we spoke to one another.

Then all at once I felt the island move under me. I said so. The others stared as if they thought my reason had left me. But a moment later they felt it too. It moved again. This was beyond all natural laws. No wind, however mighty, should move a rocky five-acre island. On the back of our necks the hair rose.

But now the natural cause revealed itself. To our lee was a great pine. Many of its large branches had been stripped from it, but though the stout trunk was curved in a rigid arc by the hurricane it had thus far resisted the fury of the wind. That pine was now being literally torn up by its roots, and its roots extended out

twenty or thirty feet—beneath the very ground on which we lay.

Just in time we rolled and scrambled to safety as a giant blast sent the pine roaring over, its root system lifting starkly twenty feet or more into the air, taking with it tons of stone and grass, including the very spot of earth on which we had been lying a moment before. That seemed to be the climax, after which it became a simple case of endurance. The Weather Bureau later recorded that the wind blew more than one hundred miles an hour—a super-hurricane, for hurricane force is rated at seventy-five miles—and continued with unabated fury for six hours, with only slightly less heavy winds twelve hours longer. Throughout the hours we lay there, enduring the ceaseless pounding of that storm.

Damage in the millions of dollars was wreaked that day on forests, crops and property. Some islands were completely denuded of trees. At least three men—two Indians and a white man—were drowned in different parts of the lake.

The only miracle was that the number was so small. We on our island at least lived it out, but we did not get back to McKeever's camp that night. Beaten and clinging like lizards to our wet rocks, we abided the tempest, until very late we managed to run our boats around the lee of the island to Helldiver Bay, and portaged three-quarters of a mile—in spite of trees still crashing all about us—to Machin's Camp, where we were fed and sheltered for the night.

Next day, though the seas were still perilous, we made our way back to McKeever's about noon. Our magnificent fish, of course, were spoiled and had to be jettisoned. This we regretted as, haggard and weary, we staggered into camp and encountered McKeever.

If there was a faint gleam of joy in his eye when he saw us safe, nothing else in his manner showed it. "I don't see any walleyes," was all he said.

How could we reply to this sardonicism? It is hard to deal with McKeever, especially if you are a friend of his.

—June, 1955

By Chuck Morgan

TERROR
with Your Trout

HELPLESS AND HOPELESS IN THE CANYON BOTTOM, THEY WATCHED THE MOUNTAIN OF WATER ROLL INEXORABLY DOWN UPON THEM.

RAW NATURE IS A CONSTANT CHALlenge to me, probably because in it I escape dull routine and tiresome monotony. It's uncertain, unpredictable, and uncertainty is what I like—within limits. One quick decision can snatch you from yawning disaster; another, perhaps thoughtlessly made, can plunge you into wild outdoor drama. That's the way it was in West Clear Creek Canyon, on Arizona's Mogollon Rim.

Bob Overbend and I were fishing a wilderness trout stream in the canyon bottom with Virgil Hoke, a local trout expert. It was almost noon of a fine May day, cool and invigorating among the 7,000-foot pines, and Virgil was about to leave with a limit of beauties. "Hey," he said, "you guys better come along and forget that notion of staying down here in this bear-and-lion den overnight. Why not climb out with me? I've got enough fish to go round."

I looked at Bob, my fishing friend from Los Angeles. "What do you think, Bob?" I asked. "Shall we quit now or lay over and catch that big brown that Virgil lost?"

Bob looked downcanyon at the deep pool where the heavy, leg-long trout still sulked. "I'm going to make old Hoke feel sick," he grinned, "by catching that big trout myself. Let's stay and siwash here tonight under this big fir tree."

Virgil is an old Arizona hill native who operates a trading post in the heart of the great, canyon-cut Coconino Forest that surrounded us.

Naturally he knows every mood of that vast country. Now he shook his head doubtfully, gathered his string of huge browns and rainbows and prepared to start upcanyon to his own private trail, a secret exit out of the 1,500-foot-deep, rock-bound gorge.

He looked up at the flawless May sky, bounced the big trout teasingly and said: "Got a hunch it's going to rain. If it does, a lot of water will come down this old canyon."

Virgil was joking, of course; May rain is extremely rare in Arizona.

"You're just afraid we'll catch that big old trout and ruin your reputation," Bob said. "Nope, we're staying. So long, Hoke. I'll show you some real fish tomorrow." Virgil toiled up out of sight.

Later I got to thinking about Virgil's warning. He undoubtedly was half serious. "Hey, Bob," I said, waking him from an after-lunch snooze. "Maybe Virgil had something. You know, it *could* rain. This canyon drains lots of high country and really floods out after a storm. And we can't get out after dark."

Bob only half heard me. He rolled over sleepily, put his hat on backward, groped for his rod and got up. "Come on," he said. "Let's catch our supper. Old Hoke just wants us to quit."

HE WENT DOWNCANYON to the big pool and tied on a small gold Colorado spinner and a tiny Black Gnat, then eased out line for a cast at the big ledge overhanging the huge old brown's lair. I knew he'd stalk that fish until dark. I worked down to the lower pools and cast idly here and there, catching five pan-size rainbows, but my heart wasn't in it and I quit.

I dozed in the warm sun, enjoying the spring flowers and wild wonderland about me, and the hours raced. Then, leaning on a big rock, I watched a water ouzel crisscross my boot toe as it worked the pool for minnows. Falling rocks from the rim above disturbed me. Forty feet above the present water level I saw a big shelf of drift trash. Not long before, water had covered this very spot higher than a two-story house. As Virgil had said, this canyon was a ripsnorter in a flash flood.

Then I heard Bob. "Yippee, wa-a-a-h-h-hoo-o-o-o!" he yelled. The echoes reverberated like a parade of idiots invading the wild, deep canyon.

Suddenly the uproar stopped. When I reached the pool, Bob was waist-deep in the cold dark water, gazing ruefully at the butt half of what had been a fine fly rod. He looked at me sheepishly.

"I had him in the shallows and reached down to beach him," he said. "Durn the luck—my hat fell off. Scared him silly. He took off for Wilshire Boulevard like Juan Fangio, then blooie—the line tangled and I tried to horse him."

"Looks like he horsed you," I said. "Better get out of that icy water before you catch pneumonia. Let's quit. I've got enough fish for supper anyway."

In silence we tramped back upcanyon to our packs. I cut through the willows to the south wall, intending to walk a hidden ledge I'd often used to avoid fording the slippery riffle, which was now probably under water from the snow-melt rise. There were still old snow packs in the deep shade. So far I'd kept my feet dry. Bob was wet enough for both of us. He walked thoughtfully along behind and ran into me when I suddenly stopped.

"What's the matter?" he said, looking blankly at the big boulder that now blocked the trail. The boulder surprised me too. But I'd already noticed that winter floods had changed the streambed.

"It's cut us off," I said. "We'll have to go back." Then I stopped and looked carefully at the rock. Somehow it seemed familiar. It was huge—the size of a small house—at least eight feet tall, worn rounded, yet rough by long stream erosion.

Then I remembered. This rock had been near the foot of the aerial tram that my local game club built to stock the inaccessible canyon with fry and fingerlings. Now it was uncounted yards downstream. "The current washed it down here," I said and walked on.

Bob stared at the huge boulder in disbelief. "Boy, some current!" he said. "That rock weighs fifty tons. Whew! Some current." He followed in silent thought back to our packs just as the brief high-country twilight ended and thick darkness filled the deep, narrow canyon like spilled ink. A damp chill bit into our tired bodies. Somehow the fun had gone out of our trip.

—◦—◦—

I STARTED A small fire from the driftwood and dead fir we'd rustled for lunch, and the beans, fish and hominy were soon ready. We ate silently, knowing it was too dark for us to attempt the nebulous, slippery elk trail we'd followed down into the abyss. It was vertical in places, with bluffed ledges, dangerous dropoffs and hidden turns. Strenuously hard to follow at noon, it was now unthinkable.

Bob gulped his beans uneasily, then asked, "Hey, were you kidding about that rock?"

My mind was elsewhere. "What rock?" I said. "Kidding about what?"

"Did high water really move that huge rock so far downstream?" Bob persisted. "If it did, a man wouldn't have a chance down in this boxed-in chute."

I'd tried to forget the uncertainty ahead. I work better that way. But now the whole thing stretched my nerves. "Bob, my boy," I said, in what I hoped was a fatherly tone, "I've been coming down to this canyon for fifteen years. I've photographed it and written stories about it. I've helped plant fish in here, helped repair that fish tram you saw on the rim a third of a mile above us. I've hunted lions, bears and elk down here. And I've seen driftwood piled forty feet up on the wall above us. But I've never been down here on the bottom when it really rained, and I don't want to be. I'm willing to let Clear Creek run its own business. Let's just hope this is a typical, dry, cold, star-filled May night and your big trout is still hungry tomorrow. What do you say we just stop talking about it? We can't do anything until daylight anyway. Let's spread our bunks and turn in." It wasn't a tough speech. I was just trying to put everything in honest perspective.

Bob looked moodily at the fire. "I've designed some crazy jet planes," he said, "for other guys. But I don't fly them. I don't take chances; I ride automobiles. I'm insured for almost everything. But now look at me." He fumbled around for a cigarette, kicked his bed over into some soft sand, pulled off his wet clothes to steam on sticks by the fire, and turned in. We both were tired and soon sound asleep.

I woke up damp and chilled at 12:40 and piled more wood on the smoldering fire. Bob coughed, got up for a drink and walked back from the fire glow. Then he padded up close to me in the damp, cold gloom.

"You know what?" he said. "No stars. It's as dark up there as it is down here. Clouds everywhere." He got a chocolate bar out of the pack, squatted by the fire's glow and looked off uneasily into the dark. A trout flipped in the hidden stream and he held out his hand. "Hey," he said apprehensively. "Was that a raindrop?"

Wisps of vapor walled us and the dim fire into a damp, gloomy room. I didn't feel calm and collected myself. I've lived in this remote mountain country since V-J Day, and I've seen my share of outdoor drama. But most of my tough moments have been alone, just looking after myself, or with old hands far cooler than I'll ever be. They'd always bucked up my nerves if I faltered for a moment. But Bob was now my responsibility. He couldn't be blamed for being jumpy. We were in a spot if things went wrong.

"You've seen too many tired TV dramas, Bob," I said. "Forget the things that *could* happen. Let's just wait and see what comes next— one thing at a time. It's simpler that way."

"Okay," Bob said. "But this dark hole gets on my nerves, that's all."

—◦—◦—

WE BOTH TURNED in and drifted off into fitful sleep. Something woke me at 2:15 A.M. I felt tense, trapped, vaguely disturbed. I sat up in the cramped mummy bag and struck a match. Then I knew. The first drops hit me, and suddenly a steady patter beat down from far above.

At first I hoped it might be just a passing shower. But the drizzle changed to a lashing downpour, then a cloudburst. I awoke Bob, and we collected our outfit by the dying fire and pulled it under a bushy spruce which grew where the sloping canyon floor joined the vertical wall that hung over us a thousand feet up into the storm-locked night. My soaked flashlight and Bob's cigarette lighter were puny sparks in the black deluge, hardly lighting our feet. The gloom smothered us with chill wet hands.

"Maybe she'll let up shortly," Bob said uneasily. "It would take half a day to make any difference down here—I guess, huh?"

I let him hang onto this thin hope, but I knew better. Soon he found out for himself. At first it sounded like a distant express train, a dull, faint pounding, more felt than heard. Then it grew rapidly louder, to drown our voices in terrifying, thunderous sound. This culminated in a terrific splash fifty feet in front of us across the canyon, followed by the overpowering sound of wild, rushing water. I could barely hear Bob's voice yelling into my ear.

"What's that?" he shouted.

Before I could answer, another splattering cascade bounced off the overhanging wall far above our heads, foamed outward, and launched a new waterfall that pinned us back farther under the gnarled spruce. There must have been a world of water falling up there to make the gutters and downspouts fill up so fast. We were right in it and saw it firsthand. You probably read about it in the papers as a freak west-coast hurricane that brought unprecedented moisture to all the Southwest.

I looked at my soaked watch by the flashlight's fading flicker. "It's 5:47," I yelled to Bob. "Daylight soon. That'll help—I guess."

He just shook convulsively and wormed in under the spruce in a futile effort to avoid the widening waterfall above us.

We'd gone to bed a good twenty feet above water level, as far up the sloping canyon floor as the vertical wall at our back would let us go. Now I could see the rushing torrent angrily devouring the narrow slope left below my feet. There were undoubtedly higher spots and better bed grounds. We hadn't found them. We'd just taken this spot for modest protection, convenience to the trail, and not as our final stand in a flooded world. But who can solve all of life's problems in advance? I've stopped trying.

Already the black night was fading to a murky gray, then to a sickly white, as seething luminous vapor filled the desolate canyon. "I'm standing in water," Bob shouted in fright, and scrambled out from under the spruce to shiver beside me in the dripping dawn.

The rain slacked and we could hear a thousand waterfalls splashing down from the steep walls above. Periodically we heard the express-train roar of rockslides or the booming thunder of a tremendous undercut boulder jackrabbiting down to the canyon floor. It was a moment of almost hopeless terror. But at least our overhanging ledge gave us protection from almost everything but the stream itself. It was the strait-jacketed feeling of futility that got me.

⊷ ⊷⊰⊱⊹ ⊶

NOW, FAINTLY, I heard a new disturbing sound, like a distant, splashing rock crusher. I delayed saying what I thought it was, but the liquid crushing-grinding noise rapidly grew louder, and Bob knew without asking. Already water was ankle-deep. Our soaked backs pressed the canyon wall, and we must move. But where? Fifty yards downstream a huge boulder stood encouraging feet above the flood. Alongside it was a sizable alder, precariously rooted in the shifting sands. Which was safer? Where else could we go when the crisis fell? I didn't debate for long.

The canyon bent sharply three hundred yards upstream. I knew I'd see the dreaded sight there soon. Studying the far side of this bend through the first lifting vapor, where a trail came down, I weighed the chance. But it was too late. A deafening roar filled my ears and the seething wall of water, towering above stream level, foamed around the bend like a slow-motion picture of volcanic lava.

"Run for the tree, Bob," I yelled, dashing forward.

He was faster and was climbing frantically when I reached it. It would hold but one. Only the rock remained. I clawed the big boulder's slippery sides, tearing my hands without feeling, and pulled until my shoulders edged over the top. I was still on my belly, scrambling the last stretch, when the crushing waves hit, splashing foam and drift about me.

It was like being on a wild seawall during a big blow at high tide as the torrent pounded the rock with deafening fury. Like a marble in a giant's fingers, the boulder rolled uneasily, swinging slowly around, rocking gently like a mammoth easy chair. Then, with a sinking heart, I felt irresistible force grab the boulder, wrench it loose, and tilt it steeply for the tumbling, crunching roll that meant disaster. Lying flat on it, I clawed for new holds and waited helplessly. Then the boulder lurched steeply and balanced precariously as fierce waves tore at my weakening body.

I had a fleeting thought of Bob. As if in reply, from somewhere behind me his piercing scream reached my ears even above the flood's roar. Suddenly, whipping tree branches slashed my back, crushed me against the rock; then, brushing me fleetingly, they were gone. There was a sodden thump alongside, and Bob joined me—stretched flat on the slick, slanting surface, clawing frantically to hang on. There we lay, silent, overpowered by the rushing water, waiting for the worst.

It seemed like eternity but was probably no more than twenty minutes. The roar diminished, the waves inched down from the rock top, which had been awash, and we got weakly to our knees, then stood up on the crazily tilted surface. Awed relief claimed us for long moments before Bob could bring himself to speak.

"I could stand a dry cigarette right now," he said. "I'm weak as a sick mouse." His voice shook uncontrollably.

I couldn't think of anything appropriate.

With indescribable relief I watched the torrent slowly quiet to a noisy rush, saw the angry flood recede until a thin sandspit showed where the vanished alder tree had stood. In the gray morning light I watched thankfully until the resilient bankside willows lifted their muddy tops above the flood.

In another hour we crossed the creek in a waist-deep rapid that nearly swept us away. Two hours later we were out of the canyon and beside the clean-washed Jeep in the sweet-scented little grove of pines by the fish-tram house. The sun burned through the thinning overcast, and we sat silent in its warmth, eating apples and candy bars, unwilling to tell each other exactly what we thought or felt.

⊸——⊰❖⊱——⊷

FINALLY BOB BROKE the silence. He stuck out his hand and gave mine a firm shake. "Thanks for not gigging me," he said. "I was scared silly, but not any more. Maybe I don't look it, but I feel older and bigger—maybe 40 and 6 feet tall—able to walk away from that one like you did—just like I'd done it a hundred times before, easy, calm, old stuff." He sounded as though he meant it.

I had no answer. What could I say? I got up stiffly. "Come on," I said. "Let's head for Long Valley and tell old Virgil Hoke we caught his big brown trout and ate it for supper. Maybe we can fool him. He might even think we're real fishermen and stake us to a good hot breakfast. Then we'll ask him if it ever rains up here on West Clear Creek in the dry month of May."

—November, 1958

By Bud Jackson

Fresh-Water
ROUGHNECK

NOODLING FOR GIANT CATFISH IS AN EXCITING AND DANGEROUS BUSINESS REQUIRING PLENTY OF KNOW-HOW AND NERVE.

THEY TELL A STORY down in the White River country of Arkansas about "Hooker John," a one-handed hill man who wore a hook on the stump of his brawny right arm and was one of the section's most widely renowned "noodlers." A noodler, in case you don't know,

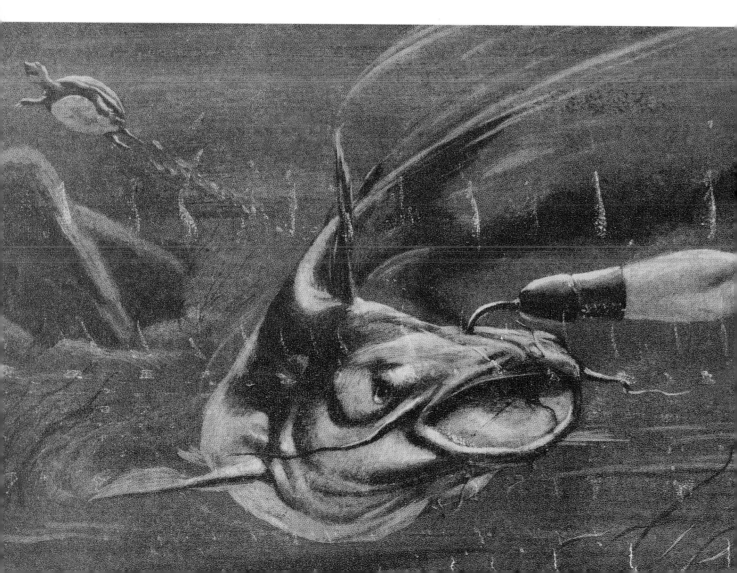

is one who specializes in catching large fish with his bare hands, or, in the case of Hooker John, with one bare hand and a hook-hand.

The hook was far from a handicap to the mountaineer, for it was a first-class asset in handling big catfish. Hooker John would wade or dive into a pool which he knew, or suspected, to hold a large fish. When he located his quarry, he caught it by the simple expedient of driving the razor-sharp hook into its head and dragging it out onto the bank.

The one-handed man failed to return home after one such expedition, so the legend goes. They found his body a few days later, bobbing in an eddy, and still caught on the hook at the end of that right arm was the carcass of a tremendous catfish. They theorized that Hooker John had caught a tartar, a fish too heavy even for his strength, and had been unable to free the hook; hence he was dragged under and drowned.

I cannot vouch for the authenticity of the tale, but I can vouch for the soundness of the theory that there are plenty of catfish in the world of water that are big enough and mean enough to drown you if you grab one in such fashion that you can't turn loose. The big cat is the rough-neck of fresh water, strong as a bull, usually as awkward, but always an antagonist worthy of respect in any man-to-fish battle.

When you get right down to cases with an old river cat weighing 45 to 50 pounds, you're at grips with a foe that carries three sharp saw-toothed daggers, a maw large enough to enable him to swallow a good-sized pig and a skin as slippery and hard to hold onto as the proverbial eel. Mostly the real big boys are yellow river cats, but occasionally you'll find a blue or a flathead running well up toward 50 pounds and, if anything, he's meaner still.

George Bradley, who as caretaker of City Lake at Pawnee, Oklahoma, has had consider-

able experience particularly with behemoth flatheads, tells a story which illustrates the danger in regarding them too lightly. Some years ago George rowed his small boat to a spot in the river where he had fastened a trot-line. Accompanying him was a 13-year-old neighbor, and as they neared the line and perceived that something large had been hooked the boy became wildly excited.

Finally George paddled the boat alongside the spot, some twelve or fourteen feet from the shore, where the water was being lashed to a froth and discovered a great catfish, hooked solidly. George instructed the youth to reach for the staging which held the big one and then try to bring the fish over the side of the boat. The boy went him one better and got a hand in the fish's gill-slit, whereupon the monster promptly closed down the gill cover, crushing the boy's hand painfully, and then lunged away, pulling the youngster half-way over the side of the boat. The small craft immediately swamped, and its two occupants were pitched off into deep water.

The boy managed to free his hand and swim to the bank. George struck out for the boat, which the current was tugging away, caught it and towed it to the bank. They bailed it out, paddled again to the spot where the fish was hooked, and this time boated it without difficulty as the lad handled the paddle and George settled with the fish. But that 47-pound flathead might easily have caused two people to drown.

In the bluffs of the Grand River a few miles below Pensacola dam in Oklahoma, is a large cavern. I've never seen it, but Charley Cohea, mayor of the small town of Ketchum, and a lifelong resident of the Grand bottoms, has told me of it. Back in the days of his youth, Charley and his young friends used to play around this cave, which extended back about ten feet into the rock at a spot which they chose for a swimming hole.

One afternoon a crowd of kids was frolicking around the pool. One of the more adventurous ones entered the cave and discovered therein a blue cat of good size. Most of the young people wanted no part of the whiskered torpedo when informed that he weighed perhaps 40 pounds. Three of them, including Charley, decided to try to catch him, however. That they succeeded without someone's being badly hurt was undoubtedly due to the grace of a kind providence.

After some discussion it was decided to form a human chain. Charley volunteered to serve as the unenviable bottom link by diving down and catching hold of the rocks at the entrance of the cave. One of his two co-conspirators then followed until he could catch Charley's ankles. Third man in the chain grasped the ankles of the second man, whose feet protruded from the water. Link No. 3 sat down and braced his feet. It was well that he did.

Charley, feeling his way into the cavern, made contact with the enemy, which turned to face him. The boy then did something that took a lot of raw courage. He closed on the old lunker, reached beneath it and tickled its belly until it opened its mouth. Non-noodlers undoubtedly will begin grinning at this point in my story, thinking that I'm fooling; noodlers will know I'm not. Then Charley Cohea rammed his right fist into that great open mouth, closed his fingers over the narrow base of the throat and started backing out with his trophy.

For a few seconds that must have seemed like as many years, it looked as though he'd never make it. All hell broke loose down there in the cavern as the tortured blue twisted and turned in his frenzy to be free. Through it all young Charley clung to his hold like grim death and, fortunately for Charley, so did his mates.

The boy ran out of wind at last and turned loose, but the great cat had clamped his mouth shut as tightly as a vice and Charley was caught. He tried to breathe, and the water rushed into his lungs. In that instant the fish yielded. There was help in plenty now, and the youngsters gathered around to lend a hand in pulling the purpling Charley and the still fighting fish out on dry land.

The fish weighed 37 pounds, and Charley was a hero. But for a moment, he confesses, he thought he was going to be a dead one. As it was, his arm, where the cat chewed savagely upon it, was a raw mass of mangled flesh and skin for many weeks.

Back in the early days of what I am pleased to call a radio-broadcasting career I read an item on a newscast one night to the effect that one Waldo Ball, living in a small town on the Lake of the Ozarks in Missouri, had been killed by a huge catfish. Ball had dived into a river pool where he had cornered a large yellow cat, and in the ensuing melee had been finned squarely in the eye, the sharp fin pushing up into his brain.

A little dubious, I drove the forty miles down there the next day to check up. The story, repeated to me by three or four residents of the community, tallied in every detail with the one phoned in by our correspondent and read on the air. Ball had indeed been killed by a giant cat, how large they discovered that evening, when, after having mined the Niangua River pool, they took therefrom a catfish weighing 79 pounds.

Almost as unpleasant to contemplate as the case of Waldo Ball is that of Oscar Beck, a fishing crony of mine back in those same days. "Becky" had been trot-lining in the Osage River below Bagneil Dam, which impounds the above-mentioned Lake of the Ozarks, and had hooked a heavy flathead cat. As he reached for the staging to boat the fish the line broke and Oscar made a frenzied grab, caught the trailing line in his hand and was dragged from the boat in an instant.

Reluctant to turn loose, he groped for a handhold on the fish itself and was finned clear through the palm of the right hand. If you have ever been gigged by a catfish—however large or small—you'll concur in the statement that it is a most painful thing. The spines of the catfish, located one on each side and one on his back, are serrated with tiny, needle-sharp projections, curving backward like tines. They go in easily, but they come out grudgingly, and in coming out they lacerate the flesh unmercifully.

Unable to free himself and in some agony, Becky cried for help. A near-by fisherman heard his desperate call, and but for his prompt action Oscar Beck would have met a tragic death. As it was, the fellow hurried to the scene, hooked the fish with a small gaff, and held it steady until Oscar, summoning his nerve, jerked his torn hand off the jagged fin.

Oscar's troubles were yet far from over, for a piece of the fin broke off in his hand. A doctor had to perform a minor operation to remove it. Beck did no nut-cracking with that hand for some days thereafter.

<hr/>

CLARK JORDAN, A chap who lives on the lower reaches of the Missouri River, is a "big-cat" fisherman who'll take 'em just about any way they come—trot-lining, jugging, hand-fishing or what-have-you. "Cee," as they call him, once showed me a scar on his torso that starts on his belly just beside the navel and runs clear around to the right side. There it breaks off, only to begin again after a couple of inches and run four more inches on around toward his backbone.

"A big cat done that," he confided, and told me the story.

Cee and his oldest son, a 16-year-old, had set a throw-line in the river, and when they came to it one morning the small willow tree to which they had fastened it was whipping like a reed in a gale. At length they managed to haul a Gargantua of a yellow catfish into the shallow water by the bank.

Examining the fish at close range, Cee discovered that only a tiny wisp of skin in the top of its ugly broad head held the big fellow. In drawing him to the bank they had somehow pulled the hook free, and by some freak of luck it had then lodged in his head. Now, not daring to try to beach the monster by dragging him the rest of the way, Cee waded into knee-deep water, hoping to get hold of the fish and some-how keep it from escaping.

As he reached for it the catfish lunged and the hook tore free. The man, faced with the prospect of losing his prize, launched himself in a desperate leap which brought him down squarely upon the leviathan's back and virtually impaled him on the long dorsal spine. For a moment—a split fraction of a second—agony blotted out Cee Jordan's consciousness. Then he fought back to awareness and to the knowledge that he must, at all costs, keep his antagonist in shallow water where he could retain the advantage of leverage against the ground.

That must have been an epic struggle in many respects as man and fish fought it out there in the foot-deep water, their movements stirring up great clouds of silt from the muddy bottom to mingle with Cee's blood darkening the water. As the cat quieted for an instant Cee made an effort to lift himself off its back. In a sense he succeeded, for the yellow one was galvanized into twisting action that tore the spine free from Cee's stomach—then pitilessly drove it back into his side!

At this point the boy, who had run to summon help, reappeared with a neighbor. Again the action lulled, and this time the newcomer waded into the water, put a .32 pistol against the big cat's head and fired a shot into its brain. Clark Jordan lost consciousness again as the fish, in its death struggle, ripped the spine free from his side. His two companions lifted him, nearly dead from loss of blood and shock, from the river and took him at once to a small town near by.

It was many months before he could walk. He tells me that the doctor who patched him up still shakes his head when he sees Cee coming down the street. The medico just can't understand how a man could have taken what Jordan took and still live.

The catfish? He weighed 86 pounds, and you could almost put your head in his mouth. I saw the dried and shrunken head, and it was still enormous after several years.

Luckily for my peace of mind, my own particular adventure with a hulking catfish occurred long before I heard of or ran down any of the above-told stories. At the tender age of seventeen, I once dived into a pool in the Moreau River of Missouri, swam to the bluff which formed one bank and squeezed through a small hole in that wall into a large subterranean room. I carried with me a large hook to which was attached one end of a stout rope.

The two schoolboy companions with whom I had collaborated in discovering this to be the den of an enormous blue cat held the other end of that rope, ready to do their share when I'd finished my part of the task. That, in brief, consisted of tickling the blue until he opened his cavernous mouth, setting the hook therein with a savage downward jerk, and getting out of there but quick.

Up to a point things went smoothly. I found the monster, scratched his belly, felt the mouth pop open, and drove the hook home. Then I turned to flee.

They say that animals cannot reason. That ugly devil had never heard it, and in the light of what came next I shall always harbor my own doubts as to the truth of it.

The fish shot past me and, to my horror, stopped in the small entrance to his den, effectively blocking my exit. My lifted hands found only solid rock above my head—no air space. There was no time to look for another passage out.

In that instant I had literally to force myself to keep calm. It was a moment of horror, for the catfish cavern would become a tomb unless I worked swiftly. Nerving myself, I moved deliberately toward the fish, reached for the rope leading to the hook in his mouth, caught the rope and jerked it frantically.

The boys on the other end bent to their job and, inch by inch, the heavy blue, struggling against them all the way, was drawn through the hole and out into open water. I was a scant yard behind him, and air never felt cooler or tasted sweeter than the lungfuls that I gulped in when my head broke water.

I'm glad that I didn't know then what I know now—that a husky river cat is an antagonist fully capable of killing the man who has cornered him. That one weighed a mere 36 pounds, and I've seen 'em three times as big. The wicked-looking, razor-sharp, six-inch spine of that catfish has served me as a letter opener for many years. Of those thrilling moments in the underwater cavern with that almost prehistoric-looking foe it is my sole memento. I shudder when I stop to think how readily I might have had others—a cut tendon, a blinded eye, a jagged scar in the abdomen. I was luckier than some!

—August, 1947

By Zane Grey

World-Record
TIGER SHARK

BATTLING AND CONQUERING HALF A TON OF BUCKING, FIGHTING MAN-EATER.

FASCINATING PLACES to fish have been a specialty of mine, and there are many where no other fisherman ever wet a line. This always seemed to be a fetish for me. New and lonely waters! My preference has been the rocky points of islands where two currents meet.

Fishing off Sydney Heads, Australia, is as far removed from this as could be imagined.

Great scarred yellow cliffs, like the colored walls of an Arizona cañon, guard the entrance to Sydney Harbor, which, if not really the largest harbor in the world, is certainly the most wonderful. These bold walls, standing high and sheer, perhaps a mile apart, look down upon the most colorful and variable shipping of the seven seas. I passed through this portal on the *S. S. Mariposa* gazing up at the lofty walls, at the towering lighthouses and the slender wireless stands, black against the sky, never dreaming that the day would come when I saw them above me while fighting one of the greatest giant fish I ever caught.

At the end of three months' fishing on the south coast of Australia, during which my party and I caught sixty-seven big fish, mostly swordfish, we found ourselves at Watson's Bay, just around the corner of the South Head, within sight of all Sydney and, in fact, located in the city suburbs, for the purpose of pursuing further our extraordinary good luck. I hoped, of course, to catch the first swordfish off Sydney Heads, and incidentally beat the shark record.

I was introduced to this Sydney fishing by Mr. Bullen, who held the record, and who had pioneered the rod and reel sport practically alone, and had been put upon his own resources and invention to master the hazardous and hard game of fishing for the man-eating tiger shark.

In angling my admiration and respect go to the man who spends much time and money and endurance in the pursuit of one particular fish. Experiment and persistence are necessary to the making of a great angler. If Mr. Bullen has not arrived, he surely is far on the way. For three years he fished for tiger sharks from boats which in some cases were smaller than the fish he fought. His mistakes in method and his development of tackle were but steps up the stairway to success. I want to record here, in view of the small craft he fished out of and the huge size and malignant nature of tiger sharks, that after a desperate battle to bring one of these man-eaters up to the surface he was justified in shooting it.

This shooting of sharks, by the way, was the method practiced in Australia, as harpooning them was, and still is, prevalent in New Zealand. In America we have sixty years' development behind big-game fishing; and all the sporting clubs disqualify a harpooned or a shot fish. The justification of this rule is that the opportunity is presented many times to kill a big fish or a shark before it has actually waked up. This is not fair to the angler who fights one for a long time.

In Australia, however, the situation is vastly different. There are thousands of sharks. In the book I am writing, *Tales of Man-eating Sharks*, I have data on three hundred tragedies and disasters.

—————✠—————

I EXPECT THIS book will be a revelation to those distinguished scientists of the United States who do not believe a shark will attack a human being. Certainly it would be better to fish for sharks and shoot them on sight than not to fish at all, for every shark killed may save one or more lives.

While I have been in Australia there have been several tragedies, particularly horrible. A boy, bathing at Manly Beach, was taken and carried away in plain sight.

Somewhere in South Australia another boy was swimming near a dock. Suddenly a huge blue-pointer shark seized him and leaped

clear of the water with him before making off. Such incidents should make a shark-killer out of any angler.

Before I reached Sydney I had caught a number of man-eaters, notably some whalers, a white death shark and some gray nurse, those sleek treacherous devils believed by many to be Australia's most deadly shark. I had had enough experience to awaken all the primitive savagery to kill that lay hidden in me. The justification, however, inhibits any possible thought of mercy.

Nevertheless, despite all the above, I think gaffing sharks is the most thrilling method and the one that gives the man-eater, terrible as he is, a chance for his life. If you shoot a shark or throw a Norway whale harpoon through him, the battle is ended. On the other hand, if by toil and endurance, by pain and skill, you drag a great shark up to the boat, so that your boatman can reach the wire leader and pull him close to try to gaff him, the battle is by no means ended. You may have to repeat this performance time and again; and sometimes your fish gets away after all. Because of that climax I contend that all anglers should graduate to the use of the gaff. Perhaps the very keenest, fiercest thrill is to let your boatman haul in on the leader and you gaff the monster. Thoreau wrote that the most satisfying thing was to strangle and kill a wild beast with one's naked hands.

It was only a short run by boat round the South Head to the line of cliff along which we trolled for bait. The water was deep and blue. Slow swells heaved against the rocks, burst into white spray and flowed back into the sea like waterfalls.

A remarkable feature was the huge flat ledges, or aprons, that jutted out at the base of the walls, over which the swells poured in roaring torrent, to spend their force on the stone face and slide back in glistening maelstrom. Dr. Stead assures me this apron is an indication of very recent elevation of the coast. The Gap was pointed out to me, where a ship struck years ago on a black stormy night and went down with all of the hundreds on board, except one man who was lifted to a rock and, crawling up, clung there to be rescued. Suicide Leap was another interesting point, where scores of people had gone to their doom, for reasons no one can ever fathom.

⊰⊱

TROLLING FOR BAIT was so good that I did not have much time for sightseeing. Bonito and kingfish bit voraciously, and we soon had plenty of bait. We ran out to sea dragging teasers and bonito in the wake of the Avalon, and I settled down to that peculiar happiness of watching the sea for signs of fish. Hours just fade away unnoticeably at such a pastime. In the afternoon we ran in to the reefs and drifted for sharks.

I derived a great deal of pleasure from watching the ships pass through the harbor gate and spread in all directions, according to their destinations. Airplanes zoomed overhead. Small craft dotted the green waters outside, and white sails skimmed the inner harbor. Through the wide gate I could see shores and slopes covered with red-roofed houses, and beyond them the skyscrapers of the city. Dominating all was the great Sydney bridge, with its fretwork span high above the horizon.

It was a grand background for a fishing scene. At once I conceived an idea of photographing a leaping swordfish with Sydney Heads and the gateway to the harbor and that marvelous bridge all lined against the sky behind the leaping fish. Our efforts were futile, however, much to Mr. Bullen's disappointment. The next day was rough. A hard wind ripped out of the northeast; the sea was ridged blue and white. The boat tipped and rolled and dived until I was weary of hanging on to my seat and the rod. We trolled all over the ocean for hours, until afternoon, and then came in to drift off the heads. Still, somehow, despite all this misery, there was that thing which holds a fisherman to his task. When I climbed up on the dock, I had the blind staggers and the floor came up to meet me.

The third morning dawned warm and still, with a calm ocean and blue sky. Starting early, we trolled for bait along the bluffs as far south as Point Bondi. I had engaged the services of Billy Love, market fisherman and shark catcher of Watson's Bay, to go with us as guide to the shark reefs. We caught no end of bait, and soon were trolling off Bondi. We ran ten miles out, and then turned north and ran on until opposite Manly Beach, where we headed in again to run past that famous bathing beach where so many bathers had been attacked by sharks. On down to Love's shark grounds, directly opposite the harbor entrance between the heads, and scarcely more that a mile outside.

We put down an anchor in about two hundred feet of water. A gentle swell was moving the surface of the sea. The sun felt hot and good. Putting cut bait overboard, we had scarcely settled down to fishing when we had a strike from a small shark. It turned out to be a whaler of about three hundred pounds.

Love was jubilant over its capture.

"Shark meat best for sharks," he avowed enthusiastically. "Now we'll catch a tiger sure!"

That sharks were cannibals was no news to me, but in this instance the fact was more interesting. Emil put a bonito bait over, and Love attached a little red balloon to the line a fathom or two above the leader. This was Mr. Bullen's method, except that he tied the float about 150 feet above the bait, and if a strong current was running he used lead.

For my bait Love tied on a well-cut piece of shark, about two pounds in weight, and added what he called a fillet to hang from the point of the hook. I remarked that this bait looked almost good enough to eat. Then he let my bait down twenty-five fathoms without float or sinker.

This occurred at noon, after which we had lunch. Presently I settled down to fish and absorb my surroundings.

⊰⊱

THE SUN WAS hot, the gentle motion of the boat lulling, the breeze scarcely perceptible, the sea beautiful and compelling. There was no moment when I could not see craft of all kinds, from great liners to small fishing boats. I sat in my fishing chair, feet on the gunwale, the line in my hand, and the passage of time was unnoticeable. In fact, time seemed to stand still.

The hours passed. About midafternoon our conversation lagged. Emil went to sleep, and I had to watch his float. Peter smoked innumerable cigarettes, and then he went to sleep. Love's hopes of a strike began perceptibly to fail. He kept repeating, about every hour, that the sharks must be having an off day. But I was quite happy and satisfied.

I watched three albatross hanging around a market boat some distance away. Finally this boat ran in, and the huge white and black birds floated over our way. I told Love to throw some pieces of bait in. He did so, one of which was a whole bonito with its sides sliced off.

The albatross flew toward us, landed on their feet a dozen rods away, then ran across the water to us. One was shy and distrustful. The others were tame. It happened, however, that the suspicious albatross got the whole bonito, which he proceeded to gulp down, and it stuck in his throat. He drifted away, making a great to-do over the trouble his gluttony had brought him. He beat the water with his wings and ducked his head under, shaking it violently.

Meanwhile the other two came close, to within thirty feet, and they emitted strange, low, not unmusical cries as they picked up the morsels of fish that Love pitched to them. They were huge birds, pure white except across the back and along the wide-spreading wings. Their black eyes had an Oriental look, a slanting back and upward, which might have been caused by a little tuft of black feathers.

To say I was in the seventh heaven was putting it mildly. I awoke Emil, who, being a temperamental artist and photographer, went into ecstasies.

"I can't believe my eyes!" he kept exclaiming, and really the sight was hard to believe for Americans who know albatross only through legend and poetry.

Finally the larger and wilder one that had choked over his fish evidently got it down or up, and came swooping down on the others. Then they engaged in a fight for the pieces that our boatman threw over. They ate a whole bucketful of cut bonito before they had their fill, and one of them was so gorged that he could not rise from the surface. He drifted away, preening himself, while the others spread wide wings and flew out to sea.

FOUR O'CLOCK FOUND us still waiting for a bite. Emil had given up. Peter averred there were no sharks. Love kept making excuses for the day and, like a true fisherman, saying, "We'll get one tomorrow." But I was not in a hurry. The afternoon was too wonderful to give up. A westering sun shone gold amid dark clouds over the heads. The shipping had increased, if anything, and all that had been intriguing to me seemed magnified. Bowen, trolling in Bullen's boat, hove in sight out on the horizon.

My companions had obviously given up for that day. They were tired of the long wait. It amused me. I remarked to Peter, "Well, old top, do you remember the eighty-three days we fished without getting a bite? "

"I'll never forget that," he replied.

"And on the eighty-fourth day I caught my giant Tahitian marlin?"

"Right, sir," admitted Peter.

Love appeared impressed by the fact, or else what he thought was fiction, but he said nevertheless: "Nothing doing today. We might as well go in."

"Ump-umm," I replied in cowboy parlance. "We'll hang a while longer."

Fifteen minutes later something took hold of my line with a slow, irresistible pull. My heart leaped. I could not accept what my eyes beheld. My line paid slowly off the reel. I put my gloved hand over the moving spool—old habit of being ready to prevent an overrun. Still I did not believe it. But there—the line slipped off slowly, steadily, potently. Strike! There was no doubt of that. And I, who had experienced ten thousand strikes, shook all over with the possibilities of this one. Suddenly, sensing the actuality, I called out, "There he goes!"

Peter looked dubiously at my reel—saw the line gliding off. "Right-o, sir!"

Love's tanned image became radiant. Emil woke up and began to stutter.

"It's a fine strike," yelled Love, leaping up. "Starts like a tiger!"

He ran forward to heave up the anchor. Peter directed Emil to follow and help him.

Then I heard the crack of the electric starter and the sound of the engine.

"Let him have it!" advised Peter hopefully. "It was a long wait, sir. Maybe—"

"Swell strike, Pete," I replied. "Never had one just like it. He's taken two hundred yards already. It feels under my fingers just as if you had your hand on my coat sleeve and were drawing me slowly towards you."

"Take care. He may put it in high. And that anchor line is long."

WHEN LOVE AND Emil shouted from forward and then came running aft, the fish, whatever it was, had out between four and five hundred yards of line. I shoved forward the drag on the big reel and struck with all my might. Then I reeled in swift and hard. Not until the fifth repetition of this violent action did I come up on the weight of that fish. So sudden and tremendous was the response that I was lifted clear out of my chair. Emil, hands at my belt, dragged me back.

"He's hooked. Some fish! Get my harness!" I sang out.

In another moment, with my shoulders sharing that pull, I felt exultant, deeply thrilled, and as strong as Sampson. I quite forgot to look at my watch, which seemed an indication of my feelings. My quarry kept on taking line even before I released the drag.

"Run up on him, Pete. Let's get close to him. I don't like being near these anchored boats."

There were two fishing boats around, the nearer a little too close for comfort. Peter hooked up the engine, and I bent to the task of recovering four hundred yards of line. I found the big reel perfect for this necessary job. I was hot and sweating, however, when again I came up hard on the heavy weight, now less than several hundred feet away and rather close to the surface. I watched the bend of my rod tip.

"What kind of fish?" I asked.

"It's sure no black marlin," answered Peter reluctantly.

"I couldn't tell from the rod," added Love. "But it's a heavy fish. I hope a tiger—"

Emil sang out something hopeful.

I said, "Well, boys, it's a shark of some kind," and went to work.

With a medium drag I fought that shark for a while, watching the tip and feeling the line. It was true that I had never felt a fish just like this one. One instant he seemed as heavy as a rock, and the next, light, moving, different. Again I lost the feel of him entirely, and knowing the habit of sharks to slip up on the line to bite it I reeled like mad. Presently I was divided between the sense that he was little, after all, and the sense that he was huge.

Naturally I gravitated to the conviction that I had hooked a species of fish new to me, and a tremendously heavy one. My plan of battle, therefore, was quickly decided. I shoved up the drag on the great reel to five, six, seven pounds—more drag than I had ever used. But this fish pulled out line just as easily as if there had been none. I could not hold him or get in any line without following him. So I cautiously pushed up the drag to nine pounds—an unprecedented power for me to use. It made no difference at all to the fish, wherefore I went back to five pounds. For a while I ran after him, wound in the line, then had the boat stopped and let him pull out the line again.

"I forgot to take the time. Did any of you?"

"About half an hour," replied Emil.

"Just forty minutes," said Peter, consulting his clock in the cabin. "And you're working too fast—too hard. Ease up."

I echoed that forty minutes and could hardly believe it. But time flies in the early stages of a fight with a big fish. I took Peter's advice and reduced my action. And at this stage of the game I reverted to the conduct and talk of my companions, and to the thrilling facts of the setting. Peter held the wheel and watched my line, grim and concerned. Love bounced around my chair, eager, talkative, excited. Emil sang songs and quoted poetry while he waited with his camera.

The sea was aflame with sunset gold. A grand golden flare flooded through the gate between the heads. Black against this wonderful sky, the Sydney Bridge curved aloft over the city, majestic, marvelous in its beauty. To its left the sinking sun blazed upon the skyscraper buildings. The black cliffs, gold-rimmed, stood up boldly far above me. But more marvelous than any of these—in fact, exceedingly rare and lovely to me—were the ships putting to sea out of that illuminated gateway. There were six of these in plain sight.

"Getting out before Good Friday," said Peter. "That one on the right is the *Monowai,* and the other on the left is the *Maunganui.* They're going to come to either side of us, and pretty close."

"Well!" I exclaimed. "What do you think of that? I've been on the *Monowai,* and have had half a dozen trips in the *Maunganui.*"

These ships bore down on us, getting up speed. The officers on the bridge of the *Maunganui* watched us through their glasses, and both waved their caps. They must have recognized the *Avalon,* and therefore knew it was I who was fast to a great fish—right outside the entrance of Sydney Harbor. The deck appeared crowded with curious passengers who waved and cheered. That ship steamed by us, hissing and roaring, not a hundred yards away, and certainly closer to my fish than we were. The *Monowai* passed on the other side, almost even with her sister ship.

——— ❈ ———

CLOSE BEHIND THESE loomed a ship twice as large. She appeared huge in comparison. From her black bulk gleamed myriads of lights, and vast clouds of smoke belched from her stacks. Peter named her the *Rangitati,* or some name like that, and said she was bound for England via the Suez Canal. Then the other ships came on and passed us, and soon were silhouetted dark against the purple sky.

All this while, which seemed very short, and was perhaps half an hour, I worked on my fish and I was assured that he knew it. Time had passed, for the light house on the cliff suddenly sent out its revolving piercing rays. Night was not far away, yet I seemed to see everything almost as clearly as by day.

For quite a while I had been able to get the double line over the reel, but I could not hold it. However, I always tried to. I had two pairs of gloves and thumb stalls on each hand;

and with these I could safely put a tremendous strain on the line without undue risk, which would have been the case had I trusted the rod.

By now the sport and thrill had been superseded by pangs of toil and a grim reality of battle. It had long ceased to be fun. I was getting whipped, and I knew it. I had worked too swiftly. The fish was slowing, and it was a question of who would give up first. Finally, without increasing the strain, I found I could stop and hold my fish on the double line. This was occasion for renewed zest. When I told my crew, they yelled wildly. Peter had long since got out the big detachable gaff with its long rope.

I held on to that double line with burning, painful hands. And I pulled it in foot by foot, letting go to wind in the slack.

"The leader—I see it!" whispered Love.

"Whoopee!" yelled Emil.

"A little more, sir," added Peter tensely, leaning over the gunwale, his gloved hands outstretched.

In another moment I had the big swivel of the leader in reach.

——— ❈ ———

"HANG ON—PETE!" I panted as I stood up to release the drag and unhook my harness. "Drop the leader—overboard. Emil, stand by. Love, gaff this fish when I—tell you!"

"He's coming, sir," rasped out Peter, hauling in, his body taut. "There! My Gawd!"

Emil screeched at the top of his lungs. The water opened to show the back of an enormous shark. Pearl-gray in color, with dark tiger stripes, a huge rounded head and wide flat back, this fish looked incredibly beautiful. I had expected a hideous beast.

"Now!" I yelled.

Love lunged with the gaff. I stepped back, suddenly deluged with flying water and blindly aware of a roar and a banging on the boat. I could not see anything for moments. The men were shouting hoarsely in unison. I distinguished Peter's voice. "Rope—tail!"

"Let him run!" I shouted.

Between the up-splashing sheets of water I saw the three men holding that shark. It was a spectacle. Peter stood up, but bent, with his brawny shoulders sagging. Love and Emil were trying to rope that flying tail. For I had no idea how long, but probably a brief time, this strenuous action took place before my eyes. It beat any battle I recalled with a fish at the gaff.

The huge tiger rolled over, all white underneath, and he opened a mouth that would have taken a barrel. I saw the rows of white fangs and heard such a snapping of jaws as never before had struck my ears. I shuddered at their significance. No wonder men shot and harpooned such vicious brutes!

"It's over—his tail," cried Love hoarsely, straightening up with the rope.

Emil lent a hand. And then the three men held that ferocious tiger shark until he ceased his struggles. They put another rope over his tail and made fast to the ring-bolt.

When Peter turned to me, his broad breast heaved, his breath whistled, the corded muscles stood out on his arms—he could not speak.

"Pete! Good work! I guess that's about the hardest tussle we've ever had at the gaff."

We towed our prize into the harbor and around to the dock at Watson's Bay, where a large crowd awaited us. They dragged the vast bulk of my shark upon the sand. It required twenty-odd men to move him. He looked marble color in the twilight. But the tiger stripes showed up distinctly. He knocked men right and left with his lashing tail, and he snapped with those terrible jaws. The crowd, however, gave that business end of him a wide berth. I had one good long look at this tiger shark while the men were erecting the tripod, and I accorded him more appalling beauty and horrible significance than all the great fish I had ever caught.

"Well, Mr. Man-eater, you will never kill any boy or girl!" I flung at him.

That was the deep and powerful emotion

World's record tiger shark—1,036 pounds of meanness.

I felt—the justification of my act—the worthiness of it, and the pride in what it took. There, I am sure, will be the explanation of my passion and primal exultance. Dr. Stead, scientist and official of the Sydney Museum, and Mr. Bullen of the Rod Fishers Society weighed and measured my record tiger shark. Length, 13 feet 10 inches. Weight, 1,036 pounds!

—February, 1937

By Sgt. Mathias Wanzung
as told to George Cullicott

FOXHOLE FISHERMAN

WHETHER HIS LUCK IS GOOD OR BAD, THE AMERICAN FIGHTING MAN FINDS IN FISHING A HAPPINESS NO OTHER SPORT AFFORDS.

ALONG THE ISLAND road on which the Yanks were driving northwest from the Solomons to the Philippines are some of the finest fishing spots in the world. In the pause between battles combat-fatigued soldiers and marines crawl out of foxholes and find in the calm blue water of the inlets a sport that relaxes their shattered nerves.

From the Battle of Guadalcanal on through the campaigns in New Guinea and New Georgia, I saw fighting men drop their hot guns in exhaustion after routing Jap troops and turn to rod and reel for comfort. My experiences were typical of the many hundreds of G. I. Joes in the Southwest Pacific who are carrying on the traditions of Izaak Walton despite front-line perils and lack of equipment.

It was on the transport that brought us to Australia from the States that I first discovered the morale value of fishing. Later I was to learn the diet value, too, after subsisting on rations in the jungles. The ship was several days out, and as we neared Jap-infested waters the men grew restless and many became jittery.

In order to get my own mind off the thought of lurking subs I turned to dreaming of my favorite recreation, fishing. All of a sudden it struck me, like the strike of a muskie—why not try my luck right now?

A crew member loaned me a length of heavy cord for a throw line. On this I rigged a hook with ¾-inch gap and dropped it over, using a five-inch strip of pork for bait.

In no time at all I had a fight on my hands. It took me twenty-five minutes to land what turned out to be a 40-pound shark. The commotion of battle attracted a large crowd, and before long most of the fellows forgot the perils of their surroundings. Many fishing enthusiasts came forward to try their hand, and before the day was over we had pulled three fair-sized sharks up on deck.

The toughest part was having no reel. We had to hoist 'em up hand over hand—and we were fifty feet above water! We were so engrossed in the battles that we didn't notice that our hands were bleeding. The cheers of the spectators made it worth while, however, and in addition we had a swell fish dinner that night.

From then on until we landed, the ship seemed to sail smoother and faster.

In the days and months that followed there was no time for fishing. After positions had been established for the push back to the Philippines, breathing spells occurred more often and leisure time returned. How to fill in the gaps between bombing raids and battles became as tough a problem as killing off Jap snipers, but once again fishing brought the answer.

I recall the first island area we cleared away for a camp site. The fringes of the jungle had been leveled by tons of explosives. Craters gaped where once pillboxes stood, and enemy dead were sprinkled everywhere.

The men took to their tasks like the pioneers of colonial days and during their off-duty hours found time to build a fishing pier out over the treacherous coral rocks. It was on this pier that the men erased the horrors of warfare by fishing and spinning yarns. There was never a moment, day or night, when there was not at least one man out on the end of the 75-foot dock holding on to a line.

My friend, Lt. Paul A. Rogers, best describes the building and use of the pier:

"We asked for volunteers, since it was an extra-curriculum job, and in a short time enough sections of scrap mahogany, pieces of crating, salvaged nails and logs were gathered for the project. The first three sections were made of 12-foot lengths and were extended into about 3½ feet of water. A boardwalk of planking was laid on the framework. Three other similar sections were completed on shore, towed out and attached to the completed section in typical Army engineer style.

"The dock has been in use for several months now and is deeply appreciated by all the personnel. It is used not only for fishing. but for swimming, mooring of small boats and as a place for the men to do a little loafing in the evening, relaxing while taking a smoke.

"This recreation has enabled the men to keep more alert, and consequently perform their duties with superior skill and efficiency."

None of us had much in the way of equipment. My first rod was shaped from an old brush handle, with heavy paper clips bent to act as guides. A metal spool was wired down into a groove to serve as a reel. The line was medical silk of durable strength, discarded by the medics because mildew had made it unfit for use. A large hook was inserted along the hollow of an old silver mess spoon with handle cut off. The spoon created an inviting twirling action when reeled through the water.

One of the favorite trolling

lures was that made from a silvery sheet of banana stalk, commonly called lily root by the Yanks. This root was rolled tightly on a trolling head with a double set of large hooks, tied and trimmed to form a fish-like appearance. It resembled a fish in motion and proved very successful.

Incidentally, it took some good salesmanship on our part to obtain this root from the natives. A mirror or a shiny quarter turned out to be the best items of all for clinching a deal.

Many fellows found that silver mullet was an ideal bait for casting. The natives caught these fish in traps or by nets. Another favorite was bonito, but some of us hated to cut up good bonito steak for fish food.

Hooks were the biggest problem. The first few we had were straightened out by the weight of the heavier fish. We finally obtained a discarded 5/16-inch steel rod from which were forged some wicked hooks, using a gasoline burner to heat the metal and a ball peen hammer and triangle file to shape the hooks. The leaders for these were made from copper-coated electric wire about 3/16 of an inch thick and capable of holding up to 500 pounds.

Several of us concentrated on shark fishing. Because of the size of this fish, plus the danger of having even the strongest of lines severed by sharp coral rocks, we had to devise a method of setting the line.

About 150 yards of old Japanese telephone wire was extended from shore to a vinegar barrel anchored with a safety device. Canteen bottles were attached to the line as floats to prevent the heavy wire from becoming entangled with the jagged rocks.

At intervals were eight of the largest hooks we could make. Each hook was baited with a two-pound chunk of fish. At the shore end of the line was rigged up a salvaged canteen containing .45 caliber slugs to serve as an alarm or signal bell.

We hadn't as yet acquired a boat; so one of us had to swim out carrying the barrel, line and heavy coral rock anchor, while another man stood on shore holding the line high above the reefs. The rough sea oftentimes just about knocked us out, but the anticipation of catching another shark kept us going.

This primitive system soon gave way to modern design, however, when we transformed the discarded belly tank of a bomber into a boat. The tank was stabilized by outriggers consisting of oxygen tanks picked up in a salvage pit. Paddling was much easier than swimming, and landing sharks from the tub, buoyant as it was, turned out to be a bit safer than going into the water after them.

Even as it was, we had many close calls. I especially remember one incident in which my buddy, Sgt. Edward R. Roberts, and I were almost turned into shark bait.

We dispatched sharks with a harpoon fashioned from heavy pipe and shaped with a murderous-looking spearhead. When once this weapon was plunged into the hide of the fish, there was no dispute as to who was the victor.

This particular time, however, the spearhead snapped, and there I was, holding a 160-pounder with but a hook and line. It happened about two o'clock in the morning, and I let out a yell that awakened the entire camp.

Sgt. Roberts was one of the first to reach the beach, and he had the presence of mind to bring along his .45 automatic. He splashed and swam out to the boat, which by now was almost full of water. He handed me the gun with one hand, and with the other he steadied the wabbling craft, keeping it from capsizing as I struggled with the frenzied shark.

Then, just as the voracious fish was about to lunge at us with what would have been a fatal blow, I pulled the trigger twice, scoring a direct hit through the head. That was the closest we ever came to being carved into shark bait.

The fellows I had awakened got a big kick out of watching the moonlight battle, but I caught hell from the CO for using the .45; so the last laugh was on me.

⤝ ⩻⬥⩼ ⤞

A THRILLING EXPERIENCE that occurred before the boat was built happened about eight o'clock one evening while my buddies and I were resting in my tent. Suddenly we heard a racket coming from the "signal bell." We dashed down to the beach to find one of our men struggling with the line. He was just about ready to let go when I grabbed it. Boy, did I sail into the water! Managing to get back on my feet somehow while still hanging on to the line, I waded out to waist-deep water.

The wild fish was now identified as a shark of uncertain weight. He ran and thrashed for fifteen minutes before I could attempt to horse him in. Meanwhile my pals had armed themselves with clubs and had crept in behind me. They handed me one club after another, but five smacks across the back of the fish's head wouldn't quiet that baby. I wish I had known then what I know now—that a tap on the snoot would have knocked the fight out of him.

Finally I lost my grip on the line, but managed to get a bulldog hold on the monster's tail. I hung on for dear life, and what a beating I took! Then one of the fellows waded out with a bayonet and thrust it through the shark's head in five places. Another lad wound up the battle by smashing a log across its head, with me still hanging on.

It took three of us to drag him ashore. That devil was more than 7 feet long and weighed nearly 200 pounds!

Lt. Rogers likes to recall one particular evening of bait-casting off the pier:

"Sgt. Wanzung and I were fishing for groupers and red snappers. I was the first to get a strike, a sort of mild tug. I thought I had hooked into a grouper, but before I could even begin pulling in the click on my makeshift reel began singing. "My thumb bled as I attempted to apply the brakes to the rapidly unwinding line. The fish finally ended his headlong lunge and began to slowly circle back and forth. I gradually pumped him in until I was able to tow him to shallow water, where Sgt. Wanzung grabbed him with bare hands and brought him in. It was a barracuda.

"From the fight he had given me, I thought he would be at least a 40-pounder. However, he was only a little more than 3½ feet long and weighed 12½ pounds. I was using a 35-pound-test line and a light bamboo casting rod."

> *"One of the fellows waded out with a bayonet and thrust it through the shark's head."*

OUR LITTLE OUTFIT has bagged more than forty sharks, ranging from 70 pounds to 180. Many smaller ones were thrown back.

Aside from the very important morale value, fishing helped solve the food problem in the early phases of the Pacific fighting. For instance, the steaking of a 130-pound shark gives approximately 125 slices of meat averaging 12 ounces per cut. Lt. Rogers, a great lover of shark-steak dinners, says: "Contrary to popular belief, shark steak is actually delicious. The meat is firm and tastes like pork."

Redfish, barracuda and grouper are among the most common of other species caught in these tropical waters. Up to the start of the fall of 1944, our outfit had brought in more than 3,000 pounds of sharks and 500 pounds of other kinds of edible fish.

During recent months modern fishing equipment has been sent to us by our families. Restrictions forbid the sending of any heavy apparatus. Navy and Air Force pilots have been especially cooperative in bringing back from civilization the equipment often requested by us.

But it was during the days of the makeshift rod and reel that we managed to find peace despite the shocks of battle. As my commanding officer, Capt. Henry B. Elkind, Jr., says: "Whether his luck is good or bad; whether it is a barracuda, minnow or nothing, the American fighting man finds in fishing a happiness that no other sport affords. The monotony of overseas life can be harmful, and fishing is one of the best and simplest ways for a man to keep a healthy mind."

And as we steadily move farther northward our gang is looking forward to some fine fishing in Manila Bay and in the waters off Tokyo before returning to the best fishing grounds in the world—the United States.

—July, 1945

By E. L. (Buck) Rogers

A Saga of SURVIVAL

THE YOUNG PEACE Corps doctor leaned across the table and put his question bluntly.

"Just how fine is the line between life and death?" he asked.

"Too fine," I answered. "The difference is much less than most of us will ever know."

"What made the difference in your case?"

I hesitated a moment as the memory of the past several days welled up in me.

"The will to live certainly had a lot to do with it," I finally said.

"Yes, but physical condition is perhaps

most important," he argued. "When the body gives up so does the mind."

We argued the subject further, but what is more important is the experience which brought this discussion about. This incident has a few lessons for all of us.

It all started when a friend and I arrived with our wives in Santa Marta, Colombia, to explore the blue Caribbean waters with rod and reel. Since boats were in short supply, we bought a big dugout canoe and assigned a native shipwright the task of rebuilding it to our specifications. When the cayuca finally was completed, we hired a native lad to run it from the mouth of the Cienaga Grande up the coast to Rodadero Beach where we would meet him and later outfit our craft for fishing and navigation offshore.

But, at the last minute our plans went awry. Instead of heading out of the Cienaga Grande toward Rodadero, the native lad beached the boat at the mouth of the pass to the open ocean and informed us that he wouldn't make the journey alone. So, I volunteered to accompany him.

BUT I DIDN'T do so without a few qualms. My intuition said no to a sea voyage with no equipment aboard, and it was only the urgency of the moment which made me consider such action. We wanted to go fishing the following day and we had to have the boat at Rodadero to equip it. There were two hours of daylight left, and according to the lad hired to run the 40 horsepower outboard, we would make the trip up the coast in that length of time. I shook off my feelings of uneasiness, handed my passport and wallet to my friend, Homer, and the native youth and I headed out through the pass into the open sea and began our journey.

I was pleased with the performance of our new boat. She took the big waves of the pass with ease and when we opened up the motor in the smooth swells outside, the 30-foot cayuca planed off at a speed which I estimated at 16 mph or better. An hour and fifty minutes later we rounded the big rock on the south end of Rodadero Bay and headed toward the beach with its brightly lighted hotels and high-rise apartments. Closer and closer came the lights, and soon I could see Homer and our two wives standing on the beach awaiting our arrival. It was too dark for them to see us, but it would only be minutes before we would be on the beach conducting the little arrival ceremony which I knew Homer had planned.

Just then, however, the husky throb of the engine changed to a high pitched whine, as the excited native boy revved it a few times before turning it off. There had been a net in the water. We had struck it and had sheared a pin.

———— ✥✥✥ ————

TO PROPERLY DESCRIBE our predicament at this moment I must explain that Rodadero Beach lies almost in the shadow of the Sierra Nevada mountains. This isolated mountain range thrusts snow-capped peaks 20,000 feet into the air a few miles inland, and generates a strong offshore breeze which at this season of the year almost approaches a gale. This phenomenon makes this stretch of the Caribbean coast delightfully cool and pleasant, but it also creates a hazard for people in a predicament such as ours. Although we were less than 300 yards from the beach, the waves were 6 feet high and the strong wind was steadily blowing us out to sea. Of course, we yelled and I even thought about jumping overboard and swimming for it. But, in the end, I decided it would make more sense to stay with the boat, replace the pin, and make another approach to the beach.

I had a pair of rusty pliers which I had picked up at the last minute and two shear pins. So I signaled my companion to try to keep the bow of the canoe into the wind with a push pole, while I endeavored to change the pin. Leaning far over the transom of the boat with the darkness and waves blinding my efforts, I struggled with a stubborn cotter key. Haste was

important, but so was care. If I dropped the pliers overboard, all was lost. I couldn't fix it leaning over the transom.

So we wrestled the big engine into the canoe and I finally tore out the rusty cotter key and removed the propeller. Then came the job of changing the pin. I have done this innumerable times and knew the tolerance was close. But, in the wind, spray, and darkness the task proved to be impossible. The native boy was screaming in my ear and pointing to the disappearing lights, so I decided on an alternate course of action. I pulled a nail from the boat, inserted it in the propeller shaft, and bent it over. It would have to do. I have come home many a time with a nail, a bobby pin, or even a wooden match for a drive pin. Care was required though.

If the motor was shifted into gear at low speed, and was not accelerated too rapidly, that eight penny nail would take us back to safety. So I cautioned the youth with a solemn *despacio* and turned the motor back to him.

But, he was more excited than I anticipated. He started the motor in neutral, but when he shifted, he literally jammed the lever into gear and accelerated simultaneously. As a result, the propeller shaft sheared the nail and without a cotter key to hold it, the propeller spun off into the depths below. Now, we were helpless. There was no paddle, no sail. The waves were growing in size and the strong offshore wind was steadily blowing us straight out to sea.

Then I became sick. Perhaps it was all the salt water I had swallowed in my ordeal with the motor, perhaps it was the motion of our rolling boat, or perhaps it was the realization that now nothing further could be done to save our lives. Regardless, I lay in the bow with my head hanging over the gunwale and heaved everything that was in me.

All that night we drifted broadside to the big waves which slammed into the sides of our canoe, and when too much water came aboard I roused the boy and we bailed with the motor cover. He said that the seas would calm with the rising of the sun, so the two of us huddled together in the bow to keep warm, and I prayed that we would last through the night.

DAWN CAME WITH no abating of the waves and for the first time I could see the 40-foot mountains of water rise from the slate-colored ocean and literally hurl themselves at us. Suddenly, the fear that had been tranquilized by the cloak of night came back to me. Most of the waves broke within a few feet of us and only gave us a wild roller-coaster ride before leaving us behind in a foam-flecked watery valley. But, every now and then a wave came extremely close and I knew that it would only be a question of time before one broke right on top of us. This realization sent a cold shiver up my spine, and it wasn't alleviated by the realization that we also had company. The long shadowy shape that came out from under the bow of our canoe and made a slow circle around us was difficult to distinguish in the dawn light, but not difficult to identify. It was an 8-foot hammerhead shark and it stayed with us for several hours.

But, a man can get used to anything. When the sun finally broke through the line of clouds on the horizon, our attitude improved. I reasoned that if the waves hadn't sunk us during the night, then perhaps we could last indefinitely. And as long as two inches of wood hull separated us from the circling shark, we would remain in one piece. Soon the wind would shift and perhaps drive us up on a beach. Certainly, planes and boats would be searching for us and it would only be a question of time until we were rescued.

So, I forced a smile that I couldn't quite feel and said, "No problems, eh."

But, my companion didn't agree. As he watched the dorsal fin of the shark cutting the surface of the water a few yards away, he said distinctly, *"gringo loco...muchos problemos."*

Three airplanes flew over that morning, but in the wild white-cap flecked surface of the ocean our low silhouette dugout canoe was impossible to see. The same situation applied to the several boats that put out from Santa Marta that morning to search for us. With 40-foot waves blocking the horizon they didn't have a chance of spotting us, and their search was further complicated by the fact that the men who went aloft all got sick. Of course, I didn't know these things at the time, but when the third airplane finally appeared on the horizon, I realized that there was the possibility that we might not be found and I began to make plans for surviving on our own.

NATURALLY, I COULDN'T help thinking and dreaming about the store of equipment I had back in my room at Rodadero Beach. There I had a plastic drop cloth which I could have used as a solar still and distilled enough fresh water to keep us alive indefinitely. There was a stout nylon line and a sea anchor which would have kept our bow into the wind and would have almost eliminated the danger of swamping. I dreamed of the knife which would have allowed me to carve a good propeller, or the sail which we could have rigged to blow us southward to the shore which I knew was there. My supply of stores contained flares, a signaling mirror, life preservers, complete first-aid kit; everything necessary for us to stay alive and bring rescue planes to our side. Particularly, I dreamed about all the fishing tackle that was stacked in the corner of my room, because fish were everywhere. Several other sharks joined the first one and kept us company throughout the rest of the day. Schools of bonito and other bait fish swarmed just beneath the surface and attracted schools of mackeral and dolphin which churned the water to a frenzy in their feeding sprees. With a hook and line I know I could have caught enough fish to feed us well.

But, the stark reality of our desperate situation kept coming back to me. I had nothing; not a knife, hook, match; nothing. My only tools were the pliers and a nail, so we put them to use.

With the nail I carved a propeller from a piece of the boat. It took nine hours, and my hands were bleeding before the job was done. But, it was something to do, and there was the possibility that this stick revolving in the water could alter our course if the waves ever subsided. I knew calm water was necessary because this was my second effort. My other crude propeller was smashed to bits by a wave during the first moment that it began to revolve in the water.

The wind continued to blow us parallel to the Colombia coast and I cursed it for not swinging to the north and bringing us up on the sandy beach that lay just beyond the haze on the southern horizon. Perhaps we would eventually end up in Panama, but land in that direction was a long way off, and I doubted if we'd be alive when we made it. But, we had to. I knew it was possible for a man to go five days without food and water if he conserved his strength and body moisture, and I vowed that I would do so.

———— ⨂ ————

IT WAS THEN that I gave serious thought to my companion. This native youth had apparently given up all hope, but in the process he was doing exactly the right thing. The only time he moved was when I roused him from his lethargy to help bail the boat. The rest of the time he huddled in the shade of the forward deck and appeared to doze. In the meantime, I was exposed to the sun and was utilizing my strength carving out the propeller. The boy didn't know as much about the art of survival as I did, but his animal instincts were serving him well.

As I pondered over this situation, I wondered what our relationship would be during the fourth or fifth day. Even after 20 hours, my veneer of civilization had worn thin, and the boy had started with a good deal less than I. From a very practical standpoint, each of us represented sustenance and life for the other, and I wondered if his instinct for survival was strong enough to prompt him to kill me for nourishment. Or how about me? Which of us would weaken first? If fate decreed that only one of us would live to tell the tale, which would it be?

While I was thinking about this some dolphin flushed a school of flying fish from the blue depths and one of them landed aboard our craft. I pounced on it before it could escape, and carefully wrapped it in a wet cloth. A few days later this little morsel would take on the significance of a full-course meal, I thought.

The waves continued to pound us unmercifully throughout the day and I decided that we were lucky to be in a heavy dugout canoe. A conventional boat would have been destroyed many hours ago. Yes, our craft was strong, but it was still a helpless thing at the mercy of the seas. How much longer could it last? As the sun began to set, the big "terror" waves began to get more frequent and for the first time since dawn, I began to worry about capsizing.

As the shadow of darkness spared us the sight of white-capped waves on the horizon, the boy and I saw lights flickering in the distance.

"*Qué es esto?*" I asked.

"Barranquilla," the youth said.

Was it possible, I thought. Could we have drifted 60 miles since our accident? It seemed impossible, but Barranquilla was the only city this size on the entire Caribbean coast. It had to be.

I didn't realize it at the time, but those lights winking in the distance indicated that we were approaching the mouth of the big Magdalena River. Here, a mighty river battled the ocean for supremacy and created a maelstrom of violence that only the experienced pilots navigated in broad daylight. We didn't know what we were getting into.

From sundown until 10 P.M. we shivered from the unrelenting wind and spray and flinched with each blow from the heavy waves. Finally, one struck us at the wrong angle and filled our cayuca half full of water. Sensing disaster, both the boy and I lurched for the motor cover and began to bail desperately. But the boy kept looking back over his shoulder as we worked, and was able to shout a cry of warning before the worst wave of all lifted our canoe, turned it slowly, and slammed it back into the ocean upside down.

———— ⨂ ————

I FOUND MYSELF under the boat and had to fight downward before I bobbed to the surface beside our capsized craft. Immediately a churning, hissing wave struck me, filled my mouth with water, and drove my head beneath the surface. Gagging for breath, I fought my way back to the slick black surface that was the bottom of our overturned cayuca, and clung there. The boy, who had been nearer to the bow when we capsized, had his legs wrapped around the bowsprit and was fairly secure. My position was more precarious. For the next two hours I clung to the side of the slick boat and tried to dodge the big waves that churned by me at 30-second intervals.

Perhaps I grew weak, perhaps I became careless, or perhaps destiny intervened. Perhaps it really was "my time." Suddenly one powerful torrent of water tore me away from the boat and in the next moment I found myself alone in the darkness, gasping for breath, and cursing the wave which had parted me from the boat. I tore off my shoes, I remember, and for many minutes thereafter I struggled to stay on the surface.

Finally, I became so tired that I could hardly lift my arms. So I asked myself, Why continue to fight the inevitable? How long could you have lasted clinging to an overturned canoe, but without it what chance do you have? I was tired. God, I was tired. My body was a limp thing that the waves tossed around at will, and even a stubborn will to live was succumbing to the inevitable. Stop fighting, I told myself. You're so tired. Relax. Close your eyes and slide downward into the depths where all is peace and quiet.

I was very close to death at this point, closer than I had ever been. My mind was arguing with my body, but as the doctor later said, the body usually wins in such cases.

Then I heard the cry, "Gringo, Gringo." It was from far away and in the spray-filled darkness, I could see nothing, couldn't even tell what direction it was coming from. But, it was something. As this cry penetrated my being, I struggled out of my lethargy and thought about life and all of the exciting things I had yet to do. I can't die, I told myself. I can't die now. I slowly lifted one arm, followed it with another, and fought my way through the heavy seas toward the sound of the boy's voice. Finally, I saw the low black silhouette of the canoe, reached its side, and clung there with renewed strength.

Back at Rodadero Beach my wife suddenly awoke from a drugged sleep and glanced at her watch. It was midnight. She walked to the balcony and looked out at the sea as she had been doing continuously since my absence. But now there was a difference. The wind had died down to a whisper and Rodadero Bay was as quiet as a millpond. "Maybe," she thought wildly, "there's still hope."

Midnight on that particular night proved to be charged with magic because it was precisely at the stroke of 12:00 when my feet touched the sand and I staggered through the surf to fall face down on the beach at Bocas de Ceniza.

The rest of the actual story is an anti-climax. We hiked 10 miles across a swamp to the nearest farmhouse, talked the man into ferrying us across the river in his dugout canoe, and I finally got to a telephone at 7 A.M. to call off the search that was getting into full swing.

<hr />

I LEARNED A few things during this little adventure which will stand me in good stead in future wilderness outings and perhaps may prove helpful to you, also. Let me summarize a few of them.

1. Always be prepared for an emergency in the field. I almost lost my life because I wasn't, and I can assure you that it will never happen again. Today, I carry a small compass, a pocketknife, and a book of matches everywhere I go; even to the office. And, when I go out in the bush I take a complete survival kit. I admit I'm more gunshy than most, but the advice is still good—include a compass, matches, knife, length of nylon cord, small first aid kit, etc., on all wilderness outings.

2. Keep in shape. As I told that Peace Corps doctor the will to live is extremely important, but if I hadn't had the strength to swim that last 100 yards, I wouldn't be here today. The fact that I quit smoking six months previously might have been a factor, too.

3. Keep fighting to survive. You must do this, because when you're tired, death represents a chance to rest, and when you're freezing, it is warmth. In a situation like this, the toughest thing you have to do is maintain your instinct to live.

4. Lack of food and water is not really the hardship that we imagine. I, frankly, just shut the lack of it out of my mind and concentrated on survival, using what tools were available to keep my attention off impending death. I believe I could have gone for another two days without extreme discomfort.

—June, 1969

By William F. McIlrath

Adventures
IN THE NIGHT

YOU DON'T HAVE TO HUNT AND FISH IN FAR-OFF PLACES FOR EXCITEMENT. THERE'S PLENTY OF IT CLOSE TO HOME.

IT IS QUIET HERE IN THE den. The kids have gone to bed. The radio is turned low. Somewhere in the kitchen or the back bedroom my wife is making busy little sounds. It's the quiet season, too. The ice is forming on the lakes.

I look out into the dark and count the days to the opening of trout season. I lift the

sixteen, take a couple of dry swings. I leaf a copy of FIELD & STREAM, but see that I haven't missed a thing. So I settle into the chair, light a cigarette, watch the smoke curl up through the lamp shade, and wonder what there is to all this hunting and fishing.

People have hunted and fished all over the world. Some travel thousands of miles to do it. Not because they're hungry, not just to kill, certainly not to satisfy themselves that they are smarter than fish and animals. They want adventure.

Adventure! Somehow the word has always aroused in me thoughts of distant places—Nairobi, the Himalayas, Point Barrow, the Amazon. But the world has gone haywire, and I discover things here tonight. I look around the den and come to know that the things we have right here at home are every bit as good, just as potent with adventure, as those greener pastures that have lured fishermen and hunters to the other side of the world in other years.

Maybe there is a man who has had a great adventure looking down his sights at a charging rhino. I had adventure the night I jumped from

the shore of Pine Lake out toward the edge of the ice and plunged through a crust into two feet of cold, wet goo.

Maybe there's another who found adventure on the side of a glacier, digging his fingers into the ice to save himself from a plunge to certain death. I had adventure enough the night I was racing after Mutt, the coon dog, and did a handless chin-up on a strand of fence-wire in Uncle Roy's woods.

Adventure comes with the night, under skies black with mystery or sparkling with unreachable beauty, in woods rustling with stealth, when there are no horizons, no up, no down. A man is on his own then. Whether it be the weight of black water smashing at his legs as he gropes for the creek bottom, the blast of blizzard snow in his face as he claws his way across the ice, the whistle of a rising storm as his boat pitches in waves that he can feel but not see, or whether it is just the fear of the unknown which he shares with all men, I don't know.

Those things are vital and heart-chilling when they happen; they leave no time for thoughts of adventure then. Frankly, when they happened to me, I was frightened. Maybe I wanted it that way; I didn't go out looking for fright, but I certainly put myself in a place where it could come. The fright came—and now it has gone. And tonight, because it's snug here and the lights are low and the music gentle, and I can lay my head back in the chair and think of them again, those things have become adventures.

All around me here in the den are my keys to adventure—adventure in the night. There's my fly rod, lying in its case beneath the bookcase. Not an expensive one, not fancy, but Old Reliable to me. It has a set in one tip. A couple of windings have been replaced in an odd color. Varnish has covered most of the scratches. I think of the night when Matt and Ernie and I—and this rod—opened the trout season at midnight on Big Creek.

The night was icy cold. We fished for two hours and caught nothing. There were still four hours to sunrise when Matt and Ernie chipped the worms from their hooks, peeled the ice from their lines, and walked off to the car for coffee and a nap.

I heard their voices die in the dark. The car door slammed and left me alone, with the creek flowing black and deep beside me. I was debating whether to follow them when a splash sounded from the stream.

A sudden eagerness, a swarm of "I'll-show-them" ideas, warmed me, and I stepped hip-deep into the water. One foot slipped off a ledge of marl, and the world lurched. The creek rolled into my boots. I grabbed for a branch, then for the bank. There was no branch, no bank, nothing anywhere in reach—only the black sky and churning water.

When at last I dug my fingers into the bank, the mud felt alive and elusive. Roots broke as I clutched them. Twice I slipped, spread-eagled. My legs were shaking and my heart pounding as I struggled up the bank at last in boots heavy and stiff with their weight of water.

I found dry wood and some matches in a water-tight container, and when the moon came up around two-thirty I had a fire crackling not far from the stream. My boots were draining and warming on stakes. Socks and pants hung, steaming, over a branch. My hat was dry.

Slowly my pulse returned to cruising speed, and the chill thawed away. I baited in the warmth of the fire and sneaked through the frost-stiff grass in bare feet to the edge of the stream. Crouching, so that my long woolens wouldn't glare in the moonlight, I fed a night-crawler into the hole below me. I had a hit, but missed. Shivering, I scurried back to the fire to warm up.

For nearly two hours I played tag with that trout until finally, after my ninth or tenth retreat to the fire, he took the hook. His brother did the same just before dawn, and when Matt and Ernie wandered along, bleary-eyed and cold, I had two nice trout.

The rest of the day was trout fishing—nice, but plain, unadorned, unadventurous. In the night, from ducking to dawn, I had had my adventure. I had it in the stream, fighting to get out. I had it at the fire in the moonlight,

and in the moments of contemplation beside my steaming boots and pants. I had it in the furtive planning, the frosty sneaks to the stream, and finally in the feeling that only I was able to catch a trout at 4 A.M. in the moonlight, in my underpants.

Tonight it's quiet and restful here in my chair. The chill of that episode has gone, but not the thrill—the adventure.

Up over the top of the bookcase I see the handle and rawhide thong of my ice spud. My wife didn't want me to bring "that rusty old thing" in here. But we have something in common, that spud and I. We've been out at night on the ice.

One night we were out on Magician Lake about two hours after sunset. With the spud I had cut two holes, about five inches across, in the ice. I sat between them, a kerosene lantern before me. Two rods were at my feet, their tips over the saucers of open water. Bobbers the size of white-oak acorns floated between spears of forming ice.

I had no more than settled on my haunches when one of the corks quivered and started to sink, slowly, as if it were waterlogged. With one hand on the rod, I let the bobber get down a foot. Then I set the hook and jumped up. Dropping the rod, I pulled the line in hand over hand until a calico bass flopped out at my feet. I baited up with another small minnow and settled back to an occasional jigging of the rod and long moments of waiting.

The circle of ice lit by my lantern became a world of my own. The flame seemed a symbol of life, and in its flickerings I read the answers to some of my problems of the day. Across the black void of the lake I saw the glow of other fishermen's lanterns, each a world of its own, satellites to my sun.

Later, as things became dull, I wandered over and swapped guesses with some of the other fishermen—Doc and Bob and a few I didn't know. Guesses about the ice, the temperature. I discovered Marvin back in a bay, and asked him how deep he was fishing and if he was doing anything. He just mumbled, "Naw."

Then I went back to my lantern and my thoughts, supreme in my world. One by one the lanterns of the others edged away, blinked into the woods at shore, and fluttered out. Then I left too, sated with the adventure of having lived for a few hours in a world of my own.

It's a different sort of adventure I share with that paint-chipped luminous plug up there on the what-not shelf.

Last summer Bob and I pushed Dan's mossy scow out into Pitcher Lake one night, about the time the sun was spinning its last rays around the spire of Silver Creek church. The red of the west was deepening into violet, and a breeze, rustling the leaves, hushed the birds.

Out on the lake, we cast where we thought there might be open water. A splash rose to our right, and Bob whipped back his favorite plug and let it ride for a mile. Or maybe two miles, I don't know—it never hit the water.

We listened. The bullfrogs baloorped and the crickets quee-eeked, and the boat rocked so gently that it might have been from our breathing. Silently we rowed toward where we thought the plug might be—and came quite unexpectedly to the shore. It was a relief to find the plug swinging daintily from a willow, ten feet from the water.

Then there was the time Pete and I were out on Coldwater Lake, rapid-firing our plugs into schools of small bass foaming in the shallows. We had our fill of fun that night—drifting in the moonlight, singing, laughing, trading confidences, sharing long moments of silence. When it was time to go in, I flipped a gum wrapper overboard. Minutes later I saw the wrapper floating beside us.

"Hey! Haul in that anchor!" I bawled.

But Pete hadn't thrown it out.

He watched the wrapper as I stroked with the oars.

"We're not going anywhere," he gulped.

It was dark. The moon had gone down. Somewhere ashore a screech-owl sounded ten miles away. Our guesses sounded weird; so we just sat. In two minutes Pete came to mean more to me as a friend, as a buddy with whom to share adventure, than in the years before or after.

At length I jerked an oar from its lock, plumbed for bottom, and hit it hard at two feet. I groped to a seat beside Pete in the stern, to let the bow ride high, and together we paddled overside with our hands. We drifted off a post that someone had driven into the lake for some fool reason, where we could float atop it in the night.

That's the kind of adventure one shares only with those who have been there. It needs no telling for them, because the thoughts live long afterward. It's an adventure in hushed silence, in comradeship, in anticipation, and in appreciation.

There is another kind of adventure, like the one I share with the scuffed, high-laced boots over there beside the gun. That is an adventure of swirling excitement.

I went out to my wife's folks one fall, and her brother, C. J., asked me if I wanted to go coon hunting. He said he had a hound, Mutt, an open trailer sort of coon dog which expected the hunter to be there when he treed. C. J. promised that Mutt, in contrast to the patient, silent-trailer type, would sing out every moment he was on a trail. He did.

C. J. carried the lantern and I the gun. We crossed the alfalfa field, and Mutt cut trail. Lord knows how much of a head start that coon had on us, but it was not enough to discourage the dog. Mutt started away from there vociferously. C. J., with the lantern, started after Mutt. I staggered along behind.

On and on through the night I crashed after them. I crossed a field of corn stubble, stumbling over the short-cut stalks, pounding my toes into long ridges of dirt. I pursued them into Aunt Katie's woods, where blackberry brambles snatched at me. An old log caught me knee-high and sent me sprawling. The devil himself lashed me twice across the face with a branch.

C. J. sensed my anguish, stopped to sympathize, then plunged on as Mutt cried again. He swung his lantern in his stride, so that one moment he blinded me with light, the next left me groping in shadow. The intermittent flashes set the woods to jumping; so the whole world seemed to jerk along a flash at a time, like a movie film run too fast in its projector.

I plunged across a small gully, plodded

ankle-deep in the muck of a cabbage patch, and stood dumbfounded in a field of standing corn while Mutt and C. J.—and, I presume, the coon—made a complete circle around me. I thought the coon might be a dozen coons, or a rabbit, or just a hope. This might be a cross-country race, or a nightmare. Then I recalled C. J.'s assurances that Mutt chased nothing but coons, and I took off through the night for another five hundred miles.

About one-thirty Mutt caught up with the coon, C. J. caught up with Mutt, and I gasped out of the darkness to find them at the foot of a beech tree. Mutt was clawing the bark, leaping to reach higher. As I came up he looked at me and wagged his tail with enthusiasm and pride. He circled the tree, nose to the ground, to show me he couldn't be wrong, then lifted his voice to the heavens again in a howling plea for a coup to end the chase.

C. J. swept his flashlight through the branches, prying into every fork. At first I had libelous doubts about it all. Then I saw two pale-green lights glow in the beam as it swept to the top of the tree. C. J. grunted. "See him?"

"Sure."

He stepped behind me and flashed the light over my shoulder. I put a cartridge into the breech of the single-shot .22, slipped the bolt home, and raised the gun.

C. J. cautioned me to hold right between the eyes, so as not to spoil the pelt. I shot and missed. I shot again, and heard the bullet hit. The lights in the tree went out, and the coon came down with a scratch and a thump. Mutt pounced on it, and, with all the growling and body-flinging of a fight with a lion, gripped it until C. J. pried his jaws apart.

I laid the coon aside as C. J. held the dog. I smoothed its fur, felt its layers of fat, hefted it and guessed eighteen pounds. Then I stuffed it into C. J.'s game pocket, and we led Mutt off to another spot.

This time I carried the lantern, and set it on a stump while Mutt ranged around us. I could hear C. J. breathing. I heard his hand whisk over the bulge at the back of his hunting coat. Neither of us talked. Mutt, too, was silent, but when I heard a branch snap and wings thunder as a pheasant took flight I knew he was running, nose to the ground.

The woods loomed before me like a great curtain. I stepped in front of the lantern to see better into the dark. Then Mutt sang again, and off we went, tripping, stumbling, cursing through the night.

In the morning I rolled over in the great feather bed and muttered, "What a gosh-awful way to spend a night."

At noon I fed on coon meat until I never wanted to move again.

That night, after supper dishes were done, I was in the kitchen with C. J., flipping ashes into the front grate of the wood range and talking of nothing special. I walked to the window and looked into the dark. The wind sounded soft and gentle. From the woodshed I heard the hound whine pleadingly.

I caught C. J. watching me. "What are you gaping at?" I demanded.

He grinned.

Through the doorway I saw my wife, leafing through last week's paper at the dining-room table. I cleared my throat. She looked first at the clock, then at me. She saw in me a guy who goes trout fishing at midnight, ice-fishing in the dark, lake fishing at sundown—and now coon hunting. She shook her head pityingly, and said, "See you in the morning, darling."

I was afraid, that night, she just didn't understand this business of finding adventure.

And now here she is again, looking into the den and wanting to know what I'm doing in here all alone. You see, she still doesn't understand.

—December, 1948

By Archibald Rutledge

Death in the
MOONLIGHT

DEATH WAS UPON ME. I WAS AT CLOSE QUARTERS WITH A WHITE SHARK OF HUGE PROPORTIONS.

*I*F AT NIGHT YOU HAPPEN to be standing up to your shoulders in salt water, when the wind is still and the tide is tranquil, in a creek not far from the ocean, and you suddenly feel a strange warm wave softly climb your neck and fondle your throat, all I have to say is, look out! I was so standing one moonlight night when just such a ghastly wave began to get intimate with me. Then terrible things happened, there in the murky water and the misty moonshine. A monster of the deep tried to do me to death—that's what happened. To this day I carry the physical scars of that encounter; and there's a scar on my mind too, a mute testimonial of my ordeal on that dread night.

My older brother and I had gone fishing down to the mouth of Ramshorn Creek. It was not sport with us, but a business. For several years we literally fished for a living. At night we used the gill seine profitably in the mouths of creeks on the young flood-tide. After setting the net entirely across the mouth of a creek, we would divide forces. I usually stayed by the seine and took out the mullets, whiting, school bass and other table fish as they gilled themselves. My brother took an oar and wandered up the edges of the creek, striking the water and otherwise disturbing the fish so that they would make a break down the estuary for the bay.

It was so on this night. I went into the water with no premonition of trouble. It was routine, and I had long been used to it. My raiment consisted merely of an old pair of trousers.

Deep night lay over the wide Carolina marshes, the mazy creeks that meandered lazily through them, the dim hummocks, the purple wall of pinewood that marked the line of the mainland to westward. Far off could faintly be heard the soft roar of the surf falling sleepily on the drowsy shores of Cape Romain. Moonlight silvered the scene, touching with tender radiance the frayed reeds, the glimmering oyster-banks, the gleaming tide. But the light was not brilliant; a lacy mist lay here and there over the dim waters and the marsh.

I could hear all the night noises, with which I had long since been familiar: the rush of a school of fish in the shallow waters on the bay-edge when a porpoise got after them; the melancholy grunting croak of a great blue heron; the mellow fluting of the willets; the weird intoning of a great horned owl from the dense red cedars on a lonely hummock. These sounds might make an amateur uneasy; but I was used to them all, and it was with our customary unconcern that my brother and I staked one end of our seine at the north side of Ramshorn Creek, and then, paying out the net as we rowed across the mouth, staked the other end at the south side. We had the long, winding estuary closed off. The boat we tied just outside the net, so that I could conveniently throw the fish in as they were gilled.

THERE WAS A lot of phosphorescence in that water that night, and I could distinctly see the pale fiery outlines of some fish as they struck. But I did not enter the water until several energetic captives had begun to make it foam wildly near the surface. By this time my brother was two hundred yards up the creek, shouting and spanking the water with his oar to frighten the fish down.

When I thought that we had about a dozen mullets and sea-trout gilled, I waded into the warm water to begin taking them out. The water at its deepest part took me about the shoulders. I worked my way to the far side of the net and was almost halfway back across, with the water up to my breast, when suddenly it happened. At the time I had my arms raised above my head, a big fish in each hand, just ready to heave them into the boat.

BEFORE THIS SINISTER stranger struck me, and just as I threw the poised fish, I was dimly aware of a monstrous show of phosphorescence and of a diabolical shape almost beside me. The next second the Thing massively brushed my left leg between the knee and the thigh, and instantly the salt water burned me like fire. When I ran my hand down in the water to see what had happened, I found that my trouser leg had been rasped away where this malignant phantom had bruised me, and that my leg was raw and bleeding.

At the same moment there came that ghoulish warm wave fondling my throat. In that creek mouth, there in the moonlight, with my brother far away, Death was upon me. I knew it. I felt it.

I was at close quarters with a white shark of huge proportions. He had drawn blood by rushing against me; his hide, as rough as sandpaper, had frayed both my clothing and my flesh. I looked wildly about and tried to discern in the water the position of this ruthless terror of the deep. I did not know which way to run. And all the while the placid moonlight slept on the world, and the willets fluted, and the faint echo of my brother's voice came to me from half a mile away.

As you can imagine, in my direful plight, all that I knew of the character and behavior of the white shark, a dread visitor from the West

Indies into our waters, suddenly rushed over me. George Eagan had been killed by a shark in Bull's Bay. I had seen his body, and was sorry that I had. In Wappoo Cut, Captain Fritz had been savagely mauled by one of these monsters, and had barely escaped with his life. By one of these prodigious brutes Charlie Deas had been killed in the surf at Sandy Point, within full sight of a dozen horrified bathers. And my own boyhood chum, Olaf Svensen, son of the keeper of Romain Light, had met the same fate in Roman Inlet—not half a mile from where I stood—literally in the jaws of death.

While every man is entitled to his opinion, I believe that a fifteen-foot white shark on a blood trail at night is about as deadly a creature as a man will ever encounter—especially since in the water, a man is out of his element. People need not talk to me about sharks being harmless. I have seen men dead by their killing. And I have had one of these burly ruffians after me.

In the midst of my wild thoughts, another wave washed me—this time going almost over my head. I plunged blindly for the shore, pulling on the seine to help me through the mud and water. While thus blundering madly toward the bank, and while I was thrusting my arms forward at full length to grip the seine to steady me and for a purchase to pull, I thrust my left hand up to the wrist full into the open mouth of the shark, now headed straight for me.

Whether he meant to seize me bodily or had his mouth partly open on account of his lust for the blood scent in the water, I do not know. But I know that I felt his cold, hard lips and the serried ranks of his fearful teeth. I jerked my hand back and floundered madly for shore, his huge bulk knocking me heavily against the seine as I passed him. I was on the slope now, but the mud and water were deep, and at every instant I expected the gray barbarian to make his final rush and drag me down.

What chance had I, or would any man have, against such an awful brute?

God knows why, but it never happened. I got out safely, and lay there on the bank in the mocking moonlight. My leg was stiff and sore; my side ached. When I looked down at my left hand, it was streaming blood. I found out after I got home that I had fourteen deep gashes in it—weird crisscross cuts and slashes from those razors in the monster's mouth. I tried to stand up and call my brother, but my voice failed me. I looked down at the seine, and suddenly saw both sustaining poles collapse violently into the water.

As the tide was flowing in, our commotion in the creek had not disturbed the waters of the bay, which shone tranquil and still. Through them now, as I gazed fascinated, I saw this murderous chimera, blazing in the lurid phosphorescence as if he were aflame, heading slowly seaward—an irresistible primal thing, cruel and cold, powerful, treacherous, ghoulish. Ghostly and pale in the haunting moonlight I saw his tall white dorsal fin cleave the water—like the periscope of some tremendous submarine about to deal death to its victim. I shivered as I watched that ponderous destroyer fade from sight. But for the mercy of God I might have been in those jaws, dead in the moonlit waters.

Whenever we went home, we hung up our net to dry. My brother did that work this night. The next morning I saw him standing by the seine, shaking his head as if to rid himself of an evil thought. As I came up he pointed to the net. Straight through the middle of it was a huge, ragged hole. When we measured it, we found it to be 2 feet 9 inches in diameter.

Although this incident happened thirty-five years ago, my scars, as I have said, are still with me, and with me still is the vivid memory of that dreadful placid night when Death stalked me in the moonlight.

—September, 1933

By C. R. Gutermuth

LIFE HUNG ON AN 18-THREAD

FATE AND FISHING SKILL WERE ALL THAT SAVED THESE THREE SAILFISH ANGLERS WHEN THEY WERE SWEPT OVER-BOARD IN A GULF STREAM HURRICANE.

THE UNCERTAIN LIGHT of a December dawn found Bess and me preparing to leave Baker's Haulover, near Miami, for another try for a record sailfish. Although the weather looked rather nasty, about like the two previous days, we were eager to get in at least one more day of fishing before heading back to work. There was no sunrise, merely a rosy hue behind a curtain of dense gray clouds. The weather signs held no promise of fair weather, neither did they forecast the nightmarish squall that, unknown to us, was sweeping landward from the middle Atlantic.

While the cabin boy was stowing things aboard and I was rigging our tackle, Shorty, the skipper of the 34-foot cabin cruiser, tinkered with the engine. Glancing up from the job of oiling my reel, I noticed a middle-aged fellow leaning on the dock railing watching our every action.

"Good morning," he said with a grin. "Sure hope you have good luck."

Everything about the fellow—his smile, cheerfulness and easy manner—stamped him as the kind of man one likes to have along as a fishing companion. Even before I knew it, I found myself inviting him aboard for the day.

He laughed. "Sailfishing's beyond me. Looks mighty good, but my pocketbook will only stand for snapper fishing from the piers." "Don't worry about that part of it," I replied. "The boat is chartered, and I have more than enough tackle for all of us. All you need to do is run up to that refreshment stand and pick up a little food to supplement what we have in the basket."

"I'll take you up on that," he said after a moment of hesitation. Without knowing it, he had made a decision that meant the difference between life and death for my wife and me.

AT 7:30, WITH Captain Shorty at the helm, the boat was nosing out of Biscayne Bay into the choppy waters of the Atlantic. Seated in the stern of the cockpit, Bess and I got acquainted with our guest who, we learned, was Ray G. Myers, a vacationing automobile dealer from Canal Fulton, Ohio.

A few miles offshore we cast over lines and began trolling for kingfish. Before reaching the Gulf Stream we had taken a dozen of these gamy speedsters, the largest of which tipped the scales at 24 pounds. Myers, new at this kind of fishing, was having the time of his life. He leaned back happily in his chair, handling the rod with the skill of an expert as one particularly heavy king stripped out line.

"Feels like a good one," he remarked.

The fish was fighting close to the surface now and the line gradually building up on Myers' reel. Then suddenly there was a swirl of white astern and a brief tug of war before the arched bamboo snapped back to normal. Myers' grin faded as he reeled in and lifted aboard the mangled head and dangling inwards of a kingfish that would have weighed 30 pounds.

"Porpoise, or maybe sharks," said Shorty laconically, glancing back from the wheel. "Tough luck. He got the eating part."

A short time later we were in the Gulf Stream, eleven miles offshore, and on word from the captain we rigged for sailfish. It was good fishing weather, even though the clouds grew heavier and the low scud swept by, driven by increasing winds.

We had dragged the teaser only a few minutes when Bess shouted "Strike!" and flicked the free-spool lever, letting the bait fall back. After counting to ten, as Myers and I reeled in our baits to prevent fouling, she set the hook. The fish sped away, pulling against the heavy drag, and then zoomed out of the crest of a wave and, with fin high and shaking head, tail-walked along the frothy surface. The bait shot into the air and Bess fell back, her expression of anticipation giving way to one of disappointment.

The clouds grew darker and the wind sharper during this brief fight. A few sea birds hurried toward land, flying in low silent flocks. I went into the wheelhouse, put on a leather jacket, and threw an oilskin around Bess' shoulders. Myers struggled into a raincoat. A few minutes later a squall-driven cloud of mist swept in and the rain poured down upon us, beating the seas to milky white.

Just as I was about to suggest that we start for shore another fish struck my bait. The count and strike was right, and he stripped out the line. Through the spray we saw him dimly as he took to the air to free himself from the hook. The wind drove the spray and rain into our faces as the fight continued. One, two, three, four—he broke water seven times. A half hour later, as the captain grasped the bill of the exhausted fish and we hauled the shimmering six feet ten inches of silver and blue aboard, the wind was commanding attention.

Shorty turned a worried face to us. "We've got to run for it," he shouted to make himself heard. "This is worse than I thought."

We had two choices, Shorty explained to me as I went forward. We could try to make the main channel to Biscayne Bay, but that would put us on a course parallel with the mounting waves; or we could quarter away from them toward Baker's Haulover. Wisely he decided to take the latter course.

From the northeast, behind us, a low-hanging black cloud was bearing down at incredible speed. Almost as soon as we saw it, it was upon us. Violent seas lifted our small craft and tossed it as a pinecone might bob in a trout-stream rapids. The surface of the water churned from gray to white. A wave would tower twelve feet above us one moment, and in the next we would be on a foaming crest, the propeller chattering clear of the water.

Yawing and writhing, the boat labored shoreward. Four miles yet to go, then suddenly a wall of black water swept toward us from the mists. I saw it tower, almost perpendicular above the boat—a "line-wave," riding the crest of another comber.

Then it struck. The boat was lifted like a chip and I heard screams. Lowering my head, I clutched at the chair. The boat suddenly seemed to fall from under me, leaving me suspended for a moment in the air before I sprawled into the raging sea. Fighting my way to the surface, I struggled for breath. I tried to shout, but the wind tore the words from my lips. Salt water choked me and spray filled my eyes.

Suddenly, a short distance away against the green wall of a wave, I saw Bess. The boat was nowhere to be seen. As a wave raised me I saw Myers, and beyond him the pitching boat. Futilely cursing Shorty for not having fastened his chairs to the deck, I swam to the side of Bess, who was pawing desperately. As I reached her she grabbed me around the neck.

"You must let go!" I screamed and, contrary to all rules, domestic and otherwise, she obeyed. Later we found that she had struck the gunwale with such force when she went over the side that the muscles of one thigh were severely crushed. If the skin had been broken, the sharks might have ended the story right there.

Myers, a strong swimmer, who could have gone for the boat, proved his mettle by fighting his way to our side. "Can she swim?" he shrieked. "No," I said as we struggled to keep her up between us.

Swimming frantically, each with one arm, we waited for the boat to turn and rescue us. About five minutes passed. Shorty, on the drifting boat, sixty yards away now, was futilely throwing life-preservers toward us. Why doesn't he come back? Choking under incessant waves, spray and rain, we stroked and stroked with aching arms. Ten minutes went by, then fifteen. Bess had passed out. In the distance, another

boat was going for shore. Shorty waved his arms and the cabin boy yelled, but the occupants either did not see us or did not care to risk their own lives in a rescue attempt.

Twenty minutes—how long will one arm keep moving? I passed out once, but as I slowly descended into the storm-roiled waters the other arm brought me up again. We could see Shorty and his helper frantically moving around deck, and with mounting panic realized that the boat was disabled. Four miles from shore without life-preservers in a tropical hurricane with nothing substantial in sight except a disabled and powerless boat, which was getting farther and farther away. Despair came closer as hope of rescue faded. It was no longer a matter of life and death, but one of time.

AS I PEERED after the boat, something which spanned the crest of the waves attracted my attention. For an instant I failed to recognize it as the trolling line still dangling from the one rod that had not been thrown from the boat when the wave struck. Eighteen-thread line tests only 54 pounds, but it was our one hope of rescue. Leaving Myers to keep Bess afloat, I fought my way toward it and finally grasped the slender thread. Vaguely I remember telling myself that if this did not save us it might take a meal away from the sharks. As I swam back to Bess and Myers I wrapped the line around my arm with each stroke. From the boat, Shorty had seen the maneuver and had presence of mind enough to pay out line instead of trying to save me alone.

Renewed hope vanquished thoughts of fatigue. In a weakened but determined effort, without releasing the line from my arm, we wrapped a number of hitches around Bess' limp body, and Myers threw a few turns of it around his wrist. Slowly the slender green cord tightened. Shorty was beginning to reel us in as he might have brought in a completely beaten sailfish. The line and light rod strained with the pitching of the boat. This line, which less than an hour ago meant death to a sailfish, could mean life to us now.

We moved forward slowly, the line biting into our wrists as the combers lifted us.

Minutes later, an eternity to us, we were near enough to the boat to see Shorty's anxious, tight-lipped face as he pumped and reeled, pumped and reeled, bringing us nearer and nearer to the tossing boat. There are several blank spaces in my memory of what happened as the gap between us and the boat gradually narrowed until the rolling white side of the boat loomed above us.

The cabin boy ran forward for a rope as we clawed the smooth painted wood for something to grasp. The rope slapped across my arm, and I quickly tied it about Bess' body. Shorty, who couldn't have weighed more than 125 pounds with a pocket full of sinkers, and the lad of about sixteen somehow hauled me aboard. Nothing ever felt better than the heaving deck of that little cruiser.

Then, as we turned to pull my wife over the side, I saw that Myers was hanging submerged, motionless, by the line on his wrist. Exhausted by the long ordeal, he had sunk quietly, as I had done previously. We managed to get him aboard, where he quickly regained consciousness. Somehow, with unskilled and almost brutal artificial resuscitation treatments, we finally restored Bess' breathing.

Myers, Bess and I slumped on the drenched deck, too exhausted to move or to speak while Shorty went below to locate the engine trouble. After a few minutes, enough of my strength returned to permit me to stagger into the engine room. I realized that getting aboard didn't mean we were out of danger. The waves still were hammering at the boat as it drifted before the gale, parallel to the troughs of the waves. Another line-wave like the one that had hit us before would be certain to capsize the small boat if it came broadside.

By the light of a flashlight we examined the engine. When the wall of water had struck the boat, a cupboard door within the cabin had been flung open and the loose tools and gear on the shelves had been thrown against the motor, loosening a wire on the distributor.

Shorty made quick repairs and we stumbled out into the salt-laden air. He switched the starter and the engine churned, coughed and then caught. A white wake kicked up astern as the propeller hit into the water. Then we were under way once more, running on our quartering course toward Baker's Haulover. As we got closer to shore we saw that automobiles were lined up on the beach road for a mile watching the spectacle.

"Lord," shouted Shorty suddenly. "Look ahead!"

We were bearing down on the Baker's Haulover inlet bridge under a driving wind. A landing in the surf on either side was impossible. Yet the waves seemed to close the inlet entrance and they were breaking over the bridge. It looked as though we had escaped death in the open sea only to end things in the surf or by crashing the boat into the wave-battered bridge. The choice before Shorty was like choosing between arsenic or strychnine. He chose to head for the bridge. The structure loomed darkly ahead as a wave lifted us. Then we dropped into a trough and plunged under the span into the safe waters of Biscayne Bay.

WE FOUND OUT later what we really had been through. We had been in the southern end of one of the most severe hurricanes in years.

Somehow the fish I had taken had managed to stay aboard during the storm. It was mounted and now graces our living-room wall. Bess and I call it "Lowell" for Lowell Thomas, who featured our adventure in his Christmas broadcast.

Yes, most dark clouds have a silver lining. In this instance it's a sort of pacifier that works like a charm on my wife. Whenever she gets out of hand, or puts her foot down too hard, I always say, "Careful, now—don't forget I could have left you to the sharks."

—June, 1949

By Louis Corbeau

HE GOT AWAY!

He made his moves deliberately, waiting for just the right moment to end the fight. Sooner or later the man would make a mistake.

FISHING FOR SHARKS off Bob Hall Pier was all right when you had room. But with the tourists there in big mobs it was strictly no good. Stan needed lots of room to put out his shark bait. He usually laid the 130-pound-test out in coils on the pier and then swung the big hunk of shark meat around his head until it picked up enough momentum to take it sixty feet out from the pier. Next he'd tighten the line on the ten pounds of tough meat lying on the bottom, and sit back and wait.

Tonight he had to ask people repeatedly before they'd move enough to let him swing the bait. One fat girl in tight slacks said, "Why don't you just fish with shrimp? It's easier." And three times he'd had to reel in and let people untangle their lines from his. It was no good. He quit and headed for the cabana.

Martha was listening to the radio and soaking her long upper lip in the triangular hole in the top of a beer can. She started chattering as soon as he came in. Sometimes she irritated him just a little—like now. The beer was cold, but it wasn't what he wanted. He started to unbuckle the shark harness, then changed his mind. "I'm going to drive down the beach a couple of miles to get away from this crowd," he said.

Martha answered "I'll need the car to get some more ice and some meat for dinner, so I'll drive you down and come get you."

Three miles below the public pier the beach curved back sharply to the west, and there a man could be alone, with just the late-afternoon sun and the slow-rolling combers and a few gulls. Even the gulls were quiet, standing one-legged on the shiny sand, still wet from the slow-ebbing tide. Martha left him with two extra beers, a 4-foot shark that was already beginning to ripen, and his big canvas sack of tackle. He lit a cigarette and sat down to watch the ocean. With the tide ebbing and the gulls quiet, it didn't seem like a time for fishing in the surf. But who ever knew when it was time to go after sharks?

It was too hot for hip boots, so he skinned down to his swimming trunks. Like all Gulf Coast beaches, this one shoaled slowly to the first trough, where the waves broke and spilled their weight downward. The water was chest-high here, and Stan waded on tiptoe, carrying the rod high in his right hand. It would be shallower farther out, beyond the first trough.

After about twenty feet he found himself walking uphill, and soon the water was only knee-deep. Then, as he moved out farther, the water gradually got deeper. When it was hip-deep, he stuck the rod butt in the harness socket, hooked the shoulder harness to the reel, and took an elastic strap out of his tackle bag.

The strap went around his chest and also the rod, hooking securely. Now he had both hands free and the reel was well up out of the water.

HE WATCHED THE slowly rolling waves, judging the depths out in front by the action of the water moving toward him. Then he took a couple of deep breaths and began to twirl the shark bait around his head in a slowly widening circle until he had thirty feet of line moving in an up-and-down oscillating arc. He put everything he had into one great heave and the bait sailed out. By good luck and timing it cleared the crest of the next comber and went ten feet farther than he had expected. Soon the bait was resting on the bottom, 150 yards from shore. Nothing but a good-sized shark would take it. That's the nice thing about using a big hunk of shark for bait—lesser fish can't chew through the leathery hide.

Walking backward, he paid out the line until he reached the seaward side of the first trough. He was in knee-deep water now, with firm sand to stand upon. There was five feet of water behind him, the whole Gulf in front. Satisfied with the spot, he reeled in until his line was fairly taut.

For an hour nothing happened. Gulls wheeled around in the unbelievable blue of the late-afternoon sky, and a few fat clouds built up and headed north into the shimmering heat waves over Padre Island. The sun sank lower behind him and the sea turned slowly from bright blue to a murky brown with brassy overtones. Schools of hardheads came hurrying by his legs, circled so close that they bumped against him—then darted away in confusion when he moved slightly.

The sun had just touched the horizon when the line began to move. Acting quickly, Stan detached the elastic strap, settled the rod butt deeper in the socket, and checked the metal snaps that bound the big reel to his shoulder harness. When he flexed his shoulders, the harness lifted off his back and the breeze was cool on his sweat-soaked skin.

THE LINE MOVED steadily to the south, paralleling the beach. Stan released the drag and freewheeled it, watching the line pay off the reel. He had 400 yards of the big stuff on his reel, and he waited until about 100 of it was out. Swinging the reel handle back to engage it again, he tightened the drag and waited. When the click began to squawk, he put both hands on the rod and lifted hard. With a swinging motion he took out all the slack and struck—once, twice, three times—driving the barbed hook deeper into the mouth of whatever was out there on the other end.

There was a satisfying reaction. The water boiled in a sudden swirl and line began to smoke out of the reel, through the guides, and into the water. With the drags set as much as Stan dared, the line melted off the reel in a sustained run until he had less than fifty yards left. This was a big one—maybe the biggest he had ever taken.

Suddenly the shark reversed its course and came sliding across the crest of a wave in a fast run back to the north. Stan reeled furiously, regaining almost all the line. Almost all of it? That meant the shark was right in front of him! And it had stopped! Looming surprisingly dark in the waning light, it was a tiger about 8 feet long. He'd had better ones. Once he'd landed an 11-foot 8-inch hammerhead off Bob Hall Pier.

But somehow this was different. Stan was enjoying the fight with this big one—in the water with it. There was nobody yelling advice, no one bumping him in their eagerness to get a picture of the fish while it was still green. Nobody was around to spoil the fight, just he and the shark and the darkening sky and the slowly rolling sea.

The shark moved off slowly—still heading north, as if wondering what was tugging at it. Stan could see the line running down to the chain leader, which disappeared under the curve of the shark's head. He was surprised at the fish's actions: it showed no fear, no desire to escape. Perhaps it didn't know it was in trouble—was just curious about the situation. Then he

remembered that no sensible fisherman ever gives a shark a minute's rest, so he jerked hard on the rod, snapping the hook deeper into its mouth.

The results were electric. The shark spun as if it had been shot with a rifle and came right at Stan, sliding past him into the first trough! In doing so it came within five feet of him, but he felt that it still hadn't seen him or realized what was happening.

"The shark spun as if it had been shot with a rifle and came right at Stan."

FEELING THAT HIS chances were much better with the fish in shallow water, Stan kept his line tight, hoping to make the shark do its fighting in the restricted space of the first trough. It made its next run to the south, dragging line off the smoking, protesting reel despite his best efforts to turn it. Nobody can turn a green tiger shark, Stan thought; you only win when the fish makes an error. If all sharks ran straight and kept on running, none would ever be landed by mere man in a fair fight. When there was bare reel arbor showing between the coils of line, this one made its error: it stopped.

For five minutes it lay resting while Stan slowly pumped line back onto the reel, inch by agonizing inch. In the shallow water the shark began to swing its head back and forth, rubbing the chain leader against the sand. Afraid that this might tear a hole big enough to let the hook drop free, Stan goaded the shark into action by putting on as much pressure as he dared and then rhythmically jerking against the rod. That trick sometimes worked—and it worked this time.

The shark came back the way it had gone, right up the deepest part of the trough, dragging the line in a long, bellying curve that Stan was unable to catch up with. Again it went right by him, and stopped twenty feet away. But this time it was different. When he jerked the line taut and pressured the fish, it turned to face him. He could see its eyes and he was sure the fish saw him. It studied him with cold, expressionless eyes, then, with a deliberate sweep of its tail, came toward him. He reeled slowly, fascinated by the size of the fish, until it was only eight feet away.

Never in his life had Stan been so close to a shark—not while it was still green. And this one hadn't been dragged in; it had come on its own, apparently to investigate him. He backed slowly away. If it came closer, he thought he might be able to turn away that fearful maw by using the rod as a tether. But the shark turned and swam away.

It would soon be too dark to see, so Stan decided to move into shore and finish the fight in shallow water. He hoped Martha had the camera with her; it would be nice to have a flash picture of this one.

As the shark moved off to the south Stan stepped into the first trough and headed for the shore, a hundred yards away. The shark whirled and dashed back toward him, shooting past in front of him as he stumbled backward into the shallower water behind the bar. The crazy thing—it was almost as if it were attacking him!

After Stan got his balance he had to tighten up on the line to locate the shark, and it didn't please him any when he found it. The shark was to the north—twenty yards away and watching him. He couldn't make it out except when it moved. He socked the hook into its jaw a couple of times, but it didn't move. Then he stepped into the deeper water—and yelled in surprise as the thing came at him in a vicious, determined charge—moving so fast that it rammed its head into the sand of the shallow bar as he jumped back onto it.

THERE WAS NO doubting it—the shark was waiting, baiting him to try for the beach and planning to jump him when he did.

Planning? That was silly. Fish don't think, so how could it plan? The shark swam slowly to the south until it got to the end of the slack line, then turned and swam slowly back to the north end of its tether. Each time it went by in front of him it seemed to slow down and look at him as he perched on the bar. The tide was still ebbing and the bar was almost out of water, which gave him a comfortable feeling.

But at full ebb there would still be two feet of water in the trough—and a big shark could maneuver swiftly in eighteen inches. Even now its dorsal fin was out of water as it swung slowly on patrol in front of him.

The wind was dying with the coming of night, the sea growing oily-smooth and quiet behind him. Only the lights of Corpus Christi on the skyline gave him orientation. The dry sand of the beach was still a hundred yards away. It was strange that Martha hadn't come back yet. In a way he was glad that she hadn't. He hardly felt dignified or brave, hiding from a fish!

During the next ten minutes the changing pull on the rod told Stan what the shark was doing—swimming figure eights in front of him, between him and the beach, and keeping its head toward him. He released all tension on the line; perhaps without the tug of the line the shark might lose track of his position and move away. If he could get across the trough and into the shallows again, he'd soon put on the pressure and whip it down to size.

He felt angry toward the shark now. It was no longer a prey that he pursued—but a fearful adversary that refused to play according to the rules. The line, completely slack, slowly paid off the free-spooled reel in the tug of the light breeze. He felt the line—it was completely dry. The shark now had almost all of the 400 yards out.

Stan squatted down and tried to silhouette the line against the light of the night sky in an effort to see which way it was tending. He thought it led to the south. Taking a deep breath, he jumped into the trough and headed for shore at a splashing run. His breath was coming in great gasps, almost like sobs. Then he stumbled and fell, and the salty water rolled over his head. Gasping and spluttering, he got up and ran.

UP ON THE hard sand of the beach, free of the water's tug, Stan coughed up the last of the brine and gasped for breath. The wind had freshened and his soaking made him feel almost cold. When he got his breath back he turned to look at the sea, and it was then that he realized he didn't have the rod!

He looked at his empty hands with a stupid stare, not comprehending. Nervous, he jumped when a sand crab scuttled by his feet. Then he ran to the tackle bag and got out his flashlight. Its powerful beam disclosed the line, tossing up and down in the wash of the last comber. It was left high and dry each time a wave receded. Watching for a high one, then timing it nicely, Stan ran out, picked up his line, and got back to dry sand without even getting his ankles wet.

He pulled in the line, hand over hand, until he had a big pile at his feet and a solid, unyielding pull off to the north, where it led into the edge of the first trough. He went slowly back into the water and moved hand over hand along the line, shining the flashlight ahead of him. Soon he saw the shiny endplate of the reel; it was snagged on something just over the slant into the trough.

He could reach it and still stay in less than a foot of water. He ran toward it, reached down, and grabbed the heavy rod. As he started to lift it the water rose in front of him in a big wave—a maverick comber that came rolling in. He jumped back and stood quivering with fear as the water washed over him. Panicky, he ran back to the beach.

***

ONCE ON DRY land, he began reeling in line. It came freely, and he felt a sense of relief at the knowledge that the shark was gone. The reel grew fat with the incoming line—and then the rod tip bucked down hard. Automatically Stan set the drag and braced his feet against the pull of the fish. The line led almost straight down into shallow water, meaning that the shark was practically at his feet. That gave Stan a very bad moment; the shark was out-guessing him every time. The shark had allowed him to lead it in, coming as far as the shallow water would allow. Stan shuddered when he thought of the consequences had he waded in to retrieve the line. Anger flooded over him and he leaned back into the rod with all his strength. He was tired of being the hunted—suddenly he hated that shark and wanted to kill it. But the line melted off his reel with inexorable certainty. Against the pull of the rod, against the squealing protest of the brake and the aching pull of his own muscles, the shark went straight out to sea. The last of the line disappeared, the knot squealed as the dry line tightened a bit more—and Stan found himself moving slowly seaward, his heels sliding in the wet sand.

He was fumbling for his knife when the water reached his knees; he was still determined not to lose the rod and reel. Then the rod straightened—the line hung loose in the water. He started to reel in again, but changed his mind. He slashed the line free and turned and ran back to the dry sand. Was it his imagination, or did something big splash against the side of the first trough?

He had stopped puffing when Martha drove up, and all he really wanted was a cigarette. She asked her usual inane question, "Catch anything?"

"No," he said, "I didn't catch anything."

"You poor dear," she said. "It must have been a long, dull evening."

—December, 1961

By James Grey
as told to Brian O'Brien

Horns of the
SEA DEVIL

FIFTEEN MILES OFF-SHORE, THE GIANT MANTA TURNED TO WREAK HIS REVENGE ON THE SWAHILI DUGOUT. ONLY GOOD LUCK AND SMART SEAMANSHIP PREVENTED A TRAGEDY.

HAMID FUMBA, THE Swahili in the bow of my dugout canoe, was pointing urgently into the cloudy green water some twelve miles off Mombasa, on the coast of East Africa. *"Hapa, bwana!"* he exclaimed.

I looked down at what I first thought was a rock. But it moved and resembled a bird—no, a bat, with wide, pointed wings and a long, whiplike tail. The wingspread was all of eight yards! Then I made out the horns, and didn't need the furious yelling of the four paddlers to know I was staring at a gigantic manta ray.

The Swahilis call them devils because of

the horns, which are really scoops to rake fish into the gaping four-foot mouth and look like the horns of Old Nick himself when the brute surfaces. And the mighty batlike wings complete the picture. Swahilis foam with rage at sight of these monsters, because they gobble up tons of the food fish intended for the Mombasa market. Personally, I can take mantas or leave them alone. So I leave them alone. Except in this case, where Hamid's Zanzibar temper got the better of him and let us in for a 15-mile Nantucket sleighride behind a ton and a half of snapping, slapping nightmare.

Everyone said it was my own fault. Maybe it was. But I was only a lowly bank teller—Dominion, Colonial and Overseas, on Kilindini Road—and I couldn't afford the Sea Anglers' Association with their glossy launches. I had to make a deal with Hamid, who was skipper of a fishing zarouk, to go out with him during the northeast monsoon, when the best fish are running, and try for something modest, like dolphin or barracuda, from his dugout while the zarouk hauled her nets. But I hadn't bargained for manta. Of course, they don't eat people, but they can darned well smash them, which this one too nearly did to me.

----✦≡◈≡✦----

I WAS STILL staring down at the mottled monster when Hamid let go at it with a shark harpoon. I saw the head of the harpoon go into the brute's back, and that's all I saw for some time. The horror slanted and came *who-oshing* to the surface like a submarine. One wing scooped a ton of water into the dugout; another slapped the surface with the report of a good-sized gun, and the palmwood shaft of that harpoon shattered against our gunwale like matchwood. Hamid stood up, screeching like a maniac, and jammed a fish spear into the streaming hide. It canted until I thought it would roll on us.

"Fire, *bwana*. Fire!" yelled Hamid.

I got out my revolver and snapped a couple of .45 slugs into the beast. Blood spurted, and he submerged. I was still gasping for breath and frantically bailing our half-swamped vessel when the bow jerked around, sending three of us into the bilge and the fourth man overboard. And also all my fishing gear.

We had no chance to help, for we were off, following that frightful creature on the surface, his horns jutting like those of a buffalo and his wings turned up at the edges, while his tail, with the long spikes plainly visible, lashed the water a few feet ahead of our prow. Astern I saw the head of the steersman swimming toward the *zarouk;* so he was okay. But we weren't! Hamid had taken a turn of the rough hemp line about a cleat in the bow and was clinging to the rope like grim death, bracing himself with his foot against the gunwale and cursing as only a Zanzibari can curse. The rest of us held on, the other two Swahilis brandishing knives and yelling vengefully.

Once the monster planed right into the air like the roof of a Kansas farmhouse in cyclone time. He hit water again and skidded around like a knife around a pie plate. Then he made straight for us. I fired again, without effect. He slapped water just under our bow, and we pitched until I thought we'd go below, but the ray slid under us, lifting our keel so that we lay over and waited to capsize. But Hamid was clinging for dear life, jabbing his spear into the bloody water.

The ray veered off again, jerking us about on another course. We soused into the rollers, shipping water so fast that it was pouring out the other side of the canoe. Again the ray broached, flapping his great wings, his long, armed tail lashing, trying to shake the barb out of his back. He hit the surface with explosive force, sending spray like shot and leaving a wide patch of foam.

I began to wonder how long this would last. Hanging on for dear life, I took a quick look astern; I could not see the shore at all, and the *zarouk* was hull down. By the sun, we were headed almost due east, and there was nothing dry ahead but India, some 4,000 miles away. Also, there was no food or water in the dugout. I began to feel a bit queer. I was trying to think up a way to suggest cutting loose from this horror without losing face, but by the expressions of my fellow canoemen nothing short of death would have made them let go their enemy.

Strangely enough, in spite of my nervousness, I, too, began to catch some of the soaring fury that filled the Swahilis. I found myself howling in the bow, my revolver ready for a shot as soon as his head with its reaching horns became visible. His head came up, a flattened mound between those two greenish-white horns. I fired, and the thing jumped a yard, the tail whipping out of the water and fetching a knot of wood out of our bow as big as my fist.

A wind was coming up by now, and spray shot into our faces until we were half drowned. We rolled gunwales under, pitched until I thought he'd drag us under and skidded along like a duck while that brute sailed through the air like a 24-foot flying carpet. Yelling and gasping, we were skidding over the ocean like madmen, hanging on while the monster, his wings batting like steam paddles, yanked us along with a bow wave like that of a P-T boat. Then the line slacked. Hamid hauled in, howling for a spear, but the line straightened and slanted steep until our prow began to settle.

Seas were breaking over us as the tremendous pull held us down. But slack came again. and I saw the dark loom come shooting up from the bottom. Hamid yelled, and the paddlers worked like demons. As the ray shot up beside us, his horns hammered the side of the dugout and sent us lurching. He was standing on end, like a horrible, sour, stinking wall. Luckily for us he fell over away from our little craft and the ride was on again.

By now sharks had joined the party, attracted by the monster's blood. One, a wall-eyed gray nurse, slid past us with a purposeful look, rolled lazily and took a hunk out of the ray just abaft his starboard wing. He lashed with his tail, and I saw that shark go sliding off with a rent in him two yards long. His brothers had him in shreds in no time.

But the ray was slowing. The mighty wings beat with less energy, though the spiked tail lashed more viciously. Every time he surfaced,

"By now sharks had joined the party, attracted by the monster's blood."

Hamid gashed him with the spear, and though he still towed us fast he was weakening. Then it was that he actually gave definite, planned battle. He sounded, turned under water and came up like a volcano under our bow. Hamid jammed a mangrove pole into his wide mouth. The monster crunched it like a field hand crushing sugar cane. The awful wide head with its fixed half-moon grin and those dreadful four-foot horns slid away, and a wing came up and bashed us. As we fought for balance a wide crack appeared in our port side.

By this time I was weary. I had one shell left in my Webley, and I had little faith in that. That beast had taken five slugs, a harpoon and several spear wounds, besides losing the hunk the shark had snatched, and he was still full of fight.

Twice more he tried to flip us over, and twice Hamid lunged at him with his spear until he backed away, the toothless mouth with its solid-bone lips open in that mournful leer which was much more frightening than a mouthful of teeth. Hamid tried to haul us close. The whiplike tail flogged us, leaving splintered scars in the dugout.

Another shark slid by, so close that I could have touched him. There was a dreadful convulsion and the sea boiled, the shark's tail and the manta's mottled wings thrashing and flailing in a maelstrom of foam and bloody water. Our canoe, leaking like a sieve, plunged and wallowed. We were soaked, half drowned, breathless from yelling, our hands cut by the lines while the struggling monsters were dragging us under.

I yelled to cut loose, but no one took any notice. Hamid, his dark hawk face grinning like a demon, was stabbing wildly and screaming like a maniac. Then the manta took off again, and for an instant the mangled shape of the shark slid past as we jerked ahead like a surfboard towed by a speedboat. But the brute was almost spent, veering erratically and slapping the waves with reports like gunshot. I wiped salt from my eyes and hoped it was the end.

Suddenly the ray went into a wild flurry, came around in a wide curve and charged, horns spread, mouth open, straight at us.

We froze as he slanted out of the sea. His wings hit like thunder, and he soared out until I saw the wide, horizontal gills in his sickly belly. Hamid screeched, and I went overside just a quarter second before he slapped down right across the canoe. I went deep, my ears full of roaring. There was a gash spurting blood from my arm, but I couldn't feel it. I stroked frantically, half drowning myself in my panic at the thought of my legs in that horrible, bone-crushing mouth.

The sea was slapping into my mouth and I was choking with fatigue. Wearily I turned on my back. Hamid and the others were close by, swimming strongly; those Swahilis are like beavers. Behind us the manta was still fighting the dugout wreckage with vicious fury.

I TURNED TO stroke again, but where? The coast must be thirty miles off, and it was already late afternoon. We'd never make it even if the sharks or the barracuda didn't get us. I tried not to think of them and headed toward the setting sun. Then I heard Hamid laugh. At first I thought he was crazy. He pointed, teeth gleaming white in his streaming face. And as a roller lifted me I saw the *zarouk* heeling toward us under her immense triangular sail.

Boy I was thankful to be dragged aboard. But Hamid wasn't finished yet. Cursing again and screeching to Allah about the devil that had smashed the dugout, he jumped to the tiller and ordered the men to brace the slanting yard around. We came close to the whirling, flapping mass of manta and wreckage. Hamid snatched a gaspipe gun from its place beside the binnacle and fired into the middle of the commotion. But the brute rose like a winged dragon, horns reaching like embracing arms, mouth open, and crashed down on the wreckage, bouncing on it in frenzy, slamming it under with appalling fury.

Hamid banged another charge of potleg into him without result. The whole crew were in the act now, lining the bulwark, jabbing with spears, screeching, almost going overboard in their excitement. Four harpoons were in the creature, their lines vibrating like fiddlestrings. I hopped about the edges of the battle, wondering what I could do.

Hamid heaved a grapnel into the mess. Four men tailed onto the rope and checked it before it raced through the block on the masthead. All hands jumped at Hamid's high-pitched yells and began heaving on the line. The brute writhed and struggled. The *zarouk* listed, trembling as the wings slammed against the freeboard.

I snatched up a hatchet and chopped at the root of the slashing, spike-armed tail. At one time we had him half-way aboard, the grapnel caught in those gaping belly gills. But just as it was a tossup whether he came aboard or we went over he gave a frightful convulsion that sprayed blood and gurry all over us, the rope parted, and he was away with two yards of the rail. No time to grab the harpoon lines; he was gone, slapping the water like a paddle steamer gone crazy.

The *zarouk* rocked and shipped water, and the Swahilis screamed blasphemy after the beast. I felt glad it was over. We were all cut and bleeding. I had a bad cut in my upper arm, which later healed nice and clean. I'd lost twenty quid worth of fishing equipment, a good Webley revolver and my helmet. I was lucky not to have lost my life.

IT WAS DARK, and we had to pick our way carefully through the big ocean-going dhows that the monsoon had brought down as we made Mombasa Old Port and tied up under Fort Jesus. I got my motor bike from the Mombassa Club compound and went home to my room at Miss MacIntyre's Hotel, thankful that tomorrow was Sunday and I could sleep.

And Monday, at the bank, I had to listen to old *Bwana m'kubwa* Davidson blowing about a 7-foot barracuda he had boated after a four-hour battle with equipment that had cost him six hundred dollars. I wanted to tell the old fool about my manta that got away. But in my spot you don't tell; you just keep quiet and listen.

—April, 1955

Sidenei and his amputated pinkie; piranhas as dinner (the larger one is the fingereater); and tributaries of the Negro River.

THE AMAZON BASIN IS CALLED "GREEN HELL," AND WITH REASON. BUT IT'S HOME TO ONE OF THE MOST SPECTACULAR GAMEFISH THAT SWIMS.

By Garrett VeneKlasen

RACING *with* *the* RAINS

The author admires a *tucunaré*.

PIRANHAS HAVE THE most devilish grin imaginable—especially when they've just removed a sizable piece of your guide's finger. And that was the least of our problems . . . .

ALMOST 3,000 MILES from Miami to Manaus, Brazil; in the middle of the night via an airline named after a prominent Bolivian drug dealer. Up before dawn to fly 4 more hours in a single-engine floatplane over an endless canopy of primordial jungle. Dropped off on an obscure river hundreds of miles from the nearest human settlement—I'm somewhere in the Amazon Basin.

Adding to our concern were the impending torrential rains and, in the back of my head, all those amazing Amazonian horror stories I heard as a kid: Man-eating jaguars, *candirú* (a parasitic fish that lodges itself in the ano-genital region), electric eels, freshwater stingrays, giant spiders, swarms of ants, killer bees. Scores of poisonous snakes, and non-poisonous snakes the size of telephone poles. Malaria, dengue, chagas, yellow fever, schistosomiasis, hemmorhagic fever. Fungus, heat rash, infection, and inch-long bot fly larvae crawling under your skin.

Why? Why would anybody do this? We hopelessly addicted fishing bums are always looking for a justification to experience exotic angling, nature, and cultures far from the so-called civilized world. The epitome of this ideal is the Amazon and its extensive list of gamefish—as exotic as the land itself. Depending upon the watershed, there are as many as twenty different gamefish—all with fantastic names to match their peculiar appearances: *pirapitinga, tambaqui, aruanã, pirarucú, pirapucu, bicuda, jancundá, traida, pirarara, matrincha, peixe cachorra, pescada, arapá,* and *surubim* just to name a few. Of all the great Amazonian gamefish, though, the one that truly stands out is the giant peacock bass: what the Brazilians call *tucunaré azul.*

Tucunaré are not bass at all, but members of the *Cichlid* family—a group of highly aggressive tropical fishes that have adapted to the Amazon's harsh environment. The *tucunaré's* striking beauty starts with blazing fluorescent-red eyes set into a backdrop of green, yellow, red, orange, and black. Top it all off with a brilliant black and yellow eye spot at the base of the tail—an adaptation evolved to distract attacking schools of piranhas, who immobilize their prey by first biting their eyes out.

Concentrations of giant *tucunaré* exist nowhere else in the world except specific locations throughout the Amazon Basin. The trick is to find one of those secret rivers with the exact environmental conditions conducive to holding big fish. It often takes months of searching an area almost the size of the U.S. (with ten tributaries as large as or larger than the Mississippi) to find a worthwhile fishery.

In March of 1992 I spent two intensive weeks scouting northern Brazil with a local outfitter, Luis Brown, floatplane pilot Bennie DeMerchant, and my jungle-wise guide, Sidenei DePassos. So here I am again, two years later, ready to embark upon a second adventure.

The plan is simple. Luis and Bennie drop Sidenei and me off on the upper Preto River,

an unexplored basin that Luis thinks to be promising. While they go on to scout several other rivers, we assess the Preto as a possible site for a future fishing camp. Two days later, they pick us up for more exploring.

After a 3-hour flight from Manaus, the Preto appears in the distance like a copper-colored snake cutting its way through brilliant emerald surroundings. Bennie circles a likely-looking spot, cuts power, and descends onto the river.

The plane, a Cessna 185 Skywagon, is so loaded down with fuel that supplies are kept to a minimum. A 10-foot folding boat is strapped to the pontoons; our other gear consists of a 5-horse outboard, a 6-watt radio, two hammocks, one small tarp, one bag of *farinha* (cassava flour), one small loaf of bread, and a battered old aluminum pot for boiling water. Luis tosses me a small bag of black Brazilian coffee—he makes it seem like a real concession. We quickly assemble the boat and then unload our supplies. With that he bids me luck and safe travels, then shoves us off and climbs into the plane, which taxis into the center of the river, and roars off in a blast of water and exhaust, leaving behind an eerie silence.

Slowly the jungle comes back to life. A *guan,* the Amazon's version of a turkey, starts its jazzy syncopated call—*buh-ba-bah-bah-boom. . . boom!* A lone katydid answers with a series of high-pitched chirps from a nearby palm, and a whistling toucan joins the singalong. Two squawking macaws land atop an *abacaba* palm, while a yellow-rumped weaver bird returns to its intricate nest with an array of warbled notes. The whole jungle is soon an overwhelming chorus of booms, squeaks, roars, bellows, chirps, squawks, and cries.

———— ✦ ————

WITHIN THE HOUR some thirty fish between 3 and 5 pounds are boated. Unfortunately, they are all an assortment of the Amazon's smaller gamefish. Most of them are the *barboleta tucunaré*—a small species of peacock bass that seldom grows much larger than 8 pounds. A few *traida* are also caught and released. Sidenei calls them "*sabonete com dentes*"—fanged bars of soap.

By 5 or so in the afternoon I've landed well over 100 *barboleta tucunaré*, but still no sign of the larger *paca* or *azul* variety. By now the monsoon clouds have formed not far to the south of us, swirling and rising. Soon the rains will arrive, descending like a tidal wave, and ending all fishing until next year's dry season.

We paddle out to the mouth of the lagoon, within casting distance of a small cluster of boulders. On the first cast, my fly is taken by a fairly large *tucunaré*. The frantic fish rushes to the surface in a thrashing boil of blood and glistening silver, surrounded by a frenzied school of white piranha. Now I know why the river holds so few big *tucunaré*.

Within seconds the piranhas disembowel their victim, removing much of its flesh in a froth of blood and water. The snapping jaws are audible some 30 yards away, but the melee doesn't last long. What little remains slowly descends into the tannin-stained gloom.

One of the piranha grabs the fly. After a brief struggle the fish grudgingly comes to the boat with a dozen more of its companions greedily nipping at the protruding bucktail. Sidenei reaches down and carefully grasps the 4-pound fish behind the gills, heedlessly singing an off-tune rendition of "*Besame Muito*" to the fish. He looks away for only a split second while attempting to remove the streamer fly, and the hook pops loose.

The piranha snaps its jaws closed, neatly removing the tip of Sidenei's pinkie and a sizable piece of fingernail. The teeth are so sharp that Sidenei feels no pain whatsoever, but the white bone and spurting blood make him wince in disgust. The piranha's jaws make a sick popping sound every time they snap shut on the remains of the finger. Sidenei buries the blade of the screwdriver between the startled piranha's eyes. "We'll eat that one," he says in Portuguese, plucking the mangled fingertip from the fish's twitching jaws. Sidenei inspects the finger meat and then tosses it into the water like some useless piece of trash. It is eaten before it can settle out of sight.

We take the piranha incident as an omen, and decide to end the day's fishing. Camp is set on a sweeping white beach void of caiman and jaguar tracks. Sidenei dresses his wound while I clean and cook the piranha over a small fire. The fish seems to be staring at me with a hellish cooked-in grin.

Dinner consists solely of fish and *farinha*, and somehow that seems enough. There is something ironic about eating the finger-eater, but at this point we are both so hungry it really doesn't matter. We sit without speaking, watching the river and the thunderheads that still loom on the southern horizon.

After dinner, we pitch our hammocks and tarp, then settle in for the night. The river's high acidity prevents mosquitoes from hatching, so we need no netting.

A small band of howler monkeys moves into the nearby trees to get a close look at us. The alpha male begins his horrid territorial roaring—a clamor somewhere between King Kong and a 500-pound German shepherd—which is audible as far as 10 miles away. The roaring suddenly stops, and from somewhere far back in the blackness a jaguar moans its deep guttural call, like a demonic cello player sawing the same notes over and over. Sidenei builds up the fire and restlessly settles back into his hammock, cradling a single-barrel 12-gauge shotgun he calls *boca quente*—"hot mouth."

At dawn the howlers again commence their roaring. The jaguar has decided not to dine on *gringo* and all is well. Sidenei brews a stout pot of jungle coffee. We share a stale crust of bread, then head downriver toward the pickup location.

By noon we reach the confluence of the east and west branches of the Preto River. On the far shore a small campfire smolders next to a primitive structure of several stacked palm fronds stacked atop a skeletal foundation of thin sticks.

We boat over to the campsite and wade ashore to see if anyone is about, stopping to inspect an assortment of charred animal parts atop a crudely built grill made of green sticks. A few are recognizable: the shell and a single clenched claw of an armadillo; the torso, head still intact, of an unlucky woolly monkey. Sidenei looks about warily.

From well inside the jungle a male voice

calls out in an indiscernible language. It is soon answered by another man, and then several more people join in until the surrounding trees are full of clamoring voices. One by one they appear from the forest—tiny, stoutly built people, the largest no taller than 5 feet. Most have little or no clothing, though they all wear intricate neck-laces strung with black and red seeds of the *tento* tree, bones, feathers, and jaguar, peccary, and freshwater dolphin teeth. Sidenei says they are Pan-rá (pronounced *pan-ha*) Indians, a nomadic hunter-gatherer tribe who still lead the exact lives of their ancient ancestors.

Bows in hand, the men of the group timidly approach the river bank, bellowing at each other in their rapid dialect. The women and children remain close to the jungle's edge, nervously chattering like a clutch of scared chickens.

It is my clothing, and especially my sun-glasses, that scare them the most. I must appear to them like some giant white-skinned appari-tion from another planet. I take off my hat and glasses and try to look as *friendly* as possible. Soon their curiosity gets the better of them, and before long the whole boat is surrounded. Just as they're starting to calm down, the float plane comes roaring around the bend in the river, only 5 feet off the water, flying full throttle. When Bennie spots us he instantly cuts power and puts down, throwing up a great rooster tail. The Pan-rá bolt for the jungle in terror.

We quickly load our gear while Luis inter-rogates me about the river. I explain the appar-ent piranha infestation as we pile into the scorching cockpit. Bennie taxis us into position and we roar up over the tree line toward our next stop, the Rio Alegria, the "river of happi-ness." Luis has heard rumors of that river's giant *tucunaré*, but it's all speculative and sketchy at best. Bennie gains as much altitude as pos-sible, to give him ". . . more time to pray if the engine quits."

⊷—⊨⊹⊟—⊶

AT 3,000 FEET the jungle looks like an endless green ocean. There is not a single land-mark as far as the eye can see. Luis pulls out his hand-held GPS and takes a reading: 63 degrees 50 minutes west, 00 degrees 07 minutes north.

We're right on the equator. To the west is the setting sun and to the south the massive cloud bank, as thick and imposing as ever, gold and salmon in the fading light. Bennie is becoming increasingly edgy, nervously glancing down at several Operational Navigation Charts (ONCs), the GPS, and finally out the window. The river is nowhere in sight.

After several panicky minutes, the outline of a river appears barely discernible on the darkening horizon. We head straight for the nearest bend in the river where, by sheer luck, a small boat sits moored along the bank. The chances of running into people are wildly unlikely, but somehow we've managed to blunder right on top of them. Bennie idles back and we float down onto the river's surface. Another 5 minutes and it would have been too dark to land.

An old man suddenly comes madly pad-dling out of a nearby lagoon in his tiny dugout. He heads straight for his little boat; surely he's seen a float plane before. Luis scrambles out on the float and explains that we're sport fish-ermen from Manaus looking for *tucunaré*. The man stops his crazed paddling and looks back at the float plane as if he's just seen a ghost. He waves us over without saying a word, quick-ly docking his canoe alongside his little junk. Several worried faces peer out of the boat's open windows.

Luis rows the plane over to the boat and we exchange formal greetings. The man's name is Euodio Pizzerra de Araujo. He and his small family have boated two straight weeks from Manaus to collect *piasaba*—a type of palm frond used as bristles in industrial brushes. He tells us he plans to return to Manaus and sell his harvest when the rains make the lower part of the river more navigable.

Bennie hands Euodio a picture of himself with a 9-kilo *tucunaré*, asking him if he's seen any such fish in the Alegria. Euodio laughs, telling us that he speared and ate a *tucunaré* last night that was much larger than the one pic-tured. He says the river is full of big fish, but wants to know why we've come so far from Manaus to fish for them when they sell them in the city market. Luis explains that we want to catch them for fun and release them unharmed.

A slow smile spreads across Euodio's face. "Sport fishing" in the Amazon is an oxymoron—you catch a fish and you kill it, no exceptions. Our explanations are useless. Euodio looks at me in a pitying manner and offers me a bowl of macaw stew. I've never eaten macaw, so I ask him how they taste.

He grins his wide, toothless smile. "My son, much like parrot, but there's more meat." Euodio takes out an ancient aluminum bowl and piles various macaw parts atop a mound of cassava flour. A drumstick, with clenched claw still attached, rolls off the top of the heap. To refuse the meal would be an unforgivable insult, so with a forced smile I accept it. The macaw is delicious.

At sunrise, Euodio and his eldest son are ready to fish. Their little dugouts are only large enough for two people, so I go with Euodio while Euodio's son takes Bennie. Together we paddle upriver into a huge lagoon rimmed with towering kapok trees. Large schools of tilapia, silver dollar, and discus fish skitter nervously along the shoreline. From somewhere out of sight comes the terrific splash of a feeding peacock bass.

Euodio laughs hysterically when I pull out my fly rod and begin casting. He wants to know what on earth I plan to accomplish with the *xicote da agua*—water whip—I'm using. I do my best to make him understand, but he can't see why I won't just use live bait. The *tucunaré* always "... swallow the bait deep in their stomachs; they never escape."

From the center of the lagoon comes a great commotion. It looks like children thrashing in a pool on a hot summer day. The giant *tucunaré* have surfaced to feed.

Panicked baitfish, some 20 inches long, desperately skip across the water's surface. Three tremendous wakes follow in hot pursuit. The stampede heads straight for Bennie's boat. He flips his fly into the chaos and the water explodes where it lands. One of the peacocks engulfs the streamer, then races away, dragging the canoe along like a toy boat. Euodio paddles us over so we can get a good look at the fish. The *tucunaré* surfaces like a green crocodile with the 4/0 bucktail looking insignificant in its huge mouth. The fish doesn't even know it's hooked.

Suddenly two others appear out of nowhere and attack the hooked fish, trying to get at the protruding fly. Water shoots 10 feet in all directions. I quickly cast my fly toward the shock wave, while Euodio struggles to steady us. A *tucunaré* pounces on the fly and races toward a fallen tree. Line peels off my reel and the fish instantly snaps my 50-pound tippet under a submerged log.

Bennie's fish stays out in open water, making several deep, powerful runs before coming to the boat. It surfaces as if to get a good look at its antagonist and then boils off again, easily towing the boat another 100 yards or so before stopping. After 15 minutes of struggle, the fish finally comes up on its side. Bennie carefully tails the giant *tucunaré* and gently lays it on the gunwale of the dugout.

The fish is one of the largest *tucunaré* I've ever seen. I lay my tape measure across it. Thirty-seven inches. My scale says 24 pounds exactly. Bennie carefully lifts it up, places it in the water, and racks it back and forth. Euodio shrieks in protest. With a powerful sweep of its tail the fish disappears into the depths.

Bennie glances up and his smile suddenly disappears. A curtain of rain is bearing down on us like a Biblical catastrophe. We must return to the plane immediately or there will be no way out.

We race back to the plane. The wind has already started to pick up. Luis hastily pays Euodio with an assortment of flies, lures, hooks, and fishing line, which has more value to him than money.

Bennie taxis us out into the main river, full power, flaps down. He crosses himself and we roar up over the canopy, circling around once to wave goodbye to Euodio and his family. The river slips from sight behind the first layer of clouds. Rain blasting the windshield, we are enshrouded in a nightmarish wall of water. With any luck we'll be back in Manaus before nightfall. I sit back, close my eyes, and think about Bennie's monstrous *tucunaré*. The psychedelic fish has captured my soul.

—December, 1995

By A. J. McClane

THE LITTLE FISH
Who Eats People

THE PIRANHA CAN BE HARMLESS OR DEADLY. FINDING OUT WHICH CAN BE A HIGHLY COSTLY PROCESS.

Black Piranha

TWO YEARS AGO, A young boy fishing with his father in a canal outside of Fort Lauderdale caught a "funny looking bluegill." Its teeth clicked like Spanish castanets, but somehow the lad managed to juggle his prize into a bucket of water to take it home, his father

meanwhile insisting that it was just another "brim" with a very red belly and a dental problem. The fish was soon identified as a red piranha.

Several months later, an off-duty Florida highway patrolman went fishing in a barrow pit which joins the Snapper Creek Canal west of Miami. The trooper was still-fishing with minnows and after being mysteriously cut-off several times he finally landed what he believed was "that little fish who eats people." A positive identification was made by the Game and Freshwater Fish Commission—another red piranha.

At both locations the waters were poisoned with rotenone over an extensive area by Florida biologists. No more piranha were found. Nevertheless, these isolated events confirm the necessity of present state regulations

Red Piranha

Wimple's Piranha

White Piranha

which strictly prohibit their importation.

Like so many exotics, piranha can survive in Florida's climate and certain species might readily live in more northerly waters. The illegal release of aquarium fishes is a problem that extends all the way to Wyoming and Montana, where tropicals such as the swordtail, guppy, and platy form reproducing populations in thermally warmed ponds and streams. These live-bearers have the same temperature tolerances as the piranha. So the ban in Florida recognized a very real danger. Dumping piranha in the village pond is not the act of a rational citizen—as this *characin* is not a very rational fish.

The popular conception of piranha is that they are small, aggressive, occur in vast, water-churning schools, and that they eat man and beast alike. The facts are that at least two species reach a weight of 8 pounds, some are so shy that they seldom take a natural bait (much less an artificial), and a few species are almost solitary in habit. All are potentially dangerous to man, particularly the capaburro, dusky, and black piranhas, as many fingerless and toeless men can testify. Yet, throughout tropical South America primitive people bathe, swim, and freely wade in piranha-infested waters. The

trick is knowing where and when—a knowledge which brings forth a flood of speculation but little else. During the past twenty years I have waded among piranha for hundreds of hours while fishing and pulling seine nets in tributaries of the Orinoco, Amazon, and Paraguay Rivers. I am a devout coward, however, and the only thing that gives me confidence is when an unscarred, all-extremities-accounted-for, local Indian (preferably over eighty years old) says "Ho-Kay" and jumps in first. Even then, I wait to see if he comes up with a smile on his face.

Piranha (pronounced peer-'ahn-yah) is the name given by the Tupi speakers of Brazil and literally means "tooth-fish." Throughout most of Spanish-speaking South America it's known as *caribe,* the origin of that tribal name being the Carib Indians who were cannibals. Other Indian appellations such as *pana, perai,* and *piraya* are used in the Guianas and eastern Peru, but piranhas were first imported by tropical-fish dealers from Brazil so the Tupi name stuck.

Scientific literature is not clear on how many different piranhas exist. An educated guess would indicate about forty species in five different genera. The common names of piranha are practical descriptions translated from Indian dialects into Spanish or Portuguese. For instance, the caribe *pinche* or "kitchen boy" caribe is perhaps more friendly than most, in that several species of piranhas serve as automatic dish-washers for the Indians. The old lady simply leaves her plates in the river and the fish clean the food residue off, slick as a whistle. Actually, another characin called the "bucktoothed tetra" does the same job and, if you hold the dish under water, he will also shave the hair off your arm.

The white piranha is often called caribe *mondonguero*, which means "dealer in tripe" and by some stretch of the imagination the allusion is to this piranha's abundance around village slaughter-houses where offal is regularly tossed in the stream. It's an unforgettable sight. You'll give up swimming forever. The caribe *capaburro* or "donkey castrater" is, oddly enough, known by that name over a wide range (from Venezuela to southern Brazil) in several languages, so it may well deserve its reputation. Capaburro often weigh four or five pounds and one glance at this snubnosed piranha is enough to intimidate any jackass.

The dentation of a piranha is more wicked than a casual examination reveals. Although its canine teeth look like unicuspids with a single sharp edge, if you depress the gums and expose a complete tooth you find a tricuspid—three cutting edges which come into play when the fish clamps its powerful jaws shut. The piranha doesn't bite and chew in the manner of a shark but literally shears out chunks of flesh like an animated scalpel. People who have been bitten by piranha often say that they weren't even aware of it until they saw blood in the water. The sensation of pain is delayed as it is with a razor cut. A poultice of tobacco is the usual Indian remedy for minor wounds, which leave deep semi-circular scars.

Nobody has ever presented a definitive explanation as to when and under what circumstances piranha become man-eaters. There is

> "It is virtually impossible to catch an undamaged fish on rod-and-reel in piranha-infested waters."

ample evidence that they are dangerous in deep, swift, or turbid water, which bears out the natives' belief that they are most aggressive during the rainy season, and on any occasion when there is blood in the water. The latter is a common situation in the simple act of releasing or cleaning fish. However, it is possible to wade in piranha-filled rivers where the water is clear and slow flowing in the dry season. I have never seen an Indian do this where the capaburro, dusky, or black piranhas abound but in areas where the ruddy, white, or Wimple's occur, they enter the water with no hesitation. Wimple's piranha is an exception in having comparatively weak jaws—which may be why it's ignored. This is purely a personal observation, and certainly not a valid rule, but it would appear that knowing which species is present plays some role in deciding where and when. On numerous occasions we have been wading in a particular location and later, just a few miles away, been told to stay out of the river.

PIRANHA SPECIES DISTRIBUTION is probably not only a matter of habitat preference as to bottom type, depth, and current velocity, but also a seasonal condition. After extensive periods of collecting specimens in one Orinoco tributary, we found that our nets had taken only adult fish of a particular species and never any juveniles. This would seem to indicate a migration from the main river. It's possible that when streams flood in the rainy season the larger, more dangerous species occur in areas that the Indians otherwise consider "safe." Language is, of course, a barrier, but even on trips when we had an accurate interpreter along, with biological training, the explanations were predicated on the *acceptance* of what happened rather than any understanding of it. The sun comes up, the moon goes down, and you don't ford the Rio São Laurenco at Brown's Farm, although it's perfectly all right to wade at the village two miles upstream. Provided the water is clear. And you are lucky.

The well-publicized film demonstration of a piranha school stripping a cow to a skeleton in a matter of minutes is factual, but it is provoked in the same manner that one can create a shark "attack" by towing a tuna carcass behind a boat. I watched a French TV crew try to set this up in Venezuela. The piranha took no interest in the deceased for two hours, despite bloodying the water. When everybody started to pack up and go home, the bashful cannibals suddenly went berserk and ate the cow so fast that the cameraman barely had time to get in focus. This was a school of Natterer's piranha, which are about as unpredictable as any I've observed. I doubt if the "dealer in tripe" or white piranha would hesitate but then, fish that hang around slaughterhouses have conditioned appetites.

The fact is that cattle wade South American rivers with impunity. On rare occasions an animal with running sores on its legs will get nipped. However, in common with the shark, piranha evidently respond to panic situations. It is virtually impossible to catch an undamaged fish on rod-and-reel in piranha-infested waters. From the instant a fish is hooked the piranha go to work chopping off its fins and finally slashing chunks out of its flesh. Sometimes you'll land nothing more than the victim's head. Obviously, a struggling animal triggers the stimuli through well-defined underwater vibrations. How this differs from a quietly wading man is apparent, but the occasional piranha attacks reported in South American newspapers are probably augmented by the more numerous "drownings" resulting from accidents which are frequent in countries where all the main highways are rivers. The basic native craft is a dugout, one of the tippiest boats I've ever had the misfortune to travel in, and rollovers are commonplace.

SEVERAL YEARS AGO, I talked with an Indian on Venezuela's Cinaruco River who lost his little daughter and her dog. His dugout turned over one evening and in the commotion that followed, the child and dog disappeared. Not a trace could be found of either victim, despite the fact that the river was in an almost currentless dry season stage. Even if we assumed that his daughter drowned, the father's reasoning was that the dog could swim and, therefore, both had been lost to the piranha. This is fairly typical, although there are reliably documented cases of actual attacks on wildly splashing people. Dr. Alvarez Aguirre of the National Museum in Rio de Janeiro told me that when they were laying railroad track along the Amazon, one of the laborers jumped in for a noon swim and his enthusiastic hand splashing turned him into an armless corpse bobbing in the current. It just happened to be the wrong time, the wrong place, and the wrong piranha.

One would imagine that such an aggressive fish would be easy to catch. At times you can cast endlessly and not get a touch—despite the fact that they will apple-core any other fish you hook. Surface lures as a rule won't even interest piranha, except for a flashy silver plug. A deeply fished jig is perhaps the most effective lure but even then certain species like the white piranha are as shy as any brown trout, and Wimple's piranha *never* to my knowledge takes an artificial (and seldom a natural) bait. The dusky, ruddy, Natterer's, red, black, Holland's and blacktailed piranhas are easy marks most of the time. They are not spectacular gamefish although the larger fish of three pounds or more put up a fast bottom-boring fight. Piranha are one of the better food fishes in South American rivers, particularly when deep fried to a golden crisp. The meat is very white and delicately flavored. It's easy, just close your eyes and bite.

—*March, 1973*

LYNN
BOGUE
HUNT

Since the advent of gunpowder, nearly all wild animals—even the most formidable—have learned to give Man a wide berth. They know that men mean guns, and guns mean death. A 12,000-pound elephant can be brought crashing to the ground by a piece of metal no bigger than your little finger.

But if you attack—or worse, wound—one, then all bets are off, and you may discover, briefly, that the gun is no match for an accomplished killer with your lead in him and all his adrenalin pumping.

Or sometimes, if you're really unlucky, you'll encounter something large that just doesn't feel like giving way at that moment, and you will be in a fight for your life before you know the fight has started.

Good luck! And take comfort from this: Most animals don't know how to kill a human being, so your odds of survival are better than you might think ... unless you meet one that learns quickly.

By Frank C. Hibben

The PURGATOIRE GRIZZLY

TWO VIOLENT CREATURES OF A VIOLENT LAND—THE OLD SOUTHWEST—ARE LOCKED IN AN IMPLACABLE DUEL UNTIL A SMALL MIRACLE INTERVENES.

*I*T WAS A SPINDLY TREE of no great height, and it was about the size of Juan's waist. As the bear stood on its hind legs its mean little eyes were almost level with Juan's feet. Suddenly it reached out and its curved claw caught the sole in Juan's moccasin. The tough buffalo hide and the ankle wrappings ripped away. The grizzly reached higher, swinging his big paw from the side like a drunk in a cantina fight.

Juan de Dios pulled himself higher on the slender limbs above the forks of the tree, which swayed as the grizzly clawed at the soft wood just below Juan's bare foot. Then, apparently tiring of this, the bear reached over and bit out a section of wood and bark as big as Juan's fist. Again and again it bit at the trunk just below the fork, and a sharp ax could not have cut

more quickly. The tree shivered as the bear tore out long pieces of green wood; a few more bites and it would fall.

JUAN DE DIOS had not been hunting this grizzly. Neither he nor the dead man, Chacon, who lay by the canyon wall, had ever hunted grizzlies—or any bears for that matter. For one thing, Apache Indians have a superstitious fear of bears. And though Juan was not an Apache, he considered himself one. He had been born a Navajo in New Mexico Territory, but he'd been captured in a slave raid by Apaches from the settlements above Santa Fe and sold to the Gonzales family in Abiquiu. Being nameless he called himself Juan de Dios, or John of God.

When Juan was 21, he was freed by the Emancipation Proclamation. He became a professional hunter, hunting mostly with the Apaches, sometimes with the Utes, and sometimes with the American mountain men who were coming into the Territory to trap beaver and to trade with the Spanish settlements. The wagon trains

that came by Bent's Fort on the Arkansas River and then turned south on the Santa Fe Trail needed meat too.

Juan had a Spanish musket that he had bought on a trading trip to Mexico City. Most of the other Indians were not allowed to own firearms, but he was often taken as a Spaniard because he occasionally wore Spanish clothes. Mostly, though, he dressed like an Apache and hunted with Apaches in the plains country along the Arkansas and Cimarron.

During the Civil War, which kept the white soldiers busy, times were good on the New Mexico frontier. When it was over, many veterans came to Santa Fe and to Fort Union; two or three wagon trains a day came down the Santa Fe Trail from Raton Pass. Game became scarce and the wagoneers arrogant. When wagon drivers raped some Indian women Juan joined with Apaches and Utes in an attack on a small wagon train. Then, to escape a punitive force of Union soldiers, Juan and his friend Chacon, an Apache chief, fled to the breaks of

the Purgatoire River, south of the Arkansas. There they hid and hunted. It was good country; the hundreds of little, sharp-walled canyons and stone cliffs were impassable for cavalry. In the breaks there was game and water and wood. Many elk wintered there. There were mountain sheep and mule deer, and occasionally even a small group of buffalo.

⟶ ⟞◇⟝ ⟵

CHACON AND JUAN DE DIOS spent the winter fairly comfortably. They built a hogan of logs and stones against the wall of a canyon near a pool of water. Both men were warmly dressed in fringed buckskin shirts and leggings made by Apache women, and they had a buffalo robe for a blanket.

Juan had 200 rounds of caps and balls from his smooth-bore musket, and Chacon owned a good bow and plenty of iron-tipped arrows, so they never lacked meat. It was a good life, though both men would have liked some cornmeal cakes and the companionship of their women. In the spring, they decided, they'd cross the Santa Fe

Trail by night and go and get the families of Chacon's band to come and camp with them in the Purgatoire breaks.

When the snows had mostly melted, Juan de Dios and Chacon went out on their last hunt. Roaming the smaller canyons to the east was a band of bighorn sheep. Sheep were becoming scarce, though Juan could remember how common they'd been when he first started to hunt in the area.

———— ❈ ————

JUAN AND CHACON had already killed two sheep that winter; they preferred bighorn meat to any other kind. But on this spring morning they did not reach the area where the sheep usually fed. A short distance from their hogan the two hunters found tracks of a large bull elk that had walked on earth softened by melting snow.

The hunters swung off on the minutes-old track, moving cautiously around a bend in the canyon, and immediately saw the elk feeding on grass spring-tinged with green. It was a big bull, but thin and gaunt. Its antlers were chalky and almost ready to shed. Chacon nodded to Juan, and the latter raised his musket and steadied it on some rock. When the elk turned broadside, Juan fired. The bull jumped violently, then galloped up the bed of the canyon, apparently unhurt. But suddenly he collapsed and died.

Juan and Chacon butchered their kill on the spot, cutting out the tenderloins along the backbone. These they tied in a package of skin, which they placed in the crotch of a small tree out of the reach of wolves. Still intent on a mountain sheep, they worked hard at cutting up the carcass and caching the meat high in the cottonwoods. Next day they'd pack it all back to the hogan. It was still early in the morning when they wiped their bloody hands on the grass, cleaned their hunting knives in a little pool of water, and moved on down the canyon to the breaks where the mountain sheep usually stayed.

But the bighorns had moved. Their tracks led straight north toward the Arkansas. That evening Juan and Chacon turned back toward their hogan, empty-handed, finding what comfort they could in the thought that they had a scrawny bull elk. Just as the sun dipped behind the Spanish Peaks, the two hunters turned up the little side canyon where they'd left the elk meat. There were the bundles in the trees, and a flock of magpies scolded in the branches above them.

The grizzly came out of the shadow of the canyon wall. There was a bubbling growl and the bear was upon them. Chacon thrust out his bow and reached for an arrow behind his shoulder. The bear struck him in that instant, and Chacon died without a sound. As the grizzly reached down to bite at the fallen man, Juan ran back two or three paces, cocked his musket, and fired pointblank at the bear.

As the cloud of smoke cleared, the bear charged. Juan dropped the gun and leaped for the nearest tree. He could not remember climbing it, but suddenly he was in its forks. The grizzly reared up on his hind legs and reached for Juan's feet. A curved claw caught the sole of Juan's moccasin and ripped the whole shoe away as the hunter jerked his foot upwards. He felt a stinging pain where one claw had grooved a furrow through his flesh. When the bear took to biting pieces out of the bole, Juan could see a matted spot of bloody fur on the hump, where his shot had struck. The musket ball had not even gone through the bone of the shoulder. In a few bites, the grizzly ripped away almost half the trunk just below the crotch, and Juan could feel the tree shiver. Two or three more tearing bites and it would fall.

Juan steadied himself between two spreading limbs, since the crotch was within reach of the great claws. Then, as the tree swayed dangerously, a bundle of meat swung against Juan's shoulder . . . . The tenderloins! Holding on with one hand, Juan drew his hunting knife and cut the strip of hide that held the bundle. Then he carefully dropped it on the head of the bear. The grizzly jumped back and dropped to all fours. With a growl, it pounced on the bundle and bit it savagely, shaking it from side to side as though to kill it. Finally the brute lay at full length on its belly and ate the meat, gulping down chunks of hide and hair with it.

Now Juan had a chance to look around. The trees on which the front and hind quarters of the elk were tied showed long claw marks where the grizzly had tried to reach the meat. Chacon lay where he had fallen beside the canyon wall.

When the grizzly has fed, he will go away, Juan thought. But it did not leave, even after it had eaten the last scrap of elk skin. As dark fell, it suddenly attacked the body of Chacon, perhaps aroused by the windblown fringe on the dead man's shirt. The grizzly bit savagely at the corpse, turned it over with his claws, but did not eat it. Then it moved beneath an overhang in the canyon wall and lay down to guard the spot.

Juan removed a headband that he wore beneath his hat and tied it around his injured foot. Then he pulled his hunting shirt up around his neck against the cold night wind that blew down the canyon. By morning, he expected, the grizzly would be gone, and he could come down out of the tree and reload his gun. Then he could bury the body of his friend in some crack in the rocks, in the manner of the Apaches.

⁜

BUT AS THE long night finally gave way to dawn, Juan saw that the grizzly was still crouched beneath the overhang. The hunter was now so cramped that he'd have to shift his weight. Cautiously and slowly, he put one foot, then the other, into the crotch of the tree. Now he eased the weight on his arms and flexed them slowly. At the movement, the grizzly sprang out of the shadow and reached the tree with lightning speed. Then it reared on its hind legs and clawed at the crotch. Juan scrambled upward and jerked his feet out of the way only an instant before the hooked claws raked the wood on which he'd been standing. Then the bear sank its teeth into the wood, now almost gnawed through.

One more bite—perhaps two—and the tree would fall. Juan prayed in a low voice to the Christian God of the Gonzales family, but he did not neglect the Apache gods of the mountains. And then Juan got his miracle.

The grizzly ceased its biting and stood almost motionless against the tree. Its black muzzle wrinkled back and forth, smelling upward. Finally it dropped to all fours and walked deliberately toward one of the other trees, the one in which the other bundles of meat still hung. All that day the bear clawed futilely at the trunk. Twice it walked deliberately to the body of

Chacon, growling and biting at the stiffened corpse. After the second visit it approached the tree where Juan perched stiffly, stood erect, and rubbed its hump against the trunk—the challenge of a male grizzly toward an enemy. Juan was careful not to move, and again the grizzly dropped, returning to the tree where the elk meat was hung. Through the long hours of daylight the bear traced a three-cornered path between the two trees and Chacon's body but made no further move to attack the man.

Just at dark, the bear lay down again beneath the ledge to guard his meat, his prisoner, and his victim. Juan prepared to spend another night in the tree. He was beginning to feel weak and he needed water badly.

When morning dawned over the cliffs and canyons of the Purgatoire, Juan again saw the blurred outline of the bear, lying there and watching him. The Indian was certain that he could never endure another day in the tree. Even if the grizzly did not bite through the weakened trunk, he'd fall from sheer weakness and lack of sleep. A spring wind that freshened with the coming of the morning swayed the tree dangerously. If the wind grew stronger, the spindly trunk would buckle. That would be the end.

Late in the morning, the grizzly emerged and looked upward at Juan with bloodshot little eyes. *Now he will push against his tree,* Juan thought. *In a little while I will again be with Chacon.* But the grizzly wrinkled its nose, turned, and lurched down the canyon. Once it stopped and looked back. Then it was gone, around the curve of the rock.

It might be a trick to lure him out of the tree, but Juan did not care. He dropped to the ground. His numbed legs would not hold his weight, so he crawled to where his musket lay. Sitting there, he reloaded the musket and put a cap on the nipple.

It was a day later that Juan came back to the little canyon to bury his friend, Chacon. The grizzly had not returned, but Juan did not track it. Nor did he retrieve the elk meat from the tree. There'd be no refuge for the Apache family in the Purgatoire canyons. No Indian would ever hunt there again. The big grizzly was evil medicine.

—April, 1962

By Jesse Fowler Smith

In the
JAWS OF A TIGER

ALL MY VARIED EXPE-riences of the last thirty years have not obliterated the record of one experience in the jungles of Burma. Today I can turn back memory's pages and see again that tropical landscape of meadow, field and forest, where, by all the laws of logic, my grave should be found. The faces of my compan-ions of that day readily come back to me, and I hear again the very tones of Mr. Geis' voice as his pent-up feelings found expression in words.

The end of March, 1902, which was the beginning of my "hot-season" vacation, found me, with my wife and baby daughter, the guest of Rev. George J. Geis and his family in the Mission bungalow at Myitkyina, Burma, north-ern terminus of the Burma Railway. We had been there about a week when failure of the meat supply in the village market induced my host to plan a hunting trip in the hope of replenishing the larder with venison. Officers from the British regiment posted at Myitkyina had reported deer plentiful at a place about twelve miles down the railway, where, not long before, the soldiers had camped for a week for field maneuvers. We decided to bring back our venison from that region.

Our party also included three members of the border tribe known as Kachins: namely, Ning Krawng, a teacher in the Mission School; one of his pupils, who was to be our cook; and an older Kachin, an escaped slave from a neighboring valley who bore, as a mark of his servitude, a scar where his left ear had been lopped off by his master. The ex-slave carried a *dah*, a sort of glorified butcher knife, the only tool and weapon of the Kachins. Ning Krawng and I were armed with double-barreled shotguns loaded for deer; Mr. Geis had a rifle.

From the station-master permission had been obtained to occupy as our camp the railway bungalow which, with water tank and the huts of the "pumpers," made up all there was of the railway station nearest to Myitkyina. Except when a railway official or his guests occupied the bungalow, four native "pumpers" were the sole inhabitants of this station.

With provisions for twenty-four hours we set out by the one daily train from Myitkyina. At 9 o'clock, about an hour after our departure, we detrained at the station. It was several weeks before I saw another train on this railway. When the return train passed about 4 o'clock that day, I was five miles back in the jungle, Ning Krawng my sole companion.

Having left the cook in charge of our folding cots, bedding and food, we took our weapons and left the bungalow to look over the ground where, later in the day, we hoped to discover herds of grazing deer. Our course led down a sharp slope to an extensive meadow. A quarter of a mile by a narrow, winding path through elephant-grass that reached five feet above our heads brought us to a wooded ravine.

As we crossed this meadow, Mr. Geis said: "Here we must be on the lookout for sleeping tigers. They like to crawl into this tall grass during the day."

However, we roused no sleeping tigers. We descended the ravine, at the bottom of which trickled a dry-season stream, climbed the opposite bank and emerged from the fringe of trees, which bordered the ravine, into a large grassy plain, much like an American prairie. Through the trees above us leaped a small troop of chattering monkeys. In other trees flocks of noisy parrots were feeding on several varieties of wild fruit.

No other signs of animal life were discernible, for before us, instead of a field of lush grass that would furnish forage to scores of deer, we looked out over several hundred acres of desolation, beyond which, some two miles away, was the edge of a deep forest. A devastating fire, traceable to the soldiers, whose former camp ground we had reached, had destroyed every vestige of food for bird as well as beast.

⟶ ⟶ ⟡ ⟵ ⟵

DISAPPOINTED, WE RETURNED to the bungalow to eat our rice and curry, enjoy a siesta, and plan a campaign for deer in "the cool of the day."

Between three and four o'clock we started once more over the same route to the hunting ground. Upon reaching the ravine, we laid our plans for obtaining a good bag despite the fire-blackened feeding grounds. We decided to look for deer in the fringe of trees that marked the courses of the ravines which seemed to encircle the open plateau.

We separated into two parties. Mr. Geis and the Kachin freedman followed the border to the right, while Ning Krawng and I took the border on the left. It was agreed that both parties should continue until we met on the far side of the open area. It was also agreed that, in case of trouble, three shots fired at distinct and regular intervals would be a call for help. So we parted.

Long-legged, barefooted Ning Krawng stalked ahead at such a pace that I could hardly do more than trail him. In a short time he disappeared from view altogether among the brush and trees. With the conviction that my safety depended upon keeping him in sight, I began to run, but before I gained sight of him his gun rang out, followed almost instantaneously by the loud crashing of some animal through the brush. My first thought was that he had shot an elephant, for it seemed to me that nothing smaller could make so much noise tearing through the undergrowth.

⟶ ⟶ ⟡ ⟵ ⟵

ON REACHING NING KRAWNG, I found him a new man. The lust of the killer was in his blazing eyes as he told me by means of a few Burmese words and much use of pantomime that he had shot a tiger—"a big one, wounded in the shoulder." Excitedly he showed me the pool of blood at his feet, breathlessly he pointed to the trail of blood leading off into the underbrush. Assured that I understood his words and signs, he waited not a second, but strode off along the crimson trail. With only a moment's hesitation, but with a question in my mind as to the wisdom of this procedure, I followed him, for I reasoned that, dangerous as this course might be, it was better than being left alone in a tiger-infested wilderness.

On the green carpet beneath the trees the bright red line of blood was easy to follow. For some distance ahead the undergrowth was not dense and the trees were small and scattered. No tiger was in sight. We would be alert and quick on the trigger at the first intimation of his being in range. Moreover, both of us were impressed by the amount of blood that the tiger had spilled along the way.

Ning Krawng, with many ejaculations, repeatedly pointed to the crimson pools which showed so plainly the effectiveness of his aim. And with each ejaculation he bounded ahead on the trail. At intervals I paused to listen. In my ignorance I expected to hear the death groans of the animal that was losing his life-blood in such quantities.

After a few minutes we came to a steep but narrow gully athwart the trail. To the bottom of this the tiger had plunged headlong, then clambered up the opposite slope, leaving at the bottom a bucketful of gore. We, too, leaped into the gully and climbed breathlessly to the other side, expecting to find our quarry so weakened from loss of blood that one more well-aimed shot would make him ours. At the top of the gully, the trail of blood led into a tangle of bushes and bamboos that was too thick for our eyes to penetrate.

We looked at each other. We shook our heads. Ning Krawng turned to the right and took a few steps toward the open field. I turned to follow, but before I had taken two steps there came an angry roar from the bamboo thicket. I looked to see, not thirty feet away, the black and tawny stripes of an enormous tiger some ten feet in the air, headed straight for me. One thought flashed through my mind: "If you're going to use your gun, now is the time."

I RAISED MY gun to take aim. As the stock pressed my shoulder I drew back my right foot to brace myself for the shot. My heel caught a trailing root, and I was thrown flat on my back so suddenly that, when the infuriated tiger landed, his right forepaw came down on my left breast, his huge body covered me completely, and his fiery eyes looked into mine for one split second.

Instinctively I turned my face away. My cork helmet fell over my features; the left side of my head alone was exposed to the tiger's fangs. With a snarling bite his jaws closed on my skull. I heard his teeth crunch through my scalp, but I felt nothing. A silent prayer went up from my heart for my wife and child, to whom I had said good-by that morning. I breathed one plea for forgiveness for my folly, as I was sure that this was the end of my earthly career.

But the monster's jaws were not fatal. He had taken his bite, and I was still alive and conscious. I said to myself, "He didn't open his mouth wide enough. He'll do a better job next time." A second time he clamped his jaws upon my head; a second time I heard the crunch but felt no pain; a second time I realized that a tiger's bite had not ended my life.

My uninjured brain worked fast. "Once more," I thought. "A third time, he'll try it and complete the job." A third time, indeed, he crunched into my scalp, causing no pain.

Then, hardly realizing what had happened, I opened my eyes, raised myself on my elbow, and saw the brute's tail disappearing into the same thicket from which, but a few seconds before, I had seen him spring. I sat up and turned my face toward Ning Krawng, who was standing like one in a trance only a few paces away.

Forgetting his ignorance of the English language, I blurted out, "Well, I'm alive, but he's got my ear." I thought that his last bite had taken my ear clean off.

As soon as he saw me get up and heard me speak, Ning Krawng cried out in Burmese, "Run! Run!" and he proceeded to climb the nearest tree. In my confusion I could see no other tree; so I tried to climb after him. My exertions caused my wounds to bleed; the smell of the blood, now trickling down my face, nauseated me. Furthermore, when I attempted to pull myself up to the branch on which Ning Krawng sat, I found that my left arm was useless. Unable either to climb the tree or to get Ning Krawng to pull me to safety, with blanched face and a feeling of faintness I began to slide down the tree, murmuring: "It's no use. I can't make it."

Then Ning Krawng became alarmed for me. He descended, fired in quick succession both barrels of his gun, and with two more hurried shots emptied mine. Thus he had put us in the delightful predicament of being alone in the tiger jungle with two empty guns. Not waiting to reload, he urged me to get upon his back, but I refused. So we started on the run, out of the woods, and into the center of the open plain.

After we had covered about a half mile, Ning Krawng carrying both guns, we reached the actual camp site of the soldiers. There we threw ourselves upon the ground and panted until I had recovered my wind. Crying out for water, I followed Ning Krawng back toward the bungalow. At the point where our morning path had crossed the ravine he made a cup from a big leaf and gave me a drink of water from the stream. It was the most refreshing drink that ever wet my lips.

Back at the bungalow, I fell exhausted on my cot, where Ning Krawng left me to go for our companions. Mr. Geis had heard the quick succession of our shots, had concluded that we were finding plenty of game, and therefore made no effort to come to our help.

The sun had set when Mr. Geis arrived. He washed my wounds, dressed me in pajamas, made a stretcher out of my cot and two bamboo poles, and ordered the four pumpers to carry me on their shoulders up the twelve miles of railway track to the nearest doctor. The swaying motion which the bearers gave to my stretcher soon lulled me to sleep, and for the most of the way I slept peacefully.

Within a few minutes of our arrival at the Mission House, the regimental surgeon from the military hospital appeared. His examination showed several scalp wounds, one deep incision near the crown, my left ear hanging in three strips, and a deep wound in the left shoulder just below the collar-bone. This last was made by my fall upon a stiletto-like stump. The pressure of the tiger's right forepaw had pushed me firmly down upon this "spit," and had also left five black-and-blue footprints upon my left breast. This wound in the shoulder, fortunately, injured neither my collar-bone nor my shoulder-blade, but the laceration of the muscles had caused my arm to be temporarily useless.

Having examined all my injuries, the doctor gave me ammoniated spirits to inhale (since he had no anesthetic), and proceeded to cleanse and dress my wounds. He took thirteen stitches in my head and ear. At this point for the first time I began to feel pain, and I felt it a-plenty.

I spent the next twelve hours in my own bed. For the next five or six days the doctor visited me daily. After that I was able to ride a bicycle to the hospital for the daily dressing. Thanks to my own clean blood and the doctor's skillful ministrations, no infection developed. This was a matter of relief to my friends and of surprise to the doctor, who declared that, in all his experience as an army surgeon in the tropics, he had never known a person to survive a tiger's mauling. In those rare cases where the victim had not been killed outright, blood-poisoning had set in, and death soon resulted.

At the end of the vacation period my wounds had all healed. I returned to my work at Rangoon according to the plan made six weeks before. At that time, few scars were discernible. Today a "dent" in my head, apparent only to the touch, a scar on my shoulder and two "seams" on my left ear are the only outward evidence of my first and only attempt to win fame as a big-game hunter.

This fearful experience is called to my mind every time I enter a barber shop, for barbers always want to know what made the "hole" in my head. I tell them, but they never believe me.

—June, 1933

HE WAS IN A COUNTRY
WHERE NOBODY WOULD
LOOK FOR HIM WHEN THE
RATTLER STRUCK. THE
NIGHT THAT FOLLOWED
WAS ONE OF SICKENING
TERROR—AND HOPE.

By Frank Triem

THE BIG DARK

A GUN WAS A GUN IN the year I was fourteen. Kids that age aren't usually inclined to look below the surface, and I was no exception. That was why the Nickel-Plated Wonder seemed to me the most desirable revolver in the world. From the moment my friend Beany first showed it to me I knew it had to be mine.

I'm afraid our teacher found me more trying than usual that day. It was one of those warm still mornings in late May. Through the open window at my elbow I could see a patch of canyon wall and, through the live-oaks, patches of silvery stream. Summer vacation was just around the corner. I could picture the long, ecstatic days ahead, fishing, hunting, panning for gold—and always with The Wonder strapped to my hip. It wasn't surprising that I responded to Miss Miller's simplest questions with "Huh?" and a vacant look.

Beany and I had exchanged notes behind our books, and the deal was cut and dried when at last the bell rang. We tore into the yard two jumps ahead of the thundering herd, and we didn't stop running until we were around the first bend in the road.

Panting, we slowed. Beany crooked a forefinger and I followed him up-hill through the brush until we came to a hollow log. Here he dropped to his knees, fished inside, and when he stood up he was holding it—The Wonder.

I put on a good show of indifference. I turned it over and over; casually, as I had seen Dad do, I flipped out the cylinder—.38 Special, Conquistador, and in small letters there were some words in a tongue I couldn't read. "How does it shoot?" I asked.

Later I realized Beany had evaded my question. "It's a .38," he pointed out. "It'll drop a lion in its tracks."

I closed the cylinder, cocked The Wonder and pointed it at a squirrel. The hammer fell with a ringing snap.

"What'll you take?" I inquired.

Beany jammed his hands down in his overalls pockets. "I want a dozen of those new traps your pa bought you," he said.

I gulped. This was a stiffer bargain than we had outlined. "I'll give you six," I told him, "and six used jump traps."

"Okay," Beany agreed.

He didn't hesitate. Later I found out why. At the time I wasn't aware that he had fished the Nickel-Plated Wonder out of the creek—after his father had thrown it there.

I pocketed the .38 and we went on up the county road a third of a mile to the place where twin wheel-tracks slanted down to our right. Here, from a cache known only to myself, I dug out the traps. I watched Beany go on up the road with my traps over his shoulder. Then, wondering what I was going to say when I got home, I headed for the ranch.

I hadn't expected Dad would be overjoyed, but his reaction fell so far short that I was disappointed. He stood with his back to the fireplace, turning the shiny revolver over and over. On his face was the expression of one who scents something urgently in need of burying.

"I've heard about these babies," he told me. "They're bringing them in from Europe by the boat-load. They're made of old melted-up stove legs." He handed it back. "You understand, of course, you're not to shoot this thing—not under any circumstances?"

The living room was very still. Mom didn't look up from her needlework. My kid brother, thumbing through a catalogue, glanced slyly at me. I glowered at him. It was because of him that I had had to tell about my deal. J. D. had heard rumors of it during the morning recess, and it had been a foot-race to see which of us got home first to tell the folks. I had won by a gnat's whisker.

"Beany shot it lots of times," I muttered. "His dad knows as much as you do about guns."

That didn't sound nice, but I was mad and wanted to cut back at Dad. He should have up-ended me and hung a few hot ones where they would have done the most good. His eyes showed hurt, but he merely shrugged.

"If Beany has any fingers or hands to spare, that's his business," he said. "You have just the usual number of everything. Play with that pot-metal Special all you like—but don't shoot it."

The discussion was ended. As I took The Wonder into my room and slid it under my pillow a muscle at the corner of my mouth twitched. But I made a show of coming back into the family living room, of getting out my history book and studying the lesson I had been too excited to master during the day's session. Once I found myself staring at the green-shaded Rochester lamp.

"I *will* shoot it!" I promised myself.

There were times during those early years when Dad gave evidence of being something of a mind-reader. This was one of those occasions. Although he seemed to consider the incident closed, I know now he sensed my rebellion, and he evidently decided to take no chances.

I awoke with a jump. Moonlight slanted in through the open window, and in his bed against the far wall J. D. breathed rhythmically. I was wide awake. My head turned as I searched the half visible room. There was no one here now, but I had the conviction that someone had been here. Out in the kitchen a board creaked. Then I caught the sound of a door being softly closed.

I slid a hand under my pillow. Instantly I sat up. My worst fears were confirmed. The Wonder was gone!

I went through the silent house and eased the back door open. A silvery moon was riding high, and someone was going down through the garden. Dad vanished briefly inside the tool shed. When he reappeared, he was carrying a spade.

Tears of resentment stung my eyes. I almost hated Dad. Quite a while later I found out for myself that saving others from the fruits of their folly is always a thankless undertaking.

In a freshly spaded area just to the right of the old redwood stump Dad dug a hole. I caught the flash of moonlight reflected on a nickeled surface—and then he was shoveling the earth back. He took his time about leveling the ground off. He must have guessed there would be a determined investigation on my part. And I'll say this for him—he did a good job. If I hadn't spotted the place exactly, I'd never have been able to go back, hours later, and retrieve the Nickel-Plated Wonder.

From then on, I played my cards close to my chest. I was determined to shoot the revolver if it was the last thing I ever did. And although the subject was never mentioned again, I knew Dad was watching me. I couldn't be sure, but I suspected he had gone back to the spot in the lower garden and had found that the buried .38 had been exhumed.

It was quite a while before I managed to get hold of a handful of .38 Special cartridges. Again it was my friend Beany who helped me—if you could call it that. He demanded another six traps for a dozen cartridges—and he didn't even tell me, until it was too late, that he had loaded them himself. I often wondered what he used for powder.

One evening, as we finished clearing away the supper dishes, I brought the matter to a head. "I'd like to go over to Chet's place, for the day, before school starts," I told my father. "You know you half-way said I could."

Dad drummed on the table with his finger-tips. He wasn't looking at me—he was looking through me—but I forced myself to meet his eyes. Then he smiled faintly. "Okay, do it tomorrow," he told me. "But you better be home by dark."

I sighed my relief. I had put it over; I had the entire day to do with as I saw fit. I'd go up the canyon far enough to do my shooting without being heard, and by evening I'd be back. My trigger-finger itched. I could hardly wait.

By noon I was in a part of the great canyon that was strange to me—and a long way from home. My blue denim shirt was glued to my torso. It was hotter than blazes down here on the floor.

I was hot, hungry and thirsty. I hurried faster. I wasn't as careful as I should have been. The thing that happened was strictly my own fault.

I felt no pain. I didn't realize until I glanced down what it was that had thumped against my leg. Then it came to me that the jarring impact meant something. My eyes widened. The snake was a big one, and I had almost stepped on him. He had struck and had coiled, ready to lash out again. My heart was picking up speed. A hard fist was knotted in my stomach. Through a ringing stillness I heard my shrill cry of fear.

The big fellow rattled. It would have been better for both of us if he had done that in the first place. Overshadowing my panic was a red mist of rage. I knew I ought to be rolling up my pants leg and attending to the bite—but first there was something else.

The snake uncoiled and began to flow toward near-by rocks. I slid the Nickel-Plated Wonder from my hip pocket and lifted the hammer. The sights wavered, and my first shot was a miss. But it did the trick; once more the rattler coiled and the triangular head was briefly still. Over the sights I fancied I saw the forked tongue darting out.

The .38 jerked, and the headless trunk of the snake was thrashing in the weeds. Vengence was mine. But as I pulled off my shoe and rolled up the leg of my overalls I knew what it had cost me. The two crimson punctures were just to the left of the shin-bone. Already the flesh around them was puffing alarmingly, and my heart had quickened to a racing beat that came too fast for me to count.

Steady, steady—I said it out loud, over and over. I was in a tight spot. Home was miles away, and mostly uphill. I gritted my teeth. That insane impulse to jump to my feet, to run, yelling for Dad —I'd have to conquer it if I was to go on living. Dad couldn't hear me. Whatever was done I would have to do alone.

I had my knife out, the blade open. I had sometimes thought it would be hard to cut into

a snake-bite, but now I found it was easy. Fear gave me what it took to do the job.

I dropped the knife and looked at the thick red blood welling from the crisscross incision. I was briefly but thoroughly sick.

And now the second step. I tore a strip from the leg of my overalls and knotted it loosely just below the knee. Then I put a bit of stick through the loop and turned it until the cloth buried itself in the calf of my leg and I felt an artery down there begin to hammer. Panting, I lay back. I had done all I could.

I'd have to have help to get home, that I knew. And the ranch was far beyond shouting distance. But we had long ago arranged a signal we were to use in the event of a mishap such as this: three quick shots, a pause, and three more.

I flipped out the cylinder of The Wonder. It stuck a bit, but I was too excited to notice that. I ejected the two empty shells and replaced them with loaded ones. My heart was hammering hard, and I was oddly short of breath. My hands shook as I flipped the cylinder shut. I raised The Wonder above my head. Three quick shots—

An ear-shattering report jarred the hot stillness of the canyon floor. Something had gone wrong. I was trying to pull the trigger again, but it wouldn't budge. I lowered the weapon. The upper portion of the cylinder was gone and the strap bulged up. My thumb was crimson from a deep gash.

I flopped down and lay gasping on the hot earth. By and by I sat up. My leg was enormously swollen and beginning to have a nasty, purplish look. It was time to loosen the tourniquet and let some of the stagnant blood into the circulatory system.

The leg had been going numb, but the minute the pressure slacked off waves of pain flowed from it. I gritted my teeth, grabbed hold of my knee with both hands and hung on while the hot tears rolled down my dirty face. But I forced myself to count slowly to fifteen, before I again twisted the loop tight.

A flaming disc the size of a dish pan was dropping toward the timber. It would soon be dark. And I was unarmed, scared and far from home. My folks would miss me before long—

but they thought I had gone to visit Chet. And Chet lived in the opposite direction.

I sat on the little knoll, watching the line of black creep up the far canyon wall. It was also inching up the little rise on which I sat. I twisted my head. The sun had flattened itself on the saw-toothed ridges to the west. It was half gone—two-thirds . . . three-fourths . . . The last shimmering edge faded, and the day was done.

I lay in the warm dust, listening to the tiny sounds of birds in the live-oaks over to my left, to the murmur of the near-by creek. A breath of cool air fanned my blazing face, and I shivered. I looked up. Away up against the high foot-hills to the east, a tiny speck of red glowed. It reminded me of a malevolent eye, but I knew it for what it was, a shaft of sunlight reflected in the window of the fire ranger's lookout. As I watched it faded and was gone.

I awoke to find the sky frosted with stars. My leg felt ominously numb, and I dug a match from my pocket and struck it. The tissues around the bite were the color of a new stovepipe. I dropped the match and once again loosened the tourniquet. This time I counted to thirty before again drawing it tight.

Again I slid into a strange, half-waking and half-sleeping state, poised between two worlds. Somewhere, and I knew that it was only within my brain, a voice was singing. The clear sweet voice was that of Mom as she went about her work in the kitchen. "The night is dark, and I am far from home—"

That made me think of the folks. They'd be wondering why I didn't show up, and might be uneasy. I wished I could save them that worry. But more than that, I wished they'd come this way. They wouldn't, of course. Why should they happen to search in this direction, any more than a dozen of others? Unless—

I was on my hands and knees, crawling in the dark. I found a bit of branch, clung to it, moved on. I came presently to another—and another. Sitting in the dirt with the branches and twigs between my legs, I broke them into fragments. Then I struck one more match and touched it to the wood. As it caught I moved back. Half fainting from weakness and fear, I crawled on hands and knees about the little

knoll and brought in bits of dead wood for my fire.

It was the fire that saved me. I had started it to thrust back the dark and in the forlorn hope that some of my family would see it and come to my aid. They didn't—but someone else did.

Miles away, in the high foot-hills, a man whose business was watching for fires saw mine as, hours before, I had seen sunlight reflected in his window. While I lay alternately raving and in a death-like stupor his voice ranged over miles of single-strand telephone wire, and help came at last . . .

A cool wind fluttered the lace curtains at my elbow. Mom and Dad had insisted that I spend a couple of days in bed, and I hadn't argued. I had come, the foot-hill doctor told my parents, very close to the Big Dark.

In the kitchen Mom moved soberly about her work. Every few minutes she came to the open door of the bedroom to look in and assure herself that her firstborn was all right. And then in came my kid brother, his hair rumpled, looking mysterious and wise. He sat on the edge of my bed.

An instant later Dad, just returned from town, came in with Mom. Dad grinned at me. "Pretty soft," he told me. "I wish all I had to do was to lie around, eat like a horse, have people bring me presents—"

"But nobody's—" I began, and stopped.

Dad was holding out a box, a mulberry-colored box maybe a foot long by five or six inches wide and two inches deep. I tipped back the lid. Reverently I lifted out the softly gleaming target revolver. A .38 Special with fine sights and an action smooth as oiled glass: the proud masterpiece of American craftsmen who took their hats off to no one when it came to building a gun a man could stake his life on.

"That," Dad told me, "is to replace The Wonder—wherever it is." His eyes met mine until I blinked hard and looked away. Years later I realized that Dad knew more than he was telling. Long after we boys were grown and had left the ranch, Dad admitted he had backtracked, had found the headless snake and the shattered fragments of the Nickel-Plated Wonder and had left them there, to rust in peace.

—August, 1950

By Andy Russell

Encounter at GRIZZLY GULCH

HE DAMNED HIS CARE-
LESSNESS AND MOURNED
OVER THE DAMAGE HE'D
DONE TO HIS HOLSTER—
AND NEXT DAY IT HELD
HIS LIFE IN THE BALANCE.

JOHN EWING AND I
scrambled the last fifty feet
up onto the top of a little shoulder
that jutted from the side of Panorama Peak.
There we looked out over the tumbled expanses
of Grizzly Gulch. Peaks, canyons, big timber
and new snow blended with the blue sky and
bright sun to form a picture typical of the wild

reaches of southeastern British Columbia in September.

My outfit had been out ten days with a party of three sportsmen from Greeley, Colorado. This was Bill Farr's second trip with us, and he and his two friends, John Ewing and Bob Noffsinger, had had plenty of climbing. The weather had been hot and dry, which made hunting tough. We'd spent most of the first week right on top of the ranges, seeing many goats and several grizzlies. Bob and Bill had got billies, and Bob missed a shot at a black bear, but John had not fired a shot at anything. Now he and I were out for the day with Bill and Dave Simpson, one of the guides. We were all determined to find John a trophy.

It might seem futile to hunt an individual animal in such a huge, broken piece of country, but that was exactly what we were doing. That morning we'd left camp near the top of Starvation Pass, where we had weathered out the first snowstorm of the season. Two days before the storm, Bill had killed a huge billy goat not far from Little Bear Lake, in a hanging basin on the rim of the gulch. While he and Wenz Dvorak, the head guide, were skinning out the goat, another billy had walked out on a shelf a thousand feet above and stood looking down. He was as big as a donkey and carried an impressive set of horns. Wenz is a veteran of forty years in the mountains, and about the coolest man I know, but when he described the goat later that day there was an unusual gleam in his eyes. Any goat big enough to get Wenz excited is worth looking for, so we were out to try and find him for John Ewing.

WE'D RIDDEN THROUGH the basin near Little Bear Lake and tied up the horses in the timber half a mile or so farther up the basin. Then we split up. John and I climbed straight up the mountain, while Dave and Bill ascended into the back of the basin.

After a long hour and a half of slippery footwork through a tangle of snow-covered

blow-down timber and snow brush, John and I sat down on a dry slab of rock in the sun. We were glassing the mountainside for sign of the big billy when a curious sound drew my attention. At first I was not sure of its direction, but then it came again clearly through the still air—a distinct sharp sound, as though someone were hammering on a rock.

John heard it, too, and asked me what it was. At first I was stumped, but then I remembered that a party of oil geologists were camped in Akamina Valley, a few miles to the north. When the peculiar sound came up to us again I suddenly decided I had the answer.

"Rock hunters!" I muttered disgustedly to John. "They *would* have to show up in here. Big help on a goat hunt."

In all the years we had hunted that area, we had never run into any interference before, and I couldn't help a feeling of vast disappointment as I glassed the basin trying to locate our unwelcome visitors. I swung my glasses along the edge of the big timber that bordered the clearing around Little Bear Lake, trapped in a natural bowl at the foot of the mountain 1,500 feet below—and a grizzly walked into view! It was a big silvertip. As it walked over to our horse trail, I distinctly heard the *chock-chock-chock* of the hammering. Then the big bear let out a hair-lifting roar. Immediately afterward I heard the hammering sound again.

John had his glasses glued on the bear, and he suddenly exclaimed, "That racket we've been hearing isn't rock hunters—it's that bear chopping his teeth together! I just saw him do it!"

He was right, and for the next half hour we were treated to a sight I'd never seen before—a picture complete with sound. The bear stalked back and forth along our horse tracks, repeatedly roaring and snapping his teeth. It was an awe-inspiring sound, leaving little doubt in our minds that this particular grizzly was mighty put out with our intrusion into his territory. It was very unusual behavior for a grizzly, but the explanation was

"I think we should turn this goat hunt into a bear hunt and go down and bust that old bruiser."

obvious. He had located the carcass of Bill's goat and was laying claim to it in no uncertain fashion. We had probably ridden right past the big animal in the morning as we entered the basin, and that thought sent a little chill up my back. If he had jumped us on the trail that snaked through boulders and down logs we'd have been in trouble—real trouble.

"That's the meanest bear I've ever seen," I told John. "I think we should turn this goat hunt into a bear hunt and go down and bust that old bruiser."

"Just fine with me," John answered. Then he added, "I'll bet this is a relative of that grizzly you were telling us about the other night. Grizzly Gulch is well named!"

He was referring to a story I had told one night at the fire—a true tale of how Grizzly Gulch got its name.

* * *

IN THE SPRING of 1908, my father-in-law, Bert Riggall, who was later to become one of Canada's most famous guides and naturalists, was working with a drilling crew that was prospecting for oil near some seeps in Akamina Valley. His job as tool dresser had two attractions for Bert, who had recently come from England into the raw new land of western Canada. It paid him a fair wage in hard cash, which was a mighty scarce article at the time, and it also took him into the heart of the practically unknown wilderness mountain country of southeastern British Columbia. Bert had climbed the Alps as a boy and had an abiding love for high mountains.

So it was only natural that he spent all his spare time exploring amongst the peaks surrounding the oil camp. On every second Sunday, his day off, he'd take a lunch and head up into the wilderness country alone to explore the unmapped mountains. The only weapon he carried was a 7.63 mm Mauser pistol, one of the first semiautomatic types. It had a six-inch barrel and the magazine was a clip that hung just forward of the trigger guard. The gun was carried in a unique wooden holster with a spring-locking lid. This lid snapped open when a concealed button was pushed. The holster, made of a piece of hollowed-out walnut, could also

serve as a quick-detachable stock for the pistol, turning it into a sort of short rifle. At the time, this pistol was the last word in sidearms and Bert was mighty proud of it.

One Saturday evening in late August, Bert busied himself preparing for a Sunday wandering and exploring. He packed a lunch and carefully cleaned the pistol. After cleaning it, he placed the gun in its holster and set it on a table in the cook shack. A few minutes later he accidentally nudged it off onto the floor, and when he picked it up he was appalled to find that the holster lid had split off at the hinges. Only a man who loves fine equipment could appreciate Bert's feelings. And no one could know that the broken lid was going to save Bert's life.

Next morning at dawn, he headed up a wild, heavily timbered valley that led into the high peaks south of the camp. The narrow gulch was choked with down logs, snow brush and bogs under a heavy growth of spruces and firs. The going was heavy, and Bert used many of the down logs as pathways through the brush.

At noon he came out into the clear at the foot of a pass. Here avalanches that came down every spring had cleared a series of broad, open swaths. These natural clearings are carpeted with berry brush, and as he climbed the pass Bert counted five grizzlies feeding on the huckleberries. At the crest of the pass, the tremendous vista of Starvation Valley came into view, with its lakes, glacier and rugged flanking mountains. For two hours Bert climbed and explored, viewing the country from various ridges and shoulders. Time passed swiftly, as it has a way of doing in such country, so it was late afternoon when he finally turned back down the pass toward camp.

He traveled fast, being anxious to get through the timber in the lower valley before dark. As he went, he kept a wary eye peeled for bears. Their sign was everywhere, and in many places along the watercourse the brush and lush grass was trampled flat into broad, intercrossing bear trails. On reaching the timber he continued to travel as fast as possible, and again used the down logs for natural boardwalks so he could avoid scrambling through the interminable snow brush.

In one place he found a whole series of logs lodged; by jumping from one to another he was able to travel several hundred yards without coming to the ground. Finally he leaped up onto a particularly large fir tree and clattered along it for about seventy feet before coming to a big branch. He swung around it and continued for a few steps more, then came to another branch blocking the way. For a moment he paused undecided, then jumped down four feet into the brush.

When he hit the ground, things happened fast. Like a giant jack-in-the-box released by a spring, a huge grizzly came out from under the log right in front of him, and stood towering on its hind feet and snorting angrily. The bear was practically within touching distance, and for a moment the picture was a frozen tableau of mutual surprise. The bear had been sound asleep and was confronted by a man. The man had been in a hurry to get home and was confronted by a bear. Bert moved first by reaching for his gun. Without a wasted fraction of a second, he swept the pistol up out of the open-top holster, thumbing off the safety catch as he drew. Just as the bear was lifting a giant paw to strike, Bert rested the pistol in the crook of his upraised left elbow and fired at a spot just under the big animal's muzzle. The grizzly stiffened and then came down like a falling tree. Bert had to throw himself backward to avoid having the big animal fall squarely on top of him. For a few seconds he stood tensely with the pistol cocked and trained on the grizzly, ready to shoot at the least sign of life. But the big animal had died instantly. The little jacketed bullet had hit it in the thorax and penetrated deep into the throat, where it had smashed the atlas vertabra that joined the spine to the skull.

Bert stood for a few moments and gazed thoughtfully at the obstructing limb on top of the tree trunk. If it had been a few feet farther along, he'd have jumped squarely on top of the bear, with no chance to defend himself. He put the pistol back into the broken holster that had allowed a fast draw, when seconds were as precious as life. Feeling mighty lucky and not a little shaken, he continued through the gathering dusk to camp.

It was Bert who gave the canyon the name Grizzly Gulch, and it stuck. To this day the valley is a favorite range of the big silvertips—just as wild now as it was back in 1908.

"The bear was practically within touching distance, and for a moment the picture was a frozen tableau of mutual surprise."

JOHN AND I turned back down the slope, swinging up into the basin behind the shoulder to avoid the dripping brush. On the way we picked up Dave and Bill, and together we returned to the horses. Riding single file down the back-trail through the timber we reached a screen of alders on the edge of the clearing by Little Bear Lake, where we dismounted to look for the grizzly. Most of the snow was gone and the flat seemed to be empty. Swinging the glasses slowly along the edge of the heavy timber on the far side of the flat, I searched for some sign of the bear. The field of the binoculars had almost completed the swing, and I was scrutinizing a knoll beyond the lake when I spotted the grizzly.

He was lying like a big dog on his belly with his head up, and he was near where the horse trail emerged from the trees. The bear was over 400 yards away, so we slipped down through the alders to a washout that cut the flat in half where the overflow ran out of the lake. We had good cover as far as the lake, but once there we were still 300 yards from the bear. Our angle of view had altered; now we were looking at a small piece of him between two giant trees. Since a wounded grizzly is pure dynamite in timber, we'd have been asking for trouble in big raw chunks to try a shot from that spot. So we eased out onto the flat below him, using some small spruces for cover.

When we had gone a hundred yards he must have heard us, for he suddenly stood up at full height on his hind feet looking our way. He made a picture to remember, framed between the towering spruces against the blue sky, with the outline of a thousand-foot perpendicular cliff behind and to one side. It was a wild and beautiful sight. We froze and waited. The grizzly dropped to all fours and we heard that ominous chopping of teeth as he came walking out onto the slope diagonally toward us.

"Get set!" I whispered.

Bill and John fanned out abreast and sat down with their rifles ready. When the bear reached a patch of broken boulders fifty yards from the timber, John cut loose with his .25-06. Instantly the grizzly swiveled on his hind feet, slapping at the rocks beside him. As he slewed our way, Bill's .300 Weatherby roared. Then things came apart in a hurry. Tumbling and bawling savagely, the bear came down through the boulders like an avalanche. Both Bill and John fired at him as he came, but the bullets went high, throwing dust off the rocks. The shooting got so fast I lost track of it, but just as the grizzly cleared the rocks a hundred yards away, a bullet caught him flush in the shoulder and his roaring trailed off into a choking bawl and silence. We all sat there tensely watching, but he didn't move.

I glanced at Bill and John; both looked as though they didn't quite believe what they had just seen and heard. Little drops of sweat were standing out on their faces.

"By gosh!" John exclaimed finally. "I'm sure glad he wasn't twins!"

"You can say that again!" Bill muttered, as he stuffed more ammunition into his rifle.

We walked over to the grizzly and gingerly approached to within a few yards. Dave chucked a rock at him but he didn't move. John had his grizzly, or so we thought. We have a standing rule that when two hunters fire at the same animal, the trophy goes to the man drawing first blood. So we dragged the bear out into the sun and photographed John with it, for we were all sure he had hit the grizzly with his first shot.

Then we skinned the bear out, and found only two bullet holes. One had struck the hip and ranged forward into the body cavity lengthwise; the other had smashed the shoulder. We recovered parts of both bullets—and both were .30 caliber.

The grizzlies of Grizzly Gulch have a reputation of being ornery bears, and this one lived up to it even after he was dead. He wouldn't even stay with the man who was supposed to have had him for a trophy.

—December, 1957

By Charles E. Gillham

POLAR BEAR BRIDE

TOM WANTED THE
CHIEF'S DAUGHTER FOR
HIS WIFE, BUT FIRST HE
HAD TO PROVE HIMSELF
THE ESKIMO'S EQUAL.

CHIEF WILLIAM DIDN'T think much of white men. Presumably he had seen too many whalers or explorers. He tolerated the *kabloonas*, as they are called by the Eskimos, and did nothing to antagonize them. However, it was noted that when the natives journeyed to Aklavik each spring to see the Hudson's Bay boat, the *Distributor*, tie up and unload the season's cargo this outstanding chieftain was never present.

Below the Caribou hills, out toward the Arctic Coast, practically all Eskimos were related to William and his several wives. He was a most commanding figure, a giant of his race, with bullet head and close-cropped gray hair.

His lips were perforated for the wearing of ivory labrets.

On the particular winter day of which I write the chief sat cross-legged on a deep bed of Barren Ground grizzly, polar bear and caribou skins. He looked a bit like a Chinese Buddha. His dark Oriental eyes never left the face of the white trapper seated on the floor before him. Intently he watched Tom Jamieson's face while he spoke, although he did not understand a word the white man said. An indolent 18-year-old youth was acting as interpreter.

An old Eskimo woman entered bearing two steaming pots. In the iron pot, which was placed on the floor before Tom, there floated half a dozen boiled muskrats, the scaly tails and grinning heads still attached. Using his fingers, the trapper removed a rodent to his tin plate and fell to. Knives and forks were entirely absent. The other pot, a blue-enamel trading-post affair, contained tea from which a full pint cup, strong enough to tan a deer hide, was poured.

When William spoke, his eyes were friendly, for he thought more of Tom than any living *kabloona*.

"You're a good hunter and have a fine rifle. Nanook is very bad this winter. One particular white bear is a devil. He has broken into our fish caches and has stolen whale meat and seal blubber. At night he has killed two sled dogs tied to their stakes. He has desecrated our dead and dug them out from beneath the driftwood cairns where they sleep. On our trap-lines he has devoured many white foxes and the skins have been lost. You are fortunate he has not followed your traps and destroyed your furs."

Tom nodded as the youth repeated the statements in English. Emulating the Eskimo, he licked his fingers with a loud sucking noise to denote his pleasure with such fine food. Then he replied: "White bears sure are hell when they're hungry. Guess my cabin is too far back from the coast. I ain't lost any dry fish from my cache yet and I haven't seen a bear track along my trap-line." Peering into the back part of the igloo where a pair of large brown eyes peeked through the smoky interior, the trapper grinned and continued: "Maybe if I kill this bear you will think I am as good a hunter as an Eskimo. Maybe then you will let me marry Lila?"

Feminine squeals from another room indicated that the younger generation understood the white man's language. A flick of a long, ruffled squaw-dress and a pair of vanishing embroidered mukluks, where the brown eyes had been, were indicative of a very embarrassed young Eskimo lady. Muffled laughter and giggles by the many sloe-eyed kinfolks denoted that they, at least, were well pleased with the idea.

Chief William grunted, and a peculiar light came into his eyes. "None of my family have ever married *kabloonas*. Such usually brings much sadness. The Eskimo can never be accepted outside in your country. In the warm climate, where you live, their health fails without the seals and fish of the sea for food. We were made to live in a cold land. If I were sure you would never leave the North, you could have my Lila. Maybe—maybe if you kill the nanook—We will see!"

＋—≡↓≡—＋

TOM DEPARTED NEAR nightfall. His dogteam had been well fed. The wind had dropped and the snow was fast and crackling cold. Bundled snugly in his toboggan, with his eiderdown robe pulled around him, he sang out to his dogs. "Mush, huskies! Mush, boys! Camp is three hours away. Mush Frankie, you little devil!"

Four tails waved like plumes ahead. They were jaunty and cocky, denoting that they were attached to happy animals. The great creatures belonged to a peculiar branch of the canine family. They chose to sleep on the snow rather than in doghouses. They could devour six pounds of raw live fish with gusto—bones, scales and all. They would fight unto death with others of their kind and dismember the unfortunate loser, eating him with relish. When abused by native owners, they were sullen and could only be controlled with the lash and brutality. Sometimes they turned on men if they had a chance and crushed leg bones, or even skulls, as they might the bones of a caribou.

But Frankie was not a malemute. Named for Frank Riddell, Signal Corps sergeant, who gave him to Tom, even his name was a queer one for a dog. He lacked a plumelike tail; his was short and stood erect and defiant. The long, woolly furlike hair was missing. His was shorter and inclined to be curly. Maybe a terrier ancestor gave him this characteristic. Without doubt a Labrador was responsible for his coal-black coat and his wide muzzle—and his brains. Small for the sled, but tough as buckskin, he had fought for his right to go with Tom, had fought bone-crunching malemutes and survived. Now he was the leader.

The moon peeked forth, and only the swish of the toboggan on the frozen snow and the pat-pat of sled-dog feet broke the stillness. Snuggled deep in his robe, Tom brushed the wolverine fur trimming of his parka hood. Ice slipped from the glossy slick hair, only to be replaced again by other ice as his warm breath struck the frigid air.

Tom watched the leader, Frankie, with admiration. Half the weight of any of his teammates, he never faltered. Leaning well into the harness, he carried his share of the load and selected the smoothest part of the terrain with almost human judgment. An Arctic hare sprang from alongside the trail. Three of the malemutes dived for him, but Frankie swerved them back on a straight line in a matter of a few feet.

"Wish I could kill that white bear," Tom spoke half aloud. "Wonder how she would like living with Frankie and me. He has always slept by my side. Guess Lila wouldn't care."

Short willows now appeared. Once in a while, through the snow, the tops of small jack-pines were in evidence—the last of their race to survive so far north.

"He wouldn't stand in my way if I never left the Arctic—I ain't ever going outside again. Guess William doesn't believe me. Got no folks any more, no relatives in the world to my knowledge. If I leave a year, I can't ever get another trapping license in the Northwest Territories—that's the law. Ain't got no trade, don't belong to any union. Why should I ever leave the north country and Frankie?"

The country was hilly now and all down grade. The toboggan fairly flew. Trees were taller. In the distance an arm of the Husky Lakes appeared. The dogs whined and increased their speed, as they always did when they knew camp was near. Down, down, down, then the lake shore was reached. Cutting across on the smooth ice toward a low point dotted with scrub, the trapper whizzed toward his cabin. How he had worked fashioning the pole shack! Trees were small and scarce in this barren country.

"Whoa, Frankie! Whoa, boys!" Tom crawled stiffly from his sled. "Gee, it's cold. Hold there, Frankie, while I take the dogs out of the harness."

Rapidly Tom unhooked the malemutes and fastened them to their stakes. The black dog, stub tail wagging, watched the proceedings. "Now for you, Frankie." Slipping the collar from the leader, Tom turned to his toboggan. Throwing the eider-down over his arm, he picked up his carbine, which was sheathed in the customary home-made canvas bag, commonly used throughout the Arctic. Turning toward his cabin, he stopped short. Frankie stood between him and the open

door, his short hair erect. He growled and cast an apprehensive eye back toward Tom.

"What the devil! Some darned Siwash must have been here." Tom bent to scan the hard snow for footprints. Frankie growled again and louder. As if he had transmitted something in canine language, the nearest animal on the dog line raised his head and wailed—the wild, weird call of the malemute. In a matter of seconds a barking clamor arose that made the night ring. Towards the Caribou Hills a blood-brother Arctic wolf took up the challenge.

"Shut-up—quiet! What's the matter with you guys? Guess I was in such a hurry to see Lila I left the door open myself. Nothing to get excited about—just because the door is open."

Brushing past Frankie, Tom pushed into the dark interior, bedroll over one arm, his sheathed rifle beneath the other. Groping his way in the direction of the stove, where a candle would be found reposing in the neck of a bottle, he stopped short. An uncanny premonition gave him the feeling that something of large bulk was rising from the floor directly in front of him. Across the room, toward the single pane of ice-glazed glass in the cabin wall, a huge shadow blotted out the pale light, as a dark cloud suddenly envelopes the moon. At that same instant Frankie sprang forward with a wild yelp and the malemutes on the stakes broke into a roar. Inside the dark cabin all hell broke loose.

Knocked to his knees, Tom felt hot breath on his face. Something seemed to jerk his parka at the shoulder and leave him half-naked. Plunging to one side, he kicked himself free of the eiderdown which half covered his body. Desperately he broke the string that suspended his mittens from his neck and freed his hands of the clumsy things. Rolling away from his invisible adversary, Tom fumbled to get his now bare hand into the wide canvas scabbard, for he had not dropped his rifle.

Pans fell from the wall, adding to the din. The rude table overturned, and Frankie, dodging,

"Swinging the rifle before him, Tom sensed rather than saw the bulk of his foe."

biting and twisting, seemed to be fighting all over the place at once. Swinging the rifle before him, Tom sensed rather than saw the bulk of his foe. His thumb cocked the hammer of the little carbine and his finger found the trigger. Holding high enough that he hoped to miss Frankie, he fired through the scabbard. Orange flame sprang from the muzzle. A smell of burning canvas and hair permeated the room. With a loud "Woof!" a huge polar bear bounded through the door, the dogs on the line howling like banshees.

Tom sat up. Something warm and sticky was running down his arm. He heard Frankie whining in a far corner of the cabin. Feeling his way to the stove, he struck a match and the candle crackled into a feeble glow. He kicked the door shut and went to the black dog. Blood was flowing from a gaping wound in his side.

Jerking a blanket from his bunk, the trapper tore it into strips with numbed fingers. Tightly he bound them around the weakened animal. Tenderly he put him on the bedroll and folded it about him. Then he shoved kindling into the stove and piled driftwood atop it to heat the sub-zero room.

Black blood clotted Tom's shoulder. Two long gashes across the upper arm had made only flesh wounds. The heavy parka had been half stripped from his body with one powerful blow, but it had prevented long claws from tearing the muscle from the bone. The cabin warmed, and Frankie watched his master beat powdered milk and water in a bowl and warm it on the fire.

"Here, boy, drink. You saved my life. That was a polar bear, sure as hell. Guess I never touched him, but he had sense enough to leave when the rifle went off. Shot the whole end out of my old scabbard and set it afire for a minute. Here, boy, drink this milk. You can't cross the divide and leave me."

Gently Tom raised the black dog's head, and great was his joy when the animal lapped the milk. Feeling the bandages carefully, he discovered that the flowing blood had been stopped, for none had soaked through. Procuring antiseptic and bandage, the trapper bound his own wounds and gazed in consternation at the wreck of his cabin.

A cache of dried fish, which probably had attracted the bear in the first place, had been torn down from beneath the rafters. Much had been eaten and the rest scattered about the floor. A sack of flour that had rested upon a box in the corner had been broken, and the contents formed a white carpet several feet square. Tom bent closer to inspect this damage and gasped. Sharp footprints over a foot long were clearly discernible.

"That must have been him—the devil bear! Had him right here in my cabin, then let him get away. Guess I was lucky, though, Frankie, lucky I had you to keep him off until I got out of those mitts and cocked the old carbine. Hope you're as lucky, Old-Timer. Here, have some more milk."

Throughout the long arctic night the trapper repeatedly dozed before his fire and replenished it at intervals. Periodically he heated milk and fed the dog. "Got to build up that blood you lost Frankie. Got to save you, old pal. You're the only folks I have."

＋—＞ ≡✦≣ —＜＋

HOWLING MALEMUTES AWOKE Tom. His fire was almost out. Hastily he put on more fuel. Frankie, watching him, seemed stronger. Uncovering the dog, he noted that the stub tail was sticking up defiantly. More heated milk and a bit of chopped caribou were eagerly taken. Apparently the crisis was over and the leader would live.

Putting on an old parka with his stiffened arm was a painful ordeal, but the trapper gritted his teeth and performed the task. After gathering an armload of dry fish from the floor, he stepped outside and pitched a double ration to each of the hungry dogs bouncing at their stakes. A breeze had sprung up during the night, and fine snow had drifted across the endless expanse of white. He could see that the dogs had been partially covered by it. With their bushy tails curled over their noses, they were more comfortable when drifted over.

Tom turned his gaze across the big lake. What a monotonous stretch of utter desolation! Miniature blizzards of skittering snow, swept knee-high, chased each other across the gloomy white surface. Shivering, he turned away. Then, as something caught his eye, he looked again across the Husky Lakes. Something appeared different, not just right. A hummock or a snowdrift was not that color. Rubbing his eyes with the back of his mitt, he looked again. Yes, it had a faint yellowish tinge. Could it be—?

The trapper advanced slowly to gaze on the straw-colored pile. He stared. Half covered with drift, a very dead polar bear sprawled full length. After he had kicked the snow away, a dark red splotch was revealed, about centrally on the ribs.

"I'll be damned! If I had hit him a foot farther to the front, I'd have shot the devil square through the heart."

Only a man in love would skin a frozen bear as big as a saddle horse in the dead of the arctic winter, especially when that man had a stiff shoulder and a wounded dog to care for. Only a lover, too, would drive four malemutes across the rolling hills to Chief William's igloo,

with a black dog, rolled in an eiderdown, riding in the toboggan along with the bear hide.

Only a real Eskimo chief, one who had been decorated by the King, would have been big enough to allow Lila to marry a white man, the first to ever mix blood with his family. Proudly he gripped the hand of his white son-in-law, who was loading his toboggan a few days later before the igloos of his many shouting relatives. Only one lead dog could pilot the team and carry the blushing sloe-eyed bride of his master through the barrens, into the scrub and to the Husky Lakes.

Tom cracked his whip. Four malemutes and a black dog got up from the snow and leaned into the traces, a stub tail flicking arrogantly.

"Mush, huskies! Mush, boys! Camp is three hours away. Mush, Frankie, you little devil. Husky Lakes, here we come. We've traded a bear for a bride!"

—June, 1951

By Frank Dufresne

LUCKY LIMIT

THE BIG CEDAR STUMP
THAT HAD MADE SUCH
A PERFECT BLIND NOW
THREATENED TO SWEEP
HIM TO HIS DOOM.
ONLY A LIMIT OF BIRDS
COULD SAVE HIM.

GIVE ME A SQUALLY day on a marsh. At dusk I'll come slopping out of the muck oozing good-will to all. Ducks or no ducks, I'm relaxed and satisfied. I've had a grand-stand seat at my choice of the great outdoor shows. If I haven't fired a shot, there is still the lingering excitement, the scalp-tingling memory of wild wings stitching their mysterious patterns across the overcast.

I like to shoot, sure. I'll burn my share of gunpowder. I'll brag when I smack a high-flier dead center. Nobody will top my alibis at the misses. But I'll not make a maximum bag limit my yardstick for measuring fun in a duck blind. There'll be no straining to rack up the biggest score allowed by law. Like a lot of other water-fowlers, I'll rate a full bag limit second to the stirring sight of waterfowl racing in the skies.

And yet I remember a certain howling November day in Portage Bay when it became a matter of life and death to shoot a limit of ducks and geese. It was a lucky break for me, too, that the ducks were mal-lards instead of teal. The white-cheeked geese that came along in late afternoon filled a desperate need.

I was hitchhiking a 100-mile boat ride along the steamer lane from Petersburg to Juneau on an Alaska Game Commission vessel when a prowling sou'easter came charging out of the Stikine back channel, twisting its tail and looking for trouble. Churning the sea into white fury, the storm snarled down upon us, laid brutal hands on the 40-foot patrol vessel and started bounc-ing it around like a cocktail shaker. Skipper

Severin was a hardy Norwegian, but he knew when to run away. His narrowed blue eyes scanned the purple-black clouds rolling ominously toward us, and he swung the *Grizzly Bear* hard aport to head for the nearest shelter.

For an hour we staggered through the tide-rips, one rail and then another scooping green water while crockery crashed in the galley. Through the foaming bore that guards the entrance to Portage Bay the vessel plunged like a spurred bronco, then raced along on spume-topped swells until the water became too shallow for further retreat. Skipper Severin slacked off on his controls, turned into the wind and signaled for the deck-hand to drop the hook. He straightened his cramped fingers from the spoked wheel and helped himself to a wad of snoose.

"Aye turn no more vheels today," he declared, glaring around the pilothouse as though expecting an argument. Then he added, "Now is gude time for everybody sleeping."

With this I could not agree. Not on the last afternoon of the waterfowl season, when the ill wind that always blows somebody a little good had laid the *Grizzly Bear* alongside one of southeastern Alaska's fine duck marshes. There was not another boat in the bay. I would have it all alone, because neither Skipper Severin nor any of the three crewmen appreciated the sweet joy of standing in cold sea water facing a whistling deluge of icy rain, the perfect combination for duck shooting. But they were glad to put me ashore in a speed boat, and they told me they'd eat all the ducks I could shoot. When Severin set me on the beach with a promise to pick me up at dark, he reminded, "Gat the limit." I'm glad he said that.

It was a mile walk across the bared mud at low tide and around to a small river delta partially sheltered by a spruce-timbered point. As I neared the mouth of this salmon spawning stream williwaws ripped patches of kelp and widgeon-grass free and sent them bowling like tumbleweeds across the open flats. Ducks jumped, squawking, into the gale and went whizzing downwind. Here in the eddying gusts and down-blasts was a feeding area crawling with waterfowl. Mallards, baldpates, pintails, shovelers and green-winged teal dabbled in the puddles. Goldeneyes, bluebills, scoters, butterballs and mergansers dived for feed in the salt-water channels. They spattered aloft, filling the blustery air with the swish of their wings.

Between the forked mouth of the river where the current ran no more than ankle-deep at ebb tide I saw a ready-made, natural blind floated into perfect position by a previous high water. It was a grotesque cedar snag offering both windbreak and hiding place. I hadn't been there a minute when a greenhead came pedaling past, folded when it ran into a charge of chilled 6's and fell close enough for me to make a vest-pocket catch. I held the glossy drake by its orange feet and shook it hard. Nothing snapped out of the open bill except some seeds and green shoots. Satisfied that it had not been gorging on salmon eggs—a nasty mallard habit in late season that imparts a horrifying flavor to the flesh—I decided to try for a full bag of these handsome big drakes.

It was almost like shooting fish in a well. Given enough shells, a man could have raked down a hundred ducks on that zesty afternoon. The cedar snag seemed to have a sign on it for waterfowl only: "Portage Bay Duck Inn. Dinner now being served." It stood in the exact center of the local flyway. For every greenhead I missed, two more crossed over the snag within easy gunshot. Once they had landed, the birds didn't want to fly against the buffeting wet gales any more. They waddled around on the muck flats while more ducks bucked in to join the party, and I snapped the rain out of my eyes and swung a bead on the fat drakes.

The shooting disturbed a gaggle of geese up the river valley. After each volley from the 20-gauge autoloader I'd hear their honking complaints. Finally they lifted up for a look, then went circling around the valley against the green wall of timber, talking strategy. Next, the entire flock, two hundred strong, swung into line and headed straight for the cedar snag, touching off chords like a spread of low notes on an organ. They spotted me, though not soon enough. The lead gander had already collapsed before the white-cheeked birds flared. A tail-ender joined the downed leader, and then the thrash of wings died away in swirling mist.

While I was gathering the brace an umbrella of milling duck wings formed overhead, out of which a wing-tipped mallard came spinning down to join others on the duck strap.

The tally after this exciting action stood at seven ducks and two geese. I had three more mallards and another pair of honkers coming to fill the bag limit of that year. The tide had turned and was foaming in across the mud flats, hurried by the wind. By the time I got back to the stump with my downed birds salt water was lapping against my rubber boots. A scattering of mallards pumped past, spaced just right for a triple on drakes. I retrieved two dead birds and chased down a flapping cripple to complete the legal limit on ducks. The water had risen knee-high around the snag, a warning to which I should have paid prompt attention.

But with the incoming tide waterfowl came tumbling in from all points of the compass. A couple of hours of daylight still remained. I decided to let the tide reach its flood stage and start ebbing away before trudging the mud flats to the meeting place with Skipper Severin. After all, this was the last day of the open season. It would be a long time before I would see the likes of this afternoon again. Also, I still had two more geese to go before reaching the four-bird limit. Two of these honkers I hoped to meet again when Severin's Norway-born wife served them old-country-style, browned, tender and swimming in hot spiced pickle sauce.

Absence of exploding shells must have convinced the geese that an armistice was at hand, because what appeared like the same flock I had thinned earlier in the day now came battling the wet storm back to the river valley. Flying low to avoid the full force of the blow, the heavy birds labored over the cedar snag scarcely fifteen feet up. It was no trick at all to pull down a double.

As I waded out to gather in the plump pair I was surprised to find the water still rising, lacking only an inch or two from spilling over my boot tops. This meant, clearly enough, that out in the river channel that I would have to ford to reach the main shore the tide would be running no less than belt-high. I shinnied atop the cedar snag to wait until it started

draining away again. It seemed that simple. I hadn't a thought of danger as I crammed my pipe, blew smoke into the breeze and gave myself over to enjoyment of quacking, squawking, whistling waterfowl.

The first doubt came when a breaker smashed solidly against the snag and I felt it lurch against the bottom. Soon there was another bump, followed by an even heavier smash. The snag heeled over and rolled back again. Scrambling for holds on its slippery surface, I was jolted by the sudden suspicion of big trouble looming. Belatedly it became clear that the cedar snag, which had been deposited on the river delta in the first instance by an extremely high tide, was due to be skidded free by another—and today might be moving day.

Now I was quite sure the tide would not change in time to do me any good. This was in the full moon of November, when the maximum flood tides of the year fell due. There would be close to twenty-five feet of rising sea between minus low and peak high level. Worse yet, with a raging wind to heap it still higher there was now no question but that the cedar snag would be carried away. Then what?

I had three chances, none of them very encouraging. One was to try to stay with the floating duck blind; try to ride its wave-washed surface as it went drifting off in the salt current. What I didn't like about this plan was the certainty that tide and wind would sweep it out into mid-channel and in an opposite direction from the *Grizzly Bear.* What next, then?

Could I, by using the gun as a third leg, hold my footing as the tide rose and fell? It might take several hours. I doubted my ability to endure the test long enough to try the third choice. This was to leave the snag and attempt to win across to the main shore, now about two hundred feet away and much too deep in spots for wading. I would need help. A drifting sawlog appeared to offer the necessary equipment. It came bobbing toward the blind as though by special delivery. If I could reach it and climb astradle, it might get me over the river channel.

Shivering and anxious, I watched it draw closer. Then, while yet several feet beyond my grasp, the log started turning around in an eddy. Slowly it changed direction and moved away into the whitecaps. As it drifted away the cedar snag under me reared off the bottom again. Time was running out. It was zero hour for Operation Duck Feathers.

✦ ⎯ ⎯ ✦

HASTILY I PULLED the ten mallards and four geese together and bound them around and around into a bushel-basket-sized mass with some cod line out of my hunting-jacket pocket. The water was waist-deep when I struggled free from my rubber boots, slicker and canvas jacket. Placing these items on the ball of feathers, I added the shotgun and started pushing the odd raft toward shore.

Soon the chilly sea rose to my armpits and I was forced to rest against the bale of waterfowl to keep balanced. Then the bottom sloped off abruptly. The river channel! Could I make the next forty feet? Would the trussed birds hold under my weight? There was no turning back now. All the answers were in front of me. My wool-socked feet kicked off the squishy bottom and I started flailing the briny flood with numbed hands.

As my chest fell across the bundled ducks they spread and settled almost to the water-line. My feet rose to splash sea behind. Waves broke against my face, strangling, frightening, and the chilling shock of icy water pouring down the front of my wool shirt was almost unbearable. When I could stand it no longer, when I could paddle no farther, I stood on end to tread water. That is when two wonderful things happened. The ball of ducks and geese lifted high on the surface. My feet touched bottom. I was across the river channel!

A few feet farther stretched the weed-lined shore of the bay. Wading clear with waterfowl, gear and gun sagging across my shoulders, I struggled into the heavy timber for protection against the stinging williwaws. Soaked though I was, this was no time to stop. A game trail punched by tracks of bears, wolves and deer led along the contour of the bay under a canopy of giant evergreens. Before heading along this path I stole a glance back toward the flooded river delta. The cedar snag was gone. It was far

out in the open bay, twisting and dipping in clouds of spray.

It wasn't the first time in my Alaska experiences that I'd been thoroughly dunked, and I knew what to do about it. When I came to a dead tree that suited me, I flung off my heavy load and went to work. Where half-rotted roots branched away from the base there was a good-sized opening through which my exploring hand encountered an accumulation of pitchy splinters. Crushing a few handfuls just inside the entrance, I fumbled off the threaded top of a waterproof case and whipped an old-fashioned sulphur match into flame.

The oily chaff spluttered, smoked, fizzled and at last broke into a puny blaze. As it grew stronger most of the fire sucked back into the hollow tree and started licking on hanging splinters. It wasn't long before the standing shell of the dead giant was roaring warmly. In its red glow I stripped off my sopping clothes, wrung each garment and dried it reasonably well.

As daylight waned, the scudding clouds lowered and began spitting snow. The fire blew itself to king-size. From its open top, forty feet above the forest floor, the hollow trunk started erupting like a volcano. Now and then, as the hot flames melted out new pitch pockets, dense black smoke rings belched forth to be whisked away in the snowstorm. Since there wasn't the slightest danger of the fire spreading in such a drenched woodland, I was enjoying the fireworks.

My clothing was getting drier by the minute when the sound of an outboard motor drew closer from out in the storm-lashed bay where the *Grizzly Bear* bucked at its anchor chain. The motor cut off in the gloom below me. I heard Skipper Severin's boots smashing through a windrow of clam shells. He came up to the red-lighted perimeter of the flaming spruce skeleton, hefted the ducks and heaved them over his shoulder.

"You gat a limit, feels like," came his hearty shout over the wind as he swayed away toward the shoreline. "By golly, you vas lucky."

Lucky? Wait till he heard the rest of it!

—August, 1953

By Keith McCafferty

The Cabin Where
TERROR CAME CALLING

THE RUINED SHED WAS LITTLE BIGGER THAN A COFFIN. BEFORE THE NIGHT WAS OVER, IT MIGHT BE ONE.

THE GRIZZLY BEAR IS believed to be among the few mammals besides man which commonly dies in its sleep. Winter takes it in the end, although its fate is not that of deer shrunk to skeletons by March, nor of bighorns drowned by avalanche. It may be that a bear nearing the end of life takes to its den early one fall, and pulling up winter for its funeral shroud, lies entombed there forever.

In the Rocky Mountain West, the grizzly has made its final stand in a handful of retreats: in Yellowstone National Park, in a slender finger of Canada's Selkirk Range that juts into Washington, and in the high country of northwestern Montana, principally Glacier National Park and the Bob Marshall Wilderness. Some grizzly researchers believe the last bear to grace this country will leave its skull in a den in the Bob Marshall Wilderness, and that its bones will be finished by the rodents in time for our generation to be the voice of its history.

In the Bob Marshall Wilderness native trout teem in three forks of the Flathead River; green, transparent races of water that vein a vast roll of mountains where every other feature of land has been named for its bears: Silvertip Mountain, White Bear Creek, Grizzly Gulch.

This area used to be a favored hunting ground of timber wolves. A few can still be heard in its forests. It also was the winter haunt of pine marten trappers, just a few of whom remain.

The marten trappers were a colorful lot who defended individual creek drainages as vigorously as did the old, boar grizzlies that ransacked their camps. Like the bears they were victims of progress, finished four decades ago by Russian sable farms that exported domestic furs thickened in Siberia. Blackened scars where traps were notched into the trunks of trees blemish the older stands of lodgepole pine in the Bob Marshall to this day. Tiny log cabins the trappers built are less noticeable. Most have returned to the forest floor, although a scattering still stand, banked back into the sides of ridges for insulation. These "cabins" were little larger than coffins, and the trappers heated them with body heat. They remain as testament to a hard way of life that has all but disappeared from this country.

——— ✦ ———

THIS IS A story told by one of the last marten trappers. He is my age, thirty, but already an old hand in the wilderness. He has run a trapline up the headwater tributaries of the South Fork of the Flathead River since he was seventeen years old.

Shortly before I met him, the trapper had the misfortune of stepping on one of the decaying, nail-quilled bear doors that are strewn about various cabins constructed by the Forest Service for backcountry rangers. I had come into the Bob Marshall with a party of three to measure the spring snowpack for government records. We had traveled 90 miles by snow cat to the wilderness boundary, and gone on skis from there. The last 2 miles of the 20 we skied trailed the lopsided dinosaur waddle of snowshoe tracks. I knew whoever was up ahead had a bad left foot.

The trapper, hunched under the bulk of his pack, looked like he had journeyed to this place from somewhere considerably farther north. He had tangled hair down to his coat collar, a winter's growth of thin beard, a hawk nose. He was not a big man, yet his handshake brought blood to the tips of my fingers. His eyes, clear and green, moved as deliberately and as carefully as his speech, which sounded like that of an older man.

"I don't want to make trouble for you," he said. But he said he had been on the bad foot for a week, and the pain which radiated from the deep puncture the nail made grew worse by the hour. The nearest passable road was still on the far side of a broad belt of mountains that avalanched frequently this time of year. This was no small predicament, and the trapper well knew it.

Our party had the key to an outpost ranger cabin that sat over the river on a bench of timber, near the junction of the South Fork with Big Salmon Creek. We had to dig out the door through 3 feet of snow. The mattresses hung up under the ceiling in looping hammocks of rope. On the slab pine floor the mousetraps were all long sprung and the mice collected in them had rotted away, leaving miniscule skeletons, puffs of fur, and threads of tails.

We walked around inside like crabs on blistered feet, banging the pots for our supper. The trapper sat beside a big barrel wood heater, his boots and stag shirt dripping off 60-penny nails driven into the log center beam, his foot soaking in a dishpan of melted snow.

There is an unspoken code in the back-country that no one broaches the subject of grizzly bears until a suitable interval has passed. To speak of the grizzly too soon is a sign of insecurity. We had pumped up a lantern going into that night. But the circle of light dimmed considerably before we heard the trapper's story.

———— ⚔ ————

HE SAID THAT years ago, a grizzly bear stole an elk he had shot for winter meat. That fall he was guiding elk hunters for an outfitter who took a string of mules up the South Fork of the Flathead. The outfitter packed out Thanksgiving week, hurrying to beat the snow out of the mountains. He left the guide his best wishes. For the trapper it would be his first winter alone in the wilderness.

The bear raided the trapper's camp the following week. It took a beaver he'd left lying on top of a skinning table; stuck its head inside the tent flap to get it. It jerked the elk out of the tree where it hung nose up with a rope around its antlers. The trapper had slept through the night; he read the story in the snow in the morning. He followed bear tracks to the river. It was a grizzly all right, its long claws biting into the snow inches from the impressions of the feet. Under a heaping of branches the trapper found the torn, bloodied carcass of the spike elk. He caught himself staring at a heap of dung that spread a brown pillow in a pool of water isolated from the current of the river.

But he wanted revenge, and took up the track again, crossing the river and climbing the slope on the far side. As he climbed, smelling the rank odor the grizzly left in its wake, the fear began crowding into his mind, and the cold desire to even his score began to dissolve in sweat and dread. At the top of the ridge he turned to look down at the ruin of his camp. He saw the sagging tent and the reddened trough in the snow the bear had made dragging the elk to the river. He thought: *No more.*

In that moment the bear, which must have been lying in the shintangle, rose to its height. The trapper later recalled that when the bear put its nose on man scent the hair of its thick neck rose like a cat's. And he had heard the hissing of his own hair as it stood against the crown of his hat.

Then in an instant the bear was down on fours, bulling through the matchstick lodge-pole and gone out of sight over the ridge. The trapper never hesitated. He turned and ran, dodging through the close trees in the thicket, coming off the mountain in a flood of adrenaline to lurch against the river and stagger to the giddy safety on the opposite bank. He sat down, sucking air. His Springfield rifle was held in gripped fists, at the ready, forgotten at his moment of opportunity.

With little forethought and no real experience the trapper had set out to kill a grizzly bear. "It was the rug," he would say. "I'd always wanted a grizzly bear rug." And a little of the morning's instant courage lingered even after retreat, a thrilling, insane urge to bend once more to the tracks.

But it had been foolhardy to take a bear to task in such tough country. The trapper knew it. He faced the fact that whatever return of confidence he enjoyed with the sun up and the bear gone would desert him utterly at the close of day.

Downriver an old plank shed had weathered the snows of too many winters. There were the remnants of a corral; a few crossed logs deteriorating over the cleared ground. The trapper had this shed in mind as he heaved at the corpse of the elk. Even with its hindquarters eaten the elk was a burdensome animal which hugged the snow as the trapper worked. It took hours to move it to the higher ground. He finally dropped it outside the shed's solitary window, a black, square hole that had been crudely barred with twisted strands of barbed wire in an attempt to keep out the bears of a former era.

Quickly the trapper retraced his steps to the tent. He packed his backpack with food, sleeping bag, lantern. He had a side of bacon for cooking grease and he packed it. Upon his return to the shed he pried a nail from a plank of wood, and stepping on top of his elk for height, nailed the bacon outside and just over the top of the window.

He figured to fire on the bear soon as it stood up to take down the bacon.

It was either a brave or foolish thing to have done. But at the time the trapper felt certain the bear would return, if not that night the next, and it would keep returning until one of them was dead. He dreaded this uncertainty as much as he feared the bear.

The shed itself offered little protection against a grizzly bear. The trapper had to prop the door with axed sections of a lodgepole snag just to keep it from falling in the wind. Inside, he sat on a cut stump, facing the door. He drank coffee he made over a fire built on earth exposed by some charred floorboards. There were blackened rings where others had built fires inside this tinderbox. It was not something to make a practice of, but the trapper knew how desperate men could be in this country.

The stars came out; they shone through the window and separations in the shed walls. He thought the stars were peculiarly beautiful; remembered precisely how they had appeared to him. He fell asleep looking at them.

When he woke up the stars were gone. The night was black and the river which murmured him to sleep, despite the coffee, had a new cadence he sought to place. The window over his head was a solid square. It was blacker than the room. The trapper did not move once his eyes opened nor did he take his eyes from the window. Breath, not wind, blew in through the window, and the trapper, wide awake, felt his body break into sweat.

He had fallen asleep with his hand on his rifle but the trapper did not dare lift it. He feared that the slightest movement on his part would trigger the bear, there all along, so close he could have touched it with an outstretched arm.

Many minutes passed. Then abruptly the tiny shed flooded with starlight and the trapper heard a heavy dragging noise as the bear moved the elk away from the window. A bone cracked outside the shed door. The grizzly began to

eat, 6 feet of air and 1 inch of wood from the ridiculously small hole at the muzzle of the rifle which now swung like a compass needle to every snuffing grunt, every underwater rumbling of the bear's great belly.

Now the trapper only wanted it to be over. He pointed his rifle at the window during maddening periods of silence. Hours passed; the trapper wondered if the bear had forgotten the bacon. Then there was lingering quiet. The trapper heard the bear's heavy tread. The light went out of the window.

In the confined quarters of the shed, the report of the rifle was deafening. The trapper threw the bolt of the Springfield, his finger on the trigger. But there were no clues at all. The sky framed the window as it had before. The river murmured through the vast emptiness of the night, smothering all sounds from the forest.

At dawn the trapper removed the braces from the door. Out on the snow was his elk, a torn drag of spine with mangled flaps of skin fanned over its bones like a wedding train. Even the head was missing. (The trapper found it later in a clump of aspen saplings, tossed many feet apparently, for no tracks approached the trees.) A riot of snow showed the path the bear had taken to the river after his shot. Above the window the slab of bacon was still nailed to the shed. Below it the huge tracks of the hind feet cut deeply and the snow had iced under them.

The trapper didn't have to look far to see what happened. The bullet had cut a hole in the braided strands of wire crossing the window. He looked for cut hair, speckles of blood, and found nothing to indicate that the bear had been hit. The trapper imagined his bullet must have deflected enough to miss it entirely.

Once again he found himself standing at the river. On the far bank he could see where the bear had shaken itself before entering the forest. This time the trapper allowed himself no illusions of following.

"Breath, not wind, blew in through the window, and the trapper, wide awake, felt his body break into sweat."

The bear never returned. The trapper stayed the winter, but moved back into his tent only when he felt sure that the grizzly had gone to its den. The trapper caught beaver until the river froze in its backwaters. He continued to take marten in the creek bottoms through March, when their lustrous chocolate fur began to thin and lose its value. Then he wrapped his Springfield in the fabric of his tent and pitched it high in a tree, where it would stay safe until his return. Like many trappers, he would not be burdened with a 10-pound rifle. His pack weighed 90 pounds, and he had no fear of the woods, even unarmed.

Ten years passed. The trapper never did get his rug. In fact, he said he didn't see much sign of grizzly bears anymore. He said he wouldn't shoot one now if he had the chance.

"But that was a real silvertip," he said, "a really big bear. I'll never forget him."

SO THAT WAS the story.

Like the best of stories it had been unexpected, and I don't believe there was a man among us who did not wish it was his story to tell, who was not reminded of probings into wilderness which paled in comparison. No doubt we all seek places where the air is soured by bears and trees grow too close together.

In the morning we saw the trapper off. He said he could make it back downriver to the wilderness boundary on snowshoes. We'd catch up in a day or two, then we'd all ride the snow cat to Hungry Horse where a doctor could attend to his foot.

In the interim there was our work, my part of it being to ski to the inlet of Big Salmon Lake where I hoped to find open water and perhaps a cutthroat trout or two for our supper. Part of the trail wound up from the river passing through a thicket of lodgepole pine. In the thicket, shafts of light escaped through the tree trunks, striping the snow abstractly.

"Trees no bigger around than that," the trapper had said, making a circle with his thumb and finger to describe a country where his hair stood on end. Now, it seemed to me a measure of grizzly bears that you felt their presence even when snow covered the dens, the graves in a foretold future.

I cast out, and while the fly settled and the rings spread from the center of the pool to the ice at its edges, I searched among the trees on the shoreline for any sign of movement.

—*September, 1984*

By Warren Page

REUNION *with* LUMPJAW

A HUNTERS' REUNION, OUT ON THE ALASKA PENINSULA 600 MILES WEST OF ANCHORAGE, BECAME A MEETING WITH A COUSIN OF THE BIG BAD BEAR.

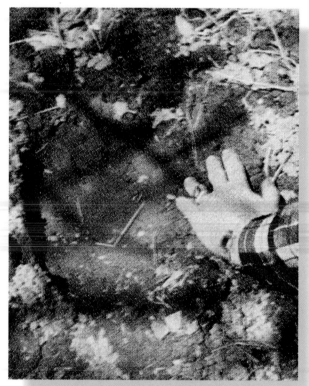

Old Lumpjaw left his track in the mud, huge as compared to Bud Branham's hand.

THE DROOP-SNOOTED, lop-eared, stilt-legged old cow moose was in a frightful tizzy. She had backed her mismatched frame out to the very tip of a peninsula stretching halfway across a shallow tundra lake. With the hair along her neck and withers bristling, she was making angry dashes, first back toward the brush and then out into the pond. Bud Branham and I watched her in puzzlement. I figured that the hot, bright May weather, unusual for the Alaska Peninsula, must be giving the Aniakchak Bay moose spring fever. Then we saw the reason for her frenzy. Two slick-haired calf moose, so wobbly legged they could be only hours old, stumbled up from their grassy bed and made an awkward effort to follow the cow.

"Darned if I know why she's in such a swivet even with the calves," Bud puzzled.

"Could be our bear went through here," I whispered.

But the bear hadn't gone through. He was lurking there in the brush all the time. We didn't know it, however, until we had topped out onto a little knoll. Then we saw the bear, a brown streak bumping himself into deeper brush away from the human scent. My rifle came up automatically.

"No—he's not good enough," said Bud, and I could see that the Alaska brownie was not in any real sense a trophy.

"The son of a gun is a meat eater, though,"

I said. "He was figuring to pick off those calves for lunch."

"Peninsula bears aren't normally meat eaters, certainly nothing like mountain grizzlies," answered the outfitter, a veteran of long years in Alaska. "But as you've already discovered, things aren't normal out here this spring. And with so many moose moving in, the bears are changing their habits."

To begin with, the 1959 spring was late in Alaska. When we began our hunt, heavy snows were still hanging on at the hibernation level, which ranges from 1,500 to 2,000 feet on the Peninsula home of the big coastal brownies. During the first two weeks of May few bears had crawled out of their dens. Then when the weather did change, it turned spring with a vengeance, day after day of brilliant sunshine. It was hot—60 degrees in the shade of the plane wing, half again hotter after we'd slogged up a couple of miles of mountain to investigate tracks shadowing across the snow. Fresh from hibernation, the heavy-coated brownies spent the warm days snoozing under alder clumps, where the sharpest binoculars or the best spotting scope couldn't find them.

The hunt, my sixth in Alaska, had started with plenty of fast action. Late on May 14, I boarded a Northwest Airlines plane in New York, stopped to swap hunting lies in Seattle that evening with Bill Niemi, the maker of Eddie Bauer down jackets, stepped down in Anchorage on the 15th at 5 A.M., local time. A commercial flight to Naknek and a charter hop brought me to Branham's base camp on Chiginagak Bay, roughly five hundred miles west of Anchorage. There an Alaskan surgeon, Dr. Hale,

and another medico, Dr. Sparks of Ohio, would hunt their brownies. Bud and I loaded up his Super Cub and flew to our own camp on Nakalilok Bay. At 6 o'clock on the evening of May 16 we were glassing a handsomely furred brownie. By 8, Bud was skinning a hide to lie before his Rainy Pass Lodge fireplace.

Thereafter matters slowed to an amble— which is about all the pace your correspondent figures to maintain for the first couple of days of Alaskan climbing with hip boots and a packboard sagging with camera gear. To begin, we hooked half a barrel of 5-pound Dolly Varden trout, tossing back all but the two we'd use for supper and breakfast. Then we made a 3- or 4-mile jaunt across Nakalilok Bay to a butte of volcanic rock to watch the high snow slopes until sundown, which comes late up there in May, around 10 P.M., with sunrise around 2:30 A.M., and no real darkness between. We saw tracks traversing the glittering white slides but no bears.

Most of the tracks were old. One set, however, stayed strong and clear under the bright sun of the next two days. "A big bear made that trail," mused Bud as we focused the 50 mm. Bushnell spotter on the high country one morning. "His tread is as wide as a Sherman tank's!"

"Then he's the guy we're looking for," I answered. "Old Lumpjaw himself."

"Who's Old Lumpjaw?"

"Remember the big bad bear in the Disney film?"

Branham remembered, all right, and the name "Old Lumpjaw" stuck. He was our meat—maybe.

We almost found him, too. A real Alaskan

williwaw cut loose somewhere west of us, and next day we were stormbound. As the storm slacked during the brief Arctic night Old Lumpjaw must have moved through our country, for when we made a 15-mile circuit of the hills lying west of camp we found his clean-edged tracks up near the snowline. The fore pads printed a full nine inches across and his hind paws dented hard gravel in a deep 15-inch print. He was on the move, stopping nowhere to chop off mouthfuls of early grass or wild celery tops, or to nip the willow buds that fattened faster every day.

In the unseasonably hot weather, the brownies were moving only during the brief night. They were bedding in rock crannies or in alder clumps throughout the day, we concluded after a 10-hour stretch of eyestrain from a butte we called Eagle Rock because we'd never seen an eagle within miles of it. The tide was nearly full down by then in the bay, and it seemed sensible to cross the Nakalilok flats back to camp for some hot grub and a few more battles with sea-run trout.

Bud suddenly punched me out of a half doze. "See him?"

I couldn't see anything but that same wall of slides and gullies and snow-filled basins we'd been watching fruitlessly all day. "Where?"

On the line of Bud's finger I picked up a spot of brown as it showed briefly on a slope far up the valley, perhaps two miles away. Too far to tell whether he was good, bad, or indifferent—Lumpjaw or his kid brother. We'd have to climb up there.

Hot and winded from fast travel, we finally made it to a knoll some three hundred yards below an alder strip into which, from the halfway point, we'd seen the bear go. Shrugging off packboards and rifles, we went to work with the glasses. No bear, not even a suspicious spot of brown.

"He must've moved while we were wading the river, Bud."

"Doubt it. He's asleep in there somewhere."

Believe me, we'd never have seen that bear if he'd stayed asleep. Only when he rolled flat onto his back, then calmly reached up and pulled down an alder branch to scratch his belly did we catch the movement. He had scraped out a cool hole in the brush roots, for all the world like a dog under a hydrangea bush, and sprawled to blend into the slope.

"Too small," said Bud. I had to agree; perhaps an 8-footer but no Lumpjaw by a long mile. "Good chance for pictures if we can get him down this way, though," Bud concluded.

Knowing he always carried a long-lensed movie camera, I suggested, "What if I slam a bullet into that rock right over him? He'll move downhill."

"Do that," said Bud, and he worked his way over to the left nearer the line the bear would take.

The clap of the 275-grain slug from the .35 Mashburn Magnum, whacking rock a foot or two over the bear's head, brought him out of there faster than any fireman ever slid down the brass pole. He burst across the slope for fifty yards in one rolling rush, whirled, and looked back toward his bed in angry inquiry, hackles high over his hump and lips pouting in a bear's piggy snarl. Then he turned again into downhill flight another hundred yards or so onto a half-acre patch of snow directly ahead of Bud, pausing there to growl and cuss at the loud noise that had disturbed his siesta, displaying himself nicely for the camera before dropping over the edge of a concealing gully and out of our sight.

So Bud got his movies and we started down the mountain. Then one of those ever-loving alders reached out and grabbed my left boot. I flipped and landed hard on a right foot that gave way with a ripping ankle tear all too easily remembered from school football days. A sprain, and a bad one, I could tell with the first few limping steps. Nothing to do about it but keep going, however. It might work itself out. But after we'd hiked the four or five miles back off the range and across the tide flats to camp, hurrying a bit to catch the 8 o'clock radio schedule maintained each night among all parts of the Rainy Pass operation, I knew it wouldn't. The swelling was coming up too fast.

I was sitting outside our camp the next morning, soaking the ankle in 35-degree sea water, when another brownie paraded out across the bay. Just over the flats he was, ambling along in broad daylight. We had the spotter on him in minutes. "Pretty bear," said Bud. "Looks like a rangy young boar, but he'll square only nine feet at best."

Foot and ankle half numb from the cold water, I hobbled over to the scope. He was a handsome bear, all right, in good coat. But even without any nearby object with which to compare him for size it was obvious that he wasn't even close to the record class—he hadn't the ponderous dignity, the belly sag, and the massive rear-end waddle of a really big old boar. I couldn't have made it over there anyway.

That evening the Chiginagak Bay transmitter told us that the two doctors, their brownie hunt over, would be flown over to Bud's lodge at Kakhonak to smash up some fishing tackle on the leg-long rainbow trout of the Iliamna area. So Bud suggested that we shift our base to the larger bay. Since the move would mean another day of rest for my gimpy ankle, that made good sense. Off we went in the morning, arriving in time to help load the float-equipped Taylorcraft that Dennis Branham, Bud's brother, was flying to ferry the doctors and their guides to Kakhonak.

"Fresh tracks showing on the snow slopes up here every day now," reported nephew Dean Branham as we waited between flights. "You fellows will find a bear, all right."

Bud and I weren't worried. We'd been yakking about finding Old Lumpjaw, but we really didn't have to find the biggest bear on the Peninsula. This hunt was a sort of reunion between a couple of characters who liked to be with each other in the wild country, to drop a quiet rock in the other guy's packsack when he wasn't looking, and to experiment with new ways of making bannock biscuits. We were in no sweat.

Wind and tide stayed right for flying only a couple of days. One day produced the encounter with the cow moose and the calf-hunting bear, another developed into a mad foot-race across the beach of Yentarny. Bruin won the race without even knowing he was in it, nonchalantly swimming the river five hundred yards ahead of us—a river too deep to wade and too cold for ordinary mortals to swim. Then the wind switched around to come from the west, straight out of the mountains. That meant bumpy flying, dips and swoops too violent to make it either safe or enjoyable.

So next morning we left the Piper lashed to waterlogged timbers, safely under the bluff that protected our camp, and started up the mountain on shanks' mare. The wind hadn't changed, nor the weather. It was still incredibly bright and sunny. The sky carried only puffy flecks of those gray masses of cloud that usually squat on the Peninsula range, when warm air from the Japan Current to the south runs into the colder flow from the Bering Sea. By the time we had reached a wind-protected spot just under the peak, we were both soaked with sweat.

We could see part way into a big valley. Enough snow was melting off its upper basins to raise its river to flood level. No bears moved there, though, and we could see no fresh traces across the high snow sweeps, save for one lightly dotted line that ended in a caribou which was grazing a mossy outcrop five hundred or a thousand feet higher than a caribou should be at this season.

It was warm there in the sun, sleepy-warm after a couple of sandwiches.

Alternately glassing the area and dozing, we spent hours in the drowsy heat, overlooking a stretch of bear country seemingly half the size of Rhode Island. No soap. I was dozing off again when Bud grunted in excitement. "A bear!" he said. "A big one. Take a line down off the right corner of that second peak. Under the snow there's a steep rock slide—gray rock. Got it?"

I had my binoculars on that slide. "Now, down and right of it there's a long escarpment, about a third of the way up from the river, with a waterfall in the middle of it, right? Just below the left edge of the rocks—"

"I've got him—feeding in that green patch. He must have parachuted in."

"More likely came up out of a gully."

It was too far to judge the bear's size with any but a wild guess, but he had that ponderous and deliberate air about him that characterizes a big boar. Chances were he'd feed out that little patch and then move slowly around the slope under the steep escarpment. Or he might just take it into his head to amble out of the country.

We had something like three miles to go. Down off our mountain, which would be easy, then down into the canyon of the river, which might or might not be wadable at this point. Finally, part way up the opposite mountain to the top fringe of alders. And for half the trip the bear would almost surely be out of our sight. In thirty minutes he could vanish. But we had to take that chance.

We waded the boiling river at a point above a rapid, and were winded and slowing down, my ankle screaming protests, when we crawled up toward the green patch. No sight of the bear for nearly half an hour, and on his side of the river the breeze was switching around, one moment cooling our brows, the next pushing gently on our packboards. Be a miracle if the bear was still out on the little flat.

He wasn't. Not there or behind any of the minor humps and gullies that chopped up the area. We could see where he had been feeding, and the softer spots showed tears in the moss and the flat-crushed traces left by a heavy brownie. Heading off below the escarpment and then downslope toward the bay flats ran a regular bear road, the broad-beamed trail the big coastal grizzlies make as they travel the country, each bear stepping more or less in the tracks of those who came before, so that the road is a double dotted line of worn spots each the size of a washbasin. He should logically have followed the road.

But he hadn't. There were no fresh tracks on it.

"Think he dropped down toward the flat?" I queried Bud.

"More likely moved left of the track and around under the escarpment, either toward the fall, in which case we may spot him, or up and completely out of this round basin."

To get a better view of the alder-grown slopes under the frowning rock cliffs, we climbed a bare knoll at the edge of the bowl. If the bear hadn't topped out or wasn't lying down up there, we should spot him. And we did, briefly— caught just a glimpse of chocolate brown moving slowly through alders a thousand yards ahead of our elevation. Again no chance to estimate size and hide condition accurately. And

the bear's direction could, if he continued moving at the feeding amble, which is fully as fast as a man can scramble through alders, carry him out of the far side of the basin.

"If I can see him from that next hump, it won't be too long a shot, Bud," I proposed.

To drop off one hill and race up the other would mean arriving too winded to shoot at any range, especially at a target that would appear only through openings. So we cut around the steep sidehill, fighting clinging alder branches every step of the way for twenty minutes. No use. When we finally staggered out into the hill clearing, the bear was not in sight. He could have dropped behind a rise of ground or into one of the gullies that ran down toward the small creek at our right. He might have topped out of the basin completely if the wind had fluked our scent in his direction, or he might still be there in the brush, sleeping or feeding.

"To climb around on top of the escarpment would take almost an hour," mused Bud, "and in that time the bear could leave the country. Probably wouldn't be able to see him from there anyway. Let's try dropping down to where we can see the whole slope, locate him properly, and see if a stalk makes sense."

We had dropped off the hill and crossed the small creek, at every step watching the left-hand face of the basin as it opened up, when the bear made his move.

Bud's shout came as I was fighting free of brush edging the creek. "There he goes!"

The brownie had fed until his belly was full, then settled down below a standing rock for a nap. He had been lying hidden only a matter of yards from our colloquy on the second hill, hadn't heard our whispers there, but had caught the human taint as sun-warmed air carried it up the side of the bowl. The bear was off and running.

My first slug from the hard-hitting .35 Mashburn Magnum caught him solidly as he showed in a room-size clear spot. Down he went, rolling twice on the steep slope. Then he was up again in dense alders and making good time slanting down across the sidehill. I caught him with a second bullet but didn't slow him much. A third turned him, though, and at sixty

It wasn't Old Lumpjaw that Page (left) and Branham finally met, but his brother or cousin, smaller but still a trophy.

or seventy yards the big brownie swung down-slope directly toward us, bellowing in pain and anger with every jump.

Not a charge, though it looked like one. He was hurt too badly to climb, and had to go downhill. It just happened that the easy path was straight down toward where Bud and I stood in a little spot of clear tundra. The bear's broad head and driving shoulders looked huge in the 4X scope as he lunged off the hill and showed clear for an instant as he broke out of a brush patch. I cut loose the fourth and last round in the rifle. It hit, but we were so close that any bullet smack was lost in the muzzle blast. The bear rolled again but recovered and plunged on a bit to our left. He finally stopped about fifteen yards away, out of sight on the other side of a clump of scrubby willows by the creek. All went oddly quiet.

Dead? Or still alive and full of steam and waiting for us to come get him? No way of telling; there was not even a patch of chocolate hair to be seen. No sound save the clicks as I slipped a couple of fresh cartridges into the Mashburn and rammed the bolt shut. Two would be either plenty or by no means enough. If he came, there'd be time for only one shot at best.

But two were more than enough. The brownie, finally running out of steam, had piled up by the creek edge. Just the faintest twitch of life remained, the last vestige of the tremendous stamina that had carried the bear fully two hundred yards on his arcing course while his forebody was absorbing three hits and over ten thousand pounds of tearing bullet energy. Tough bear.

A good bear, too, with the spread of hide that can square out at half an acre if soaked rubbery overnight in salt water and then stretched on an A-frame, as some do it. It figured a strong 9½ feet as hides should be measured, laid hair side down on the grass and not hauled out of shape. Not a record skull, alas; so Bert Kline-burger of Jonas Brothers wouldn't be calling the Seattle papers about this one. No deformation of the jaw or dental equipment; so it certainly wasn't Old Lumpjaw. But one odd thing: a toe had long been missing from the left front foot. It could just have been Old Lumpjaw's first cousin, slightly wounded in some battle between the sexes. A fine ending for a reunion of good friends and hunting companions, however—that's for sure.

—November, 1959

By Dan Holland

FIRE!

WITH TIME—AND MY LIFEBLOOD—SLOWLY
RUNNING OUT, I PRAYED THAT THE GREEDY
YELLOW FLAMES WOULD BRING HELP.

THIS WAS MY LAST CHANCE, AND I KNEW
it. I had tried three times already and failed. If I
didn't have a good share of luck this time, I figured I'd had it.
When night came and I didn't return to camp someone would start looking
for me, and I knew that particular someone well enough to be sure he would
find me in a hurry. But nightfall was a long way off. I was hurt. I couldn't wait
that long. The day had started innocently enough as far as I was concerned,
but not so far as a buck deer was concerned. Ted Trueblood, his wife Ellen
and I were camped at the end of the road in the foothills of the Sawtooths. It
was a perfect camp, located beside a clear trout stream bordered by steep grass
hillsides that were dotted with aspen groves and clumps of chokecherry. Each
day I climbed high, sat, and soaked up the autumn scenery. The higher I
climbed, the higher the hills on the opposite side of the valley seemed to grow.
The aspen leaves, quivering in the slightest breeze, had turned a rich gold, and
the sky was a deep blue, as blue as the sky can be only in the high country. I
saw blue grouse and ruffed grouse, and I sat occasionally to watch a covey of
mountain quail scurry back and forth in a brushy ravine. It was good to be
alive and in Ted's Idaho country.

Ted didn't know it at the time, but I didn't have any serious intention of
shooting a deer. After this hunt we were going bird shooting, and that was
what I was waiting for. In the meantime I was enjoying the freedom of the big
hills around camp. Ted got his deer quickly and efficiently, of course; then, on
the fourth day, Ellen made a remarkable shot with her .257 Roberts. I was on
the point of a ridge where I could watch the whole thing: see the buck jump
and see Ellen lay it down with one clean shot. I was impressed.

And that was that, I thought to myself. Now we could head down-country
and start hunting Huns and quail. I knew that Ted was more than ready to go
bird hunting too, but I didn't realize how he would feel about my not having a
deer. In camp that evening he said, "If you don't get a buck tomorrow, I'll have
to drive this meat to town, but I won't break camp until you do get one. I'll

bring back more grub, and I can work as well here as anywhere."

That was one of the best things Ted ever did for me. Being strictly a bird hunter, I didn't realize what I had been missing.

The next morning I was on the mountain as soon as the law allowed. I meant business. And I was lucky. I had been out of camp less than an hour when I spotted a buck. He wasn't a big one and he was a quarter mile away, but he was a buck. I sat down and watched him. He was on an open hillside with no cover between us; so I had to wait until he was out of sight before I could make a move in his direction. Instead of topping the ridge, he disappeared into a tiny brushy spot and didn't come out. This was ideal. He had bedded down. I waited ten minutes or more, then went after him. And for a partridge hunter I did myself proud, using the slight breeze and the lay of the land to get as close as possible.

He jumped when I was hardly fifty yards from him and started directly away from me up the grassy hillside. I was toting a .30-30 with open sights, no good for that big country; so the ordered procedure would have been to shoot fast from the rear while he was close. I didn't because I wanted to make a clean kill. Ted and Ellen had set an example for me.

To get the most out of my gun and my limited ability, I sat down to rest my elbows on my knees, then whistled sharply. The buck stopped and looked back, but by now I was suddenly excited. Before I could get the sights where I wanted them he was bounding on up the slope, as though mounted on springs. I stopped him a second and a third time. The third time I touched it off. He was 150 yards away by then, but somehow I made the clean shot I had hoped for. The deer kicked like a mule, made about three bounds, and dropped dead.

By now I was thoroughly excited, a bit proud of myself as a deer slayer, and happy. I could get him back to the valley in time to break camp that morning and go bird hunting.

I moved fast, and that's when I got into trouble. I had the deer about half dressed when, for no good reason, I decided to cut through the pelvis, the arch of bone between the hind legs, and lay the animal open. This is poor procedure under any circumstances—unless an animal is so large that it must be quartered—because it uselessly destroys good meat; so the only explanation I can offer is that I was working fast with my mind in neutral. In the process I made a discovery, one I won't forget. The forward side of this arch is solid bone, not too thick, but the last three-quarters of it is attached only by a thin line of cartilage. If the knife happens to find this seam of cartilage, it will cut through it like butter. My knife did find it, when I was applying full strength to cut bone, and the next thing I knew the blade was buried to the hilt in my right thigh.

There's no immediate pain from such a wound. I felt only shock, followed by disgust with myself for having done such a fool thing. Also, there's no blood for a moment, just a deep, bulging incision, an ugly white gash down to the bone. Then the blood gushes.

Stopping the hemorrhage in a big cut is no easy matter. I used up two bandannas, a muslin meat bag, string, and my trouser leg in dressing the cut and making tourniquets. I knew that the main source of blood to the leg is from arteries on the inside of the thigh; so I wadded a lump of cloth over the arteries and twisted the tourniquet with all my strength, using the knife in the loop of the tourniquet to gain leverage.

It was a long while before I stopped the flow. I looked at the blood around the deer, which had been heart-shot, and I looked at the blood where I sat. As far as I could see I had lost more than the deer, and it was dead.

The sun had been behind the hills to the east when I cut myself, but now the whole mountainside was in full sunlight. It was another beautiful, crisp day. The sky was the same deep blue, and above me was a small aspen grove with the same golden leaves. But I was in no mood to appreciate it.

With the flow of blood stopped, the pain set in. My leg felt as though it were welling up like a balloon, throbbing and pulsing. But at least I had the hemorrhaging stopped in time. The tourniquet was so tight that I might eventually lose my leg for lack of circulation, but that would be better than bleeding into unconsciousness, and death.

Now I was faced with a second problem, one that many hunters have had to face. When you're hurt too severely to move, what do you do? That's when you need a friend, and it explains why wise outdoorsmen have a rule: always hunt with a companion. If he is within shouting distance, there is no problem; but even if he isn't, the knowledge that he is somewhere near is comfort enough to keep a man cool in his emergency, to sustain his courage. I know.

That Idaho hillside would have been a lonely spot if I hadn't known there was a good man in the valley thirty minutes away. Even though I am not given to panic or hysteria, I might have overextended myself without his presence. As it was, each move I made was methodical and calculated. I was confident that all I had to do, once I had successfully applied first aid to myself, was to get word across to Ted Trueblood; then I could turn the whole problem over to him. Without Ted I might not have lasted the first hour, and I certainly wouldn't have two good hunting legs under me today.

How do you let someone know you are in trouble? Do you use the standard distress signal, three evenly spaced shots? Sure, if you have a lot of ammunition. Maybe it will calm you to hear the sound echo off the hills. Otherwise I have no faith in it. The next time you are on a deer stand or in a duck blind with nothing better to do, count the number of times you hear three evenly spaced shots in the course of a day. If you tried to run down every such volley looking for someone in trouble, you would wear yourself down to the knees by noon.

I knew this, but I had to try anything. I shot three times, paused, shot three times, paused, and shot three times. Ted heard me and was pleased, just as I knew he would be. I was whamming away at a big buck, he logically concluded. Later he told me that if I had waited longer between groups of shots it might have registered. I knew that I was only making noise, nothing more, and I undoubtedly did shoot too fast, but I doubt if it would have made any difference. In any case, there was no three-shot answer from the valley.

The only thing to do—the only thing for anyone in a tight spot—is to make smoke. The trouble was that I was sitting on a cheat-grass hillside with only a few scattered clumps of bitter brush and sagebrush. If somehow I could set fire to the sparse grass, it might reach the small aspen grove above me. There would be enough debris on the ground there to make a dense smoke. This was my only hope. Otherwise I would sit there all day. After dark I could direct Ted to me with my rifle, but I didn't think I could last that long. Certainly my leg, with the tight tourniquet, would be lost.

I lit three clumps of brush, but each in turn flared and went out. They didn't make any smoke and they didn't set fire to the grass. In the process of moving from one to another I started the wound bleeding again. It was an insidious thing. As soon as the warm blood flowed it eased the pressure and relieved the throbbing pain. It actually felt good, good enough to have a lulling effect. Luckily I stopped it this time before it got well started.

Then I waited quite a while before making my next move. After calculating every possibility, I decided optimistically that I could inch along gradually on my backside about four hundred yards to the top of a ridge, where I would stand a better chance of attracting attention in the valley. Less than twenty feet of this changed my mind and I quickly altered course to a tiny grove of chokecherries about fifty feet away. By the time I reached my goal I was bleeding freely. I used the remainder of my trouser leg making tourniquets and broke three of them in an attempt to stop the bleeding, but the fourth one was strong enough to hold. Twenty minutes later I eased it slightly, and the bleeding remained checked.

I knew now that I had moved as far as I was going to move. I didn't dare shift my leg so much as an inch. I had lost so much blood already that I was lightheaded and dizzy. If I bled again, I would pass out. This was it.

I sat very still with my back against a chokecherry, and I had plenty of time to think. I remembered a photograph that appeared in FIELD & STREAM about twenty years ago, when I was a young editor on the magazine. It showed the skeletons of a buck deer and of a man, a rusty gun and a rusty hunting knife. We printed the picture, and the consensus of the readers was that the hunter, about to cut the deer's throat, had been charged by the dying animal and killed. Now I knew the true solution. There was no question in my mind how that man had died. He had cut himself severely while dressing the deer, had passed out, and had died.

The dry leaves under the chokecherries were my last chance for a fire. I built a little tepee at my side out of paper from my pockets plus twigs and leaves, but I didn't light it. I waited. I was afraid. I was afraid to spend my final attempt at a signal. Also, although there were few other hunters in the area, I hoped I might possibly see someone who, in turn, would have a better chance of seeing my little fire.

I waited about three hours, which is a long time to sit and think the thoughts I had. About 10:30 A.M. I thought I heard a rock click below me. It might have been a hunter, or a deer, or my imagination. The air was stirring with a slight breeze up the draw, as it does toward the heat of day, and that would be a help. I struck a match and lit my little tepee of kindling.

The flame spread out through the tiny grove and worked uphill. It swept along efficiently, like a vacuum cleaner, sweeping up the curled yellow leaves as it went. At times it seemed to disappear completely; then it would reappear, flare up, and die down. Finally it burned all the way through the grove, and the trees didn't catch and there wasn't any smoke. That was the lowest moment of my life.

I kept looking back over my shoulder wishfully. The last dry twig finally burned out and there was no sign of a flame anywhere in the grove, only charred ground. Then I saw a clump of cheat grass above me spurt into flame, and my hopes rose with it—and sank quickly and sickeningly as it burned out.

Then another clump to the right flared and burned out. Slowly the sparse grass burned in fits up the hillside, the most fascinating and tortuous thing I have ever watched. It burned

and died, burned and died. Eventually the erratic line of fire topped a slight rise and passed from view. From my chokecherry grove in the gully I could see only the golden tops of the aspens against the blue sky far up the hill. I couldn't see whether my fire burned or not, and the suspense was agonizing.

That was a long half-hour. I waited and waited, until I had about given up hope. Then I heard the fire take off! It burned and popped and crackled and snapped, the grandest music I have ever heard, and the aspens sent a beautiful column of black smoke towering into the sky. I picked up my rifle, put it to my shoulder, shot three times with complete confidence, and relaxed.

Ted arrived carrying a shovel and blowing like a four-minute-miler, followed closely by Ellen carrying an ax. They had come to help me fight a fire, which I considered a compliment. It still hadn't occurred to them that I was fool enough to get myself into so helpless a mess.

I've always admired Ted's efficiency, and in an emergency he was just as efficient as he is at boiling a pot of coffee at daybreak in camp. In no time he had me on a travois and had dragged me to camp and the car, and before I realized it he had returned with the deer and hung it. Then we started the long drive from camp to town. We arrived at the hospital just about fourteen hours after I had cut myself.

Ted left me there, giving the doctor strict orders to keep me penned up, which he did for six days. And of course Ted reported the fire immediately, although, having checked it, he was quite certain it could go no farther than the isolated aspen grove.

That was several years ago. All I have to show for the experience today is a five-inch scar with fourteen stitch marks—and a receipted bill from the Forest Service as a result of burning some of their very own aspen trees. To be fair, the bill was actually for the expenses of men sent to check on the fire to be positive it was out. Anyway, it was the cheapest load of firewood a man ever bought!

—*August, 1960*

By Larry Bamford

LION
of a LIFETIME

MY HUNT WAS THE CULMINATION OF MUCH RESEARCH, PLANNING, AND PRACTICE PLUS AN EXHAUSTING CHASE OVER SOME OF THE ROUGHEST COUNTRY IN WESTERN COLORADO.

THE DATE WAS DECEMber 12, 1967. Before me, high in a twisted juniper tree, was one of the largest mountain lions any hunter will ever see. I gripped the string of my bow tightly. The aluminum arrow was ready. The cold wind caused my eyes to water, blurring my vision as I strained to see. The weather was 12 degrees below zero.

All of this action was the culmination of much research, planning, and practice plus an exhausting chase over some of the roughest country in western Colorado.

The hunt was my second for Felis concolor,

better known by one of his many nicknames: mountain lion, puma, cougar, painter, panther, or catamount. Bill Wallace, of Collbran, Colorado, was my guide for this trip, as he had been a year before when we'd teamed up for a lion hunt in Utah. That had turned out to be one of the most exciting adventures of my life, climaxing with the shooting of a cougar that made the Boone and Crockett record book as well as the archery records of the Pope and Young Club. I told that story in "One for the Books" in the September 1968 *FIELD & STREAM.*

Following that experience, I did not plan to ever hunt another cougar, mainly because I already had an excellent trophy. However, in the summer of 1967, I began reading everything I could find concerning this extremely shy animal that few hunters ever have the opportunity to see in the field.

I learned that cougar seldom range above 8,000 feet, their favored domain apparently being the lower foothills. The animal, which is mostly nocturnal, may travel twenty-five to thirty miles in a twenty-four hour period. Mule deer are the favorite food, though rabbits are eaten as well. If an area is short on deer, you can be sure the lion hunting will be poor.

Once a lion has made a kill, it usually goes for a quick liver or heart feast, then sleeps it off nearby. Normally the cat will lay up and visit its kill for several days before leaving altogether. It is the custom of the cougar to scratch branches, leaves, and earth over the kill between visits.

Since the lion characteristically eats only what it itself has killed, the animal cannot be baited like the black bear. This trait probably saves many cats from the poison bait stations put out by the Federal predator control agents.

According to professional hunting guides, late January or February is an excellent time to try for a large male lion. During that period, the males are stalking the countryside, visiting as many females as possible. Just after the first of the year in the high country, the temperatures are dry and cool with snow likely. These conditions are just right for tracking the elusive puma.

In March of 1965 the Colorado legislature repealed the old mountain lion bounty of $50 which was first enacted in 1924. With the price

off its head, the lion gained new stature, and in July of 1965 the state declared it to be a big-game animal, subject to regular seasons, limits, and licenses. (The resident fee is currently $25, with nonresident fee being $50.) About the same time both the Boone and Crockett and Pope and Young Clubs declared that only lions coming from states that no longer paid the bounty fee were eligible to be entered in their biannual competitions and permanent records.

My cougar research made memories of my first lion adventure even more vivid, and I decided to arrange for one additional, and final, hunt with Bill Wallace. I set the date for mid-December, several months off, so I'd have enough time to get in the right mental as well as physical condition for a hunt I wanted to be in top-notch shape for.

The previous spring, Ken Barnes, president of the Howett Archery Company of Yakima, Washington, had given me a prototype of a new hunting bow, which had a draw weight of 57 pounds and a length of 60 inches. I cut a big section out of the handle and put a coat of brown flocking on the entire weapon. The handle neck was so small that I began to wonder if it would hold together under all conditions; however, it now fit my hand perfectly, and I quickly developed confidence in the new bow. I found that every so often I could shoot a perfect score on a Professional Archery Association target with the bow. This particular target has a 3-inch bull's-eye and is shot from 20 yards.

Finally the long anticipated day of the lion hunt arrived and with it came one of the worst snowstorms of the winter. I started out by car, but was forced by road conditions to turn back, borrow a friend's 4-wheel-drive vehicle, repack my hunting gear, and start all over.

By the time I arrived in Crescent Junction, Utah, our designated meeting spot, it was 4 A.M. and the temperature registered 19 degrees below zero.

Bob Ward, assistant guide to Bill Wallace, met me inside a local cafe where we had a cup of coffee to warm up while we talked over plans for the hunt.

"Bill's been real busy," Bob told me. "He's been talking to every rancher he knows, and some he don't, trying to find some lion trouble. Yesterday he heard the government hunter was called over to check on a lion causing a ruckus with sheep down near the Colorado-Utah border. Wallace went right down there to ask if we could hunt him instead."

"Did you hear anything about its size?" I asked.

"No, just how many sheep it's been killing."

We downed the coffee and headed out with haste. Our destination was a place called Coal Canyon, between Grand Junction and Dove Creek along the Colorado-Utah border. Since we had to pick up some gear in Moab, Utah, we headed south through Moab and Monticello, and east into Colorado.

As we arrived in Dove Creek, Bill was standing in front of the post office. He was sporting his favorite dark brown Stetson hat and green insulated coat. Bill is a young, enthusiastic guy who looks like the outdoors he lives in. His job is not an easy one, but he certainly enjoys it. Because of all his guiding experience, he's got a lot of confidence in himself, and some of it rubs off on his hunters.

A big grin appeared on Bill's face as he walked up to the jeep. As we shook hands, he said, "I was out to check on the sheep kill. From the tracks, this cat is a real monster. He may be even bigger than the one you killed last time."

My first lion scored 14^{12}/16 inches. The chance of taking a larger one would be remote, I thought to myself.

———— ✦✦✦ ————

WITHOUT FURTHER DELAY, we loaded up Wallace's truck with all my gear and headed north for an hour's ride to the ranch where the lion had been reported. As we drove, I noticed that the terrain certainly looked like typical lion country. About a mile before we turned into the long ranch drive, five deer ran across the road ahead of us. This seemed like an encouraging sign. When we reached the ranch we met Jim Branch, one of the ranch hands, who was checking the antifreeze in an old truck. I asked him about the lion, and he told me he thought it must be an old one. It was his opinion that the lion had drifted into the area about a month before, possibly from Utah.

The hounds—all of the Plott strain—had been let out of their boxes, and most of them seemed anxious to get on with the hunt. Branch asked if he could come along with us; as he said, he wanted to see this "dude" try to take a cougar with a bow and arrow. He helped us load the dogs, and we all climbed into the truck.

A thirty-minute 4-wheel-drive ride over a creek bottom brought us to the head of a wide, rocky canyon with very steep walls and slightly rolling country in between. Many cedars dotted the area.

We wasted no time in unloading and heading for the closest canyon rim. I quickly tried a couple of practice shots on a stump and heard the shafts thump twice from 30 yards. The hounds were so excited that we had to exert all the strength we could muster just to hold them back.

After nearly an hour and a half of trudging through foot-deep snow, we had our first look at the track of the cat.

"That is one of the biggest lion tracks I've ever seen in all my years of guiding," Bill exclaimed.

To me the pad mark looked so large it appeared to have melted out and increased in size. However, it certainly could not have melted much in the below zero weather.

Within another three quarters of a mile, we found our first lion-killed sheep, but the tracks were not fresh.

"We've got some catching up to do," Bill informed me.

Bob Ward added, "I'll bet the lion made another kill up ahead, probably last night."

"If he stayed in this area and killed again, we've got a good chance of taking him," Bill observed. We all agreed with him.

Wallace moved out ahead as the chase warmed up, announcing, "I'm going to turn ol' Ranger loose. I think he can pick up the scent now."

As soon as the chain was released, the dog bolted forward with his nose working furiously. He disappeared over a small ridge ahead, tail wagging with excitement. All of a sudden Ranger opened up with that sweet sound of a dog on scent. Everyone was running as the barking became higher pitched. I sprinted as fast as I could but was losing ground with every stride.

As we topped a rocky cedar-covered bench, we saw the hound going around in circles with his head in the air. He was howling like crazy. Another lion-kill was lying in a shallow depression partly covered with brush and dirt. Since the kill was fresh, we all felt that our chances had just improved considerably. I had to remind myself that the cat hadn't even been seen yet. We only knew that he was somewhere in the huge canyon complex.

Ranger was having trouble untangling the maze of tracks around the sheep so Bill took the dog's collar and led him in a wide circle away from the kill. Finally, finding the lion's exit, the dog charged back into the canyon, bellowing and growling as he went. Now Bob unchained the other dogs, which fell all over themselves trying to catch Ranger. We sprinted along behind, although we could not keep up. The most we could hope for was to keep within earshot.

Fifteen minutes later, the tempo of the hound chorus reached a peak with wild yelping and barking. Wallace yelled excitedly, "They've jumped him."

I surmised that the lion had been lying on a ledge nearby, resting after gorging himself on the latest kill. By now I was plenty excited. I was trying to run faster as I heard the hounds go wild up ahead. My lungs were burning. My heart was pounding. But I kept stumbling along. We were midway up the side of the main canyon. It seemed the lion was heading downward towards a small side canyon.

I finally had to stop. Inhaling the raw, cold air was harsh on my lungs, and the rest of me felt as though I'd been running the half mile in a track meet. Just as I flopped into the snow to rest, Bill yelled, "He's treed! Come on, let's get the lead out."

IN A SECOND I was up and running downhill, dodging bushes and rocks. I worried about my camera as we slipped and slid down the slope. The footing was extremely unstable, and once three of us were down at the same time. Near the bottom of the canyon, the cat had bounded along a narrow rock ledge, then jumped into a cedar tree. Although the lion was 200 yards away, shifting from limb to limb, he looked very large.

Apparently the lion had only been resting, for he suddenly jumped to the ground and dashed away with the hounds right at his heels. Hearing a commotion ahead, we were just in time to see the lion leap up on a rock. As the hounds tried to reach him, he spat and waved a claw-extended paw in defiance. As we watched, a young Plott hound hurled himself onto the lion's perch. Within a second, the dog was knocked to the ground, having had a sample of lion teeth and claws. He had been bitten and slashed across the face. Bill treated him quickly and chained him to a tree for our return.

Jim had gone ahead and now yelled back to us, "The lion is heading for the other side of the canyon."

To do this, the animal would have to cross a flat area about a hundred yards wide. The dogs were now moving in on him. He was beginning to tire. We skidded to the bottom of the side hill and hightailed it across the flat. Branch was pointing when the rest of us caught up to him.

"He's in that juniper near the edge of the cliff."

"He's climbing right to the top," Bob exclaimed. "We better move in slow and chain the dogs off first—if we can."

Neither Bill nor Bob wanted me to shoot the lion while the dogs were loose under the tree. A wounded lion could kill the whole pack, setting Bill back as much as $500 per hound.

The lion had been watching Branch until I came up on the other side of the tree. Then he swapped ends, looking directly at me, hissing, and swatting the air.

Bob whispered to me, "They don't get any larger than this one."

The cougar looked as hefty as a full-grown man. We later guessed his weight to be between 180 and 190 pounds. His head was very large, with flashing teeth and a scarred face. I sensed that he was getting ready to jump out if he could only find space below the tree.

Without warning, Ranger broke loose from

Bob. By leaping desperately, he landed in the lower limbs of the tree. When this happened, the lion went back to the top, which gave Bill a chance to snap a couple of photographs. The other dogs were now trying to get loose and join Ranger. Branch and Ward chained them to nearby trees, while Bill managed to capture Ranger and chain him also. Since the cougar had been forced to bay three times, the dogs were tired but still very excited. The cougar suddenly moved to a lower limb.

"Shoot," Bill yelled, "he's coming out!"

Quickly I drew the bow, and I aimed the arrow. With my release, the arrow was on its way in a black-and-yellow flash. It hit the animal, then sliced through and bounced high into the air. However, it had first clipped a small twig and then ricocheted, striking the cat too far back to be a good shot.

Bill yelled immediately, "Watch out! He's coming down. Get out of there, fast."

I didn't need to be told. All I could see were teeth and tawny-colored lion coming straight for me. In our confusion, Bill and I collided, almost knocking each other down. It was every man for himself as the big cat landed on the ground in front of us, very much alive. At close range, he looked three times bigger than he had in the tree. Since the dogs were chained off, I was the nearest to the cat. As I tried to get another arrow nocked, I was all thumbs. My heart was pumping madly as I managed to draw the second arrow, fire...and miss. I flipped another shaft onto the string and released at no more than 10 yards. The arrow caught the cat through the lungs. He took about three quick bounds and slumped in the snow.

RECOVERING A LITTLE, I walked up to examine the cougar. It was a truly awesome animal, one I thought might make the top five of the Pope and Young trophy list.

Wallace began to cape the cat while I took photographs from every angle. Looking at the enormous head, I discovered the cat was very old. Its teeth were broken and worn; its ears were full of holes from fighting, and there were several big scars on his face. I tried to get some

idea of how large the skull actually was by fashioning calipers out of a piece of rusty wire I found on the ground, but the device did not work too well. As soon as I took the wires off the skull they would spring back together, giving me a smaller reading. Even so, we could see the skull was over 15 inches. For an accurate total score, one must measure the top part of the skull only, adding the width and length together.

Sixty days later, after the skull had been boiled and dried, I had it officially measured by a Boone and Crockett measurer and was amazed when the final score totaled 15 7/16 inches! At the time the minimum score recognized as a trophy cougar by the Pope and Young archery records was 12 inches. Recently it has been increased to 13.

The skull was sent to Glenn St. Charles of the Pope and Young Club. His reply was a surprise of the most pleasant type. The score exceeded the world record taken ten years before by Dr. James Smith in Arizona. That lion had scored 15 4/16 inches, and Dr. Smith's record had never been challenged in the last decade. At the 1969 Pope and Young Club awards banquet in Denver, I was awarded a plaque for my new world's record.

The Boone and Crockett record book published in 1964 shows no larger mountain lions having ever been taken in Colorado, with the exception of the famous giant world record cat shot by President Theodore Roosevelt in 1901. According to that same record book, my lion is the ninth largest ever taken by any means, and topping off my list of honors, this past May I was informed that my trophy had been awarded a medal for placing first in the 1968-1971 Boone and Crockett competition.

But it's more than medals and plaques that makes a hunt unforgettable. Every time I look at the 8-foot 6-inch cougar rug that dominates my den, I can almost hear the dogs again, feel the cold, and relive the excitement of the moment when my arrow found its mark from a 10-foot shot at that once-in-a-lifetime lion.

—August, 1971

By Art Young

MOUNTAIN SHEEP
and the Bow

THE MOUNTAIN SHEEP is considered the most elusive of America's game. He lives in a rough, hard-to-get-at country and is entitled to first place as a big-game trophy.

It is true that some sheep country affords an easier approach to the game than others; yet the hunter is eternally confronted with the problem of escaping the ever-scrutinizing telephoto eye of the sheep. Little seems to escape his sight at any distance, and he acts upon his instinct by playing safe. The distance between hunter and sheep is generally fixed and maintained by the sheep. His strategic position enables him, almost at will, to be swallowed up by a rough country such as his merely by a few jumps.

WHETHER OR NOT he is to be seen again rests entirely within the head that supports the horns. This is why the hunter, when making preparations for a sheep hunt, places at the head of his list a rifle which boasts a flat trajectory.

All this made me most anxious to try conclusions with the bow and arrow with this wary and worthy individual. If successful, I felt that I should truly have a trophy, but I never believed that two rams would fall to my arrows by such methods.

I like what Stewart Edward White has written on the chase: "There is as much difference between a hunter and a killer as there is between a sportsman and a sport. The hunter gets his game by the exercise of his wits, his woodcraft and knowledge of natural history; the killer uses merely the skill with a weapon."

THIS IS WHY I like the bow. It does call for something more than the killing of game at almost any reasonable rifle distance. With the bow you must get close. The greatest distance at which I have ever killed an animal with an arrow was 155 yards. Had I thought it possible to cut that African space between the little antelope and me by only 5 yards, I would surely have made the attempt.

If you manage to "Injun" to within 100 yards of your game, try to cut it down to 75; and if successful in this, try to reduce it again—

and as much as possible. But to get back to Alaska and our sheep.

Capt. Jack Robertson and I took our movie camera and bows and arrows and started working on sheep in a district most easily described as being northeast of the Mt. McKinley region. It took us several anxious days to locate the sheep. As we had expected, we found them in great numbers, the rams bunched together. They were holding a powerful strategic position high up, but to feed they were obliged to travel some distance below. After feeding they would again return to their rookery.

We spent many days shooting with the camera. I was becoming anxious for a try with the arrow and was studying Mr. Ram's every move. My first opportunity came rather unexpectedly, while I was alone. As I had reached a small backbone my eye caught sight of an old ram. He was traveling a faint trail and was just about to drop into a deep cut, or cañon, about 400 yards ahead of me.

I stopped short and waited until he had disappeared. Then I broke into a run along the rocky slope, trying to figure out as I ran about where he would first appear on my side of the cut. I guessed wrong by about 30 yards, for just as I slowed down to almost a crawl he surprised me by showing his horns and head almost 45 yards to my right. We both stopped short. I drew my bow and let drive. He didn't make a move until the arrow hit his horn, right where it joins the skull, but then there was plenty of action. While the old fellow was still tearing down the almost perpendicular side of the bank my arrow was flying off into space, with a steel head badly bent. This I know, for I later hunted for and found it.

Running to the edge of the bank, I saw the ram just climbing to the edge on the opposite side. My supply of arrows was limited to begin with, and I had used some of these few shooting ptarmigan among the rocks the day before. On this trip we were traveling light; therefore I needed all my shafts.

―――❈―――

AT FIRST I hesitated to shoot at the sheep in this mass of rocks that nature had so roughly thrown together, but the temptation was too great. I felt it would be an arrow or arrows justly sacrificed upon such a magnificent specimen of bighorn; so again I let one go. The sheep was walking through the one little patch of smooth ground, about 10 feet square, as the arrow tipped his rump. From all appearances it might just as well have been charged with electricity, high life, or something else equally effective, for he tore straight back down the steep bank until he reached about half way to the bottom. Then he turned sharply and fairly flew over a straight course along the side of the cañon.

I have seen an old buck hit the ground pretty hard and often, but it was nothing compared with the speed of this sheep. At times when he hit the ground or rocks, his legs would seem to break or double up under him completely. In fact, at first I thought he would be mine by reason of his breaking all four legs in one of his hammering jumps, but it was soon very evident that this was his own game and he knew all about it.

Evidently the arrow that touched his rump convinced him that his enemy was right at hand. He knew that I was on the opposite side of the gorge; so he split the difference between the top and bottom of the roughest side of the cañon in his mad flight. I stood in my tracks and watched, with the greatest admiration, that sheep leave the country behind him, headed for the mouth of the gorge a mile below. My admiration was still greater when I climbed laboriously up through the rough mass over which he had raced.

This is quite a bit to write about a fine head that got away, but the incident so impressed me that I like to tell about it.

The very next day, within only half a mile from this scene, I saw a good head about 600 yards above me. The chance for a shot looked very promising, for the ram was feeding in a rather broken country. I set right out on the job, and as I went along with much caution I felt highly encouraged. Finally I landed just where I wished and was sneaking around a small jetty of rocks when I saw a bit of white hair. It was moving and only 60 feet away.

I leaned over against the rocks to my right

to get out of sight temporarily, but before I could collect myself and straighten up, this bunch of hair came around the corner. It was a young ram. He was walking slowly as he fed and coming directly toward me. Closely following were two more young rams. I was now not more than 20 feet from three sheep that I had never seen before.

—————— ✦ ——————

IT WAS RAINING and cold. I had no hat, for a gust of wind had taken it the day before. The rain peppered my face and ran down my neck. There I was, caught redhanded but not discovered, perfectly still and a part of the landscape. The wind was favorable. I was doing the only thing that could be done—just holding my uncomfortable position and wishing for these young feeders to pass on, for I was anxious to look up the old ram that I had set my hopes upon.

It seemed that this was not to be, for at this point a fine big ram suddenly appeared on the scene, following in the tracks of the younger ones. He also was feeding, but his choice was the grass that lay at the very edge of the jetty of rocks against which I was flattening myself. He was feeding directly toward me, and I realized that his coming closer than the 15 feet which separated us would make him a very much more startled animal when the inevitable did happen.

To be within 15 feet of one of these wary old creatures, where I could see even his eyelashes, was quite some joy in itself. Of course, if he did feed up to me, I could remain fixed. But I must occasionally wink my eyes, for the rain in my face demanded that; and should he be watching me at that particular time, the result would be the instant scattering of the sheep. The effect would be the same if I remained undiscovered until he had passed and the wind should betray me.

I decided to try for a shot. The bow was strung and an arrow rested on the string, but that was all that favored a hit. My drawing hand was in an awkward position, as I was half supporting myself on it. Somehow I felt that this would be my undoing. I tried ever so hard to bring my right hand to the string

without letting the sheep detect the motion, but I failed.

The old ram raised his head to a graceful position and looked not at my hand, but straight into my eyes. From that time on I never winked. This I know. My legs and back were stiff, and my hands cold. I made a miserable attempt to draw my heavy-pulling bow for a shot at the sheep, which had suddenly stopped and was standing broadside at 40 yards.

That bow seemed to pull a ton; it was an awful exertion. As my fingers left the string of but a half-drawn bow they really pained, and continued to do so for some time. The arrow appeared to be well directed, going in a direct line with his shoulders, but it was one of those close misses and passed through the hair on his back. This was the last straw—and the last of the sheep.

To this day I do not know whether or not this was the ram that I had intended as a trophy; but I suppose it was, for I could not locate him. Another one that got away, but I like to tell about him too.

The day was not entirely ruined, for I again looked over the lost-hat ground. Just why I looked in the swift glacier stream for my hat and expected to find it I do not know, but I did. There was my perfectly good and only hat, snugly set over a rock about the size of my head, right in the middle of that stream.

—————— ✦ ——————

BACK AT CAMP, there was a rehearsing of the incidents as we ate choice sheep meat—a small ram that had fallen to the arrow before.

Our next day's work took us into the same territory, and we were successful in filming some good old rams. Just before sundown, as I was sitting on the edge of a small ditch, I noticed a small white spot about half a mile above me. My fieldglasses revealed a fine old ram, all alone, lying down on a green grassy bench. He looked to be a big one and was most likely an outcast, a whipped lord. He looked interesting, but that was about all.

As optimistic as I am in hunting, I entertained no thought at first of even making an attempt at a shot. The ram was watching me and no doubt had been watching me all afternoon.

Having nothing to do just at that time, I decided upon a try, even against such apparently impossible odds. I was in hopes of soon passing under cover and working my way up under the bench on which he lay, but this was a game in which he had been trained to be on the watch.

I buckled on my quiver, picked up the bow, and started out. I had gone but about a hundred yards when the ram rose to his feet. He was most cautious and doubtless was already planning his getaway. At that, there was not much for him to plan, for behind him lay many miles of very rough sheep country. A few jumps, and my part of the world would be blocked out. However, I had started and I wanted to see the finish.

Another hundred yards, and the whole topography of the country seemed to change. I saw that I could not keep out of sight more than half the time, and accordingly changed my plans. I decided to use animal psychology.

Applied animal psychology is the one thing in particular, I believe, that White had reference to in differentiating the sportsman from the sport. I think this psychology plays a much greater part in successful hunting than some hunters realize. White is especially good at it; in fact, I have seen none better.

THERE ARE VAST differences in an animal's actions, depending upon whether he is feeding, playing, looking for trouble, or traveling. An animal knows by a man's actions just about what he is up to, and accordingly my mission must be that of a traveler. That was my only excuse for walking almost directly into him.

As I went along in a most careless manner I took particular pains to keep in the open. This was an easy matter, for the approach favored my plan. I believe I even whistled a bit as I moved on. I was most careful to avoid turning my head, let alone look up, but I saw all that was necessary from under the brim of my hat.

As I neared the ledge on which he stood, naturally I could see less and less of the sheep. Inch by inch the animal sank below the horizon. After his eyes left mine, I was quite relieved to notice that he did not wheel and run, for that was the time for such action. Instead he stood in his tracks, 250 yards from me. This convinced me that the trick was working. It also convinced me that he wished to have another look.

I was paying close attention to my speed and maintaining as nearly as possible an even gait. Within a fraction of a minute I saw his horns appearing on the skyline. He walked out, showing only his head and neck. I could see that he carried a wonderful set of horns. On I plodded. The turning point was now getting near, for I was close for a rifle shot but too far for the arrow.

As I walked in under the ledge he again sank from view as before. As his eyes left mine he still stood there, only 150 yards away. I broke into a run. Already I had an arrow on the string. Now my face was lifted directly toward the cliff, for I wanted to get the first glimpse of his reappearing horns.

I was never more sure of an animal's showing himself than of this one. He had my pace timed and all calculations made; so he felt safe in having that one last look which he just must have. But he erred in just one thing—he had been seen. He was too curious, too certain of it all.

When I saw his horns begin to loom up again, I stopped stock-still and half drew my bow, so as to cut down as much motion as possible in making the full draw. His head appeared, but I was not where he expected to find me. Out he continued to walk in that stately, majestic stride so in keeping with the royal blood that flowed in his veins.

I should love to know what passed through his trained, calculating brain when he saw not a thing moving. Instead of my being 150 yards

> *"An animal knows by a man's actions just about what he is up to, and accordingly my mission must be that of a traveler."*

below him, as he expected, I was 80 yards to one side and ready to shoot. I did want that old ram.

He stepped right out to the very edge in his endeavor to locate me, and I could see horns, hoofs, and all. I made the final draw on my bow and loosed the arrow. He caught the action of the bow and snapped his head toward me, but he stood. The arrow's flight was lost to view in the poor light. I had a short and most intense wait, with my ears tuned and strained for the result—silence or the impact of the feathered shaft.

It struck! The ram wheeled and instantly disappeared. I raced up the ledge, putting an added effort into the last few yards. I wondered how successful the shot had been. If it had reached any part of his body cavity, there would be a trophy, for no animal so arrowed had ever been lost for my efforts.

I peered cautiously over the ledge. There was no sheep in sight at first glance. The rough country and failing light caused me to abandon any effort to locate him until morning, though I did see something that might be taken for a sheep a short distance across a small gulch. In fact, many objects began to look like sheep, but messing around in the rough and putting to flight a possibly wounded animal was not the thing to do. He could not be followed.

Jack and I returned to a clump of willows about a mile below and "siwashed" it all night, more or less uncomfortable in our effort to keep a fire going. At the break of dawn we were on the scene of the shooting and soon found the old ram, dead. He was strung lengthwise with the arrow. It had entered at the point of the shoulder, passed through his body, and come out almost between his hind legs. He had a fine big set of horns.

I firmly believe that had he not been a wise old sheep, with many years of experience in escaping from more than one form of danger, and undoubtedly capable of the most correct calculating, I should still be wishing for such a fine trophy.

—January, 1968 (reprint)

Editor's note —
Art Young is one of the most famous bowhunters in modern American history. Young and his equally famous partner, Saxton Pope, often wrote of their adventures in FIELD & STREAM *magazine, mostly during the 1920s.*

By Frederic M. Baker

Down the
ICE DOME

SEVERAL TIMES, WHILE hunting and fishing, I have thought I was facing the Big Blot-Out. On looking back at those times, I now feel I overestimated or imagined the danger. A grizzly with a face full of porcupine quills once looked ready to finish me off, but didn't. And perhaps that mule deer didn't mean it when he ripped my shirt nearly off with a horn as he plunged by on his death run. Maybe those things weren't close. Possibly I imagined the danger; so I look back on the incidents without rating them serious.

But there was one escape that was narrow. How narrow? About fifteen feet, I'd say. Not narrow? Well, judge for yourself.

In September, 1940, my companion and I were hunting in the Shuswap Mountains of British Columbia. For three days we had climbed, through brush and over logs, up the steepest side hills, until at last we reached the open meadows, at what I judged to be about 7,000 feet. We were then just about on top, as far as this part of the world goes. Here and there, sharp, bald peaks climbed another 2,000 feet or so. Among them were little plateaus—grassy, lake-dotted and inviting. Down lower, thickly wooded valleys looked dark and moist, with snaky little creeks lacing across them.

It was early in the season; so all the game, except grizzlies, which were down among the blueberries, were high. We camped as far up as we could find wood, in a clump of balsams near where the timber stopped.

In the morning we climbed the nearest peak to look around and plan our moves. There was scenery spread around below us that the words "wild" and "rugged" just attempt to describe. Rock slides, grassy steeps, peaks, lakes and creeks were jumbled in a tossed-together mass for as far as we could see with 8-power glasses in any direction.

The final touch of grandeur was made by the glaciers. In a single glance twenty could be seen. To count them all would have been a chore. The farthest, fading into the sky in the distance, was white and cold-looking. The nearest, only half a mile away, was diamond-bright and even warm-looking as the sun played on its melting shining surface. To a railway surveyor, an explorer, or a homesteader the country was hopeless. To us goat hunters it looked fine!

But three days went by without my seeing any goats, although Johnny was more fortunate. On the morning of the fifth day I packed up a husky lunch and started out for distant fields, or, in this case, plateaus. I reasoned that if I hunted far enough I'd be bound to find some goats, and new territory appeals to me; so I'd mix my hunting with exploring.

For four hours I hunted slowly, crossing bare rocky flats, circling peaks, peering over rims and gingerly crossing set-trigger rock slides. I saw no game but two flocks of ptarmigan. It was a warm day and I was hot from climbing; so when I came to a ridge of broken rock, I was ready to rest. However, I don't like resting at the bottom; I'd rather climb first and rest while looking over the other side. So up I went, wondering at the queer smell of ground stone.

As I cleared the top an icy wind zipped through my clothes. A huge glacier, shaped like an inverted bowl, lay in front of me. It was a good three miles long, and the wind from it was steady and chilling.

I was near the lower end. Looking straight across, it humped itself roundly into a flattened dome, then slowly gave way with increasing steepness until it ended precipitously in curled-over jagged lips, three hundred yards below me. The sun had melted the surface, and hundreds of tiny streams, ten to twelve feet apart and two feet wide, spider-webbed down the dome, one rushing over the edge nearly at my feet. The water was so cold that my teeth ached when I drank from it. Somewhere underneath the glacier a steady roaring was going on where a river, filthy with silt and sand, threshed its way out to freedom.

The glacier blocked my way. I didn't fancy going down below it. The lips of ice down there were twenty to thirty feet high and were honeycombed by the rushing under-torrents. Any time a slab of ice might give way. The whole bottom end of the glacier seemed to be on very insufficient foundations, for that matter. The jumble of broken rocks and precariously hanging boulders didn't look pleasant to cross, either. I decided to go any place but there.

Straight across the ice route looked best. A mountaineer would have waltzed across it, but I'm very cautious. I had only hobnails in my boots, and the ice looked greasy in places. But my main fear was hollow places. I didn't want to fall into one and sit on the ice forever in a state of perfect preservation. It was foolish to monkey around on a glacier, but I thought the goats might be on the other side. Maybe a record head!

It didn't look much more than a hundred yards to the top of the dome. The more I looked at it the safer it appeared. I decided to try it, but thought it best to go up unencumbered, to see how the going was. So I propped my rifle between two boulders, muzzle to the sky, with a red bandanna handkerchief tied to the sling strap so that I could find it easily among the rock jumble, and started up.

Instead of being slippery, as I had expected, the surface was rather rough with surface honeycomb. No signs of crevasses could I see, although I kept a sharp lookout. There was a good deal of glare, and the sky seemed painfully blue. I wished for dark glasses.

Up and up I went. It was steeper than it looked, but the hobs held well and I was gaining assurance. The top was more than a hundred yards, though. The summit of the dome seemed always just a little farther.

⊢—◄◆►—⊣

WITHIN A FEW yards of the top I stopped for a second to rubberneck at the scenery. I looked first to the right, up the glacier, marveling at its length. Then I turned to look to the left, and without thinking shifted my feet a step or two. Plumb in the middle of one of the little streams I stepped. My feet flipped from under me, and I landed hard in three inches of water that flowed over the smoothest, slipperiest sort of ice.

My head got such a violent whack that I couldn't see clearly for possibly half a minute. Somehow I thought the best thing to do was to lie still until my head cleared. I closed my eyes against the sun. But the water made me very uncomfortable, and I also had the vague feeling of sliding; so I opened my eyes and tried to get up.

My stomach was hollow with fear as I saw my position. I had slid down into a two-foot-deep trough on the side of the dome. A fair-sized head of water was doing its best to speed my descent, which was even then quite rapid.

I clawed at the ice at the edge of the chute, but got no grip, my fingers just slipping off uselessly. I drew my boots in under me, then pressed them against the sides of the trough; but neither way checked me in the least. Apparently the hobs had become clogged with slush. With as much calmness as I could force upon myself, I tried to get a footing and clamber out, but it was as impossible as climbing a glass ball. I tried to flounder out, to spring out—anything.

Wild with rage and impatience, I tried to fight and claw my way out. I can remember cursing my futile efforts, the ice, the water and the nails in my boots. Finally, exhausted, I got on my hands and knees and rested, all the while sliding down backward, faster and faster.

I was terribly tired. My strength had been used up in a few seconds. All that strength I was so proud of, that strength I had imagined pulling me out of many tough spots. Used up in a few seconds! That shows how I fought to save myself.

Sliding down backward, I saw the glacier whisk by. For a moment I thought of the waiting rocks below, ready to smash my bones when I shot over the edge on to them. They didn't seem important, somehow. What did seem important was the blue sky, the green heather and moss on the safe mountain slopes.

As I slid, helpless and hopeless, that sky got bluer and bluer, the hillsides greener and fresher, and the mountain world looked more magically enchanting than any hunter's heaven could look. It was too good and splendid to leave, and I was now racing to leave it. The glacier ice was blurring now, I was going so fast. I made a last wild, futile effort to save myself. It was no use. I turned over, sat on my rear, legs to the front, and watched the ice chute curve alarmingly down to the Big Bump.

I guess it didn't take long to slide that last hundred yards, yet a long time seemed to pass. After the first wave of awful regret to be leaving the bright sunny world, only one thought was in my mind that I can remember. It was a feeling of sympathy for Johnny. I thought of his having a miserable time hunting for me, and a still worse time getting me packed out. I remember being glad my rifle was in a conspicuous place. He would see the red handkerchief and know just about where to look for me. Surprisingly, I was more sorry for him than for myself.

The slide was nearly over now. The ice was so steep that it seemed to curve in under. I wondered why I didn't shoot into space. I saw the end of the ice and the rocks below. I shut my eyes,

rolled into a ball, held my breath, and wondered what the next few seconds would be like.

I seemed to hover, and then dropped, anticipating the impact with the rocks for what seemed minutes. With a jarring shock I hit something and my ears roared. For a second I couldn't understand; then I realized I was in water. I opened my eyes, but everything was brown. I kicked, and in a second or two came into the clear, wonderful world again.

I had landed in a pool of muddy glacier water. It was nearly round, rock-edged, about fifteen feet across and possibly eight feet deep. The cascade of water from the chute, twenty feet above, hit the rocks at its edge, spraying the pool steadily like rain.

A couple of strokes brought me to the rocks. In very short order I got away from the overhanging ready-to-crumble ice. Shivering, I climbed up to where I had left my rifle. On the way I passed about forty water-cut slides, although none of them looked as deep as the one I had gone down. Not one of them had a life-saving pool at the bottom! They just splashed and dashed on the broken boulders.

I got to camp without trouble and without serious nervous reaction getting hold of me, but for two days afterward I was continually getting jittery spells, and the nights were full of dreams a lot worse than the real thing.

I won't say I will never walk on a glacier again. That would be overdoing the caution. But I do say I will never treat one as just a big hunk of ice again. And I will carry a pair of ice creeps next time I go high up, looking for goats.

Whenever I feel fed up with things, when the trout don't rise, when the game has moved on, when life seems dull, I just think of that nice green interesting world, under that fairy blue sky, which I saw when I thought I was losing it. Then I don't feel so bad. I'm still in that same world.

—August, 1941

By Bob Brister

The ELEPHANTS of CHIRISA

THE TRACKS ARE THE size of small washtubs, and we have been following six hours since the chill of dawn. Now sweat trickles, the canteen is out of water, and September sun beats down like a blowtorch.

It is dry season in the Chirisa Safari Area in Zimbabwe, and little puffs of dust float up from each step of professional hunter Chris Hallamore ahead of me.

I do not like the looks of that dust. Sometimes it floats back as it should, but then it drifts to right or left. Eddying air currents have fatally altered the course of a lot of elephant stalks.

The three bulls have moved fast and steadily, from the sandy river climbing into rugged highlands, then into a brushy plateau of chest-high yellow grass crisscrossed by steep canyons and gullies. Elephants seem to know wind plays tricks in canyons.

Somehow they knew we were behind them.

At one narrow place in the trail where a rock ledge overhangs a drop of maybe 100 feet, a freshly uprooted tree lies across the ledge like a barrier. Not a leaf has been eaten. I have seen trees shoved across roads, clearly on purpose, since no others in the area were felled, and I have seen the wreck of a hunting car in Botswana that trip when the young bull stepped out of ambush and rammed a tusk through the cab, overturning it, and then crushed it as he fell from hunter Dougie Wright's brain shot. ...

Chris Hallamore is tapping his sock filled with fireplace ashes. One bit of dust blows one way, the next another. "They seem to know where the wind eddies like this; they can't see well but they can pinpoint us if they can get the slightest smell. We'll have to go very slowly from here. Watch me; if I suddenly drop to the ground, you do the same."

Like the heat haze shimmering over the long grass, my mind keeps shifting and wavering. ...

On four safaris I have tracked elephants, including that time in Kenya crawling into the huge herd on the Athi River with David Lunan so close that, with heart in throat, I noticed toenails on the "tree" beside me in the thick grass just before cows and calves stampeded all around us. Maybe I took more risk than those with the rifles because I had the movie camera for the TV film. By the time my partner Harvey Houck shot the big bull with the long, curving ivory, the young bull with him charged me instead of the guns because he heard the camera. ...

All those miles, and blisters, and chances, but never with the rifle in my hands. Now I have the heavy Ruger .458 with its 510-grain solids and its razor-sharp Leupold scope set on 2½ power so I can count every wrinkle in a bull elephant's trunk ... and I am having misgivings because this trip I have learned a lot more about elephants. No more fear or awe of them—there was always that—but now mystery and new respect for an intelligence I cannot fully comprehend.

At the Chirisa Wildlife Research Station and its vast surrounding safari area, new things are being learned about elephants. Forty-seven of them are being radio-tracked day and night as biologists and scientists study their movements, their habits, why some learn to become crop raiders or dangerous elephants while others do not.

We had visited the research station, seen the 12-foot neoprene collars used to attach the brightly colored radio transmitters behind the heads of dart-drugged elephants. Each unit sends out a different beep, and with three-directional receiving towers, the location of each animal can be pinpointed within a few yards. Scientists from around the world come here to study the elephants, with much of the program expense financed by the U.S.-based Mzuri Foundation, a hunters' group. The area is literally overrun by elephants crowded out of other areas by an increasing native population.

Yet relatively few elephant permits are issued for safari hunting in an area as vast as some states and so overpopulated with elephants that rangers have been methodically culling entire family groups. They may take another 1,000 before destruction of habitat is brought under control.

Why not let safari hunters do that culling? The bull license in my pocket cost $3,200; enough to pay for an anti-poaching patrol. Elephants killed by the wardens and patrols are worth much less, and the men doing that job do not relish it. The animals are located and harassed by aircraft into ambushes; fully automatic FN assault rifles cut loose on cows, calves, the whole herd. Meat stripped from their bones brings $9 a gunnysack to natives. Ivory and hides sold to traders bring far less than safari income generated for management. Why not safaris for full-time culling?

"BECAUSE," SAYS BRIGHT, highly dedicated director of the research station Tony Conway, "we have learned the hard way that the elephants can communicate. One reason we use trained culling crews is that we must kill entire family groups. If even one is permitted to escape, word is immediately out among the other elephants and after that it becomes much more difficult, and dangerous, for scientists to approach them for observation or for our crews to cull them. We cannot take those chances with human lives; there are just too many elephants here and too many natives on the surrounding tribal lands."

We went to an "elephant graveyard," big as a small city dump, where stripped carcasses of literally hundreds of elephants lie bleaching in the sun. Out of the rubble poked the small, round feet of calves alongside those of big bulls.

"I know how you feel," said Tony Conway softly as we stood there. "It is a terrible thing, if you like elephants as I do. I've lived around them, worked with them, most of my adult life. The more I understand them the more difficult it is to kill them, but it must be done if they are to survive here."

He showed me a huge map dotted with different-colored pins. "These are surrounding tribal lands," he explained. "Natives are attempting to grow crops. Here we are, in the heart of the wild area left. These pins represent poachers' camps we have apprehended, these are some we haven't gotten to yet. Poaching is mostly with wire snares.

"Here is the leg bone of an elephant; see how the snare cut completely through it and the bone calcified around it. This elephant must have lived in constant pain, and she was a very dangerous one that had to be destroyed. Once an elephant is hurt by a snare, or wounded by some primitive native muzzleloader, the odds are much higher for that one to be a dangerous elephant.

"In this area every safari hunting party is required to have one of our game scouts along, armed with an assault rifle. It is added protection for the hunters. We realize the value of safari hunting—it provides the funds we must have to deal with the poachers and to manage and study the elephants.

"I visited your country recently," Conway added, "and I couldn't believe some of the so-called documentaries on your American television, nor the attitude of some people toward hunting here. They do not seem to realize that safari hunting is the most realistic, practical hope for the survival of many African species in countries where no other monetary support for game management exists. We have more game, of all indigenous species, here in Chirisa now than existed forty years ago, and this is desig-nated as a safari area. By contrast, look at Kenya where the government stopped safari hunting and the elephant was almost decimated from the land by poachers. You must write some of this when you return. Or send some of your television people here. We can show them the real world of the African elephant in the wild."

When we were riding back to camp, 3 hours over rough country, I asked veteran professional hunter Sten Cedergren, who spent years guiding safaris in Kenya before moving to Zimbabwe, if he accepted Conway's views.

"About Kenya elephants and poachers, yes," he said. "About elephant communicating, yes. I have watched them, whole herds on different sides of a high ridge, out of sight of each other, suddenly begin moving at the same time to meet at the same place. As if they knew what the others were thinking."

"They do it by telepathy," says professional hunter Gary Baldwin, a native of Rhodesia and now Zimbabwe, "they have developed senses over the centuries man cannot fully understand. Yet they do some things that are so stupid for their survival. Look out there."

We were passing what appeared to be the path of a tornado; large trees were uprooted, others stripped of limbs or broken halfway to the ground. Yet most of the bark and leaves remained. Elephants that shoved over those trees took only a few bites and then shoved over others. If they are so intelligent, can they not see they are destroying their future food? A tree requires years to grow but one elephant can shove down a small forest in a day.

＊＊＊

ONE OF THE most important things being studied at the Chirisa Research Station is which bands of elephants move around most, create the most crop or habitat destruction. Perhaps by concentrating upon those bands for culling, there could eventually be a resident population able to live within its own habitat. . . .

My mind reverts instantly to reality. Something has moved.

"Shhh," says Chris Hallamore, on his knees testing the wind. "He's right there. Young bull. Don't look at him. We'll have to go completely around. The wind is changing. I think they somehow knew it would. They're waiting for us right there, and they have the wind. Hurry! We have to cross that canyon and come up on the other side."

We follow him doggedly, thirsty and tired, my wife Sandy's normally olive complexion is pale, and Kasare, our native Green Beret game scout who has become a trusted friend, is carrying her cameras over one shoulder, the assault rifle over the other.

Suddenly he leaves the trail, circles wide, and motions to Chris.

The elephants have moved, silently as ghosts, and somehow Kasare has anticipated that and crossed their new track. We could have been walking right into them. Again we circle, and in the heat my mind wanders. . . .

It had been the cold, windy dawn before, scouting for fresh tracks, when we met a ragged apparition of a man in the road, frantically waving us down. At first we thought he was a native; his European features were smutted by campfire ash, his clothing singed, eyes blank with cold-numbed terror.

His name was, and is, Gabriel Stoltz, and he has every reason to be terrified of elephants. I had already heard his life story from the hunters and park rangers. His father had been a ranger and elephant-control officer at Wankie National Park. One night when Gabriel was fourteen, news came that a tourist vehicle had been found inside the park overturned and crushed, its occupants dead. His father, Wilhelm Stoltz, left at first light with his elephant gun and two trackers. That night young Gabriel saw his father's body rolled into a blanket because there was not enough left to carry. The two native trackers were dead, but their bodies were unmolested. From the huge tracks and other indications, a great head had crushed Wilhelm Stoltz into the ground, time and time again.

Three years later, the body of Gabriel's uncle (for whom he had been named) was found cut almost in half, gored by an elephant.

Now, still a young man, he was showing us the remains of his fire where he had lain in the sand trying to keep warm after his vehicle broke down, and the huge elephant tracks

around it. He said they had come screaming and trumpeting and pounding the ground and he had climbed a tree where he'd shivered through the rest of the night. The fire had died but the elephants had stayed for hours.

COULD IT BE true that elephants never forget? That they can communicate past happenings in far-away places? Could they somehow have known that this was the son of Wilhelm Stoltz, the man some older Wankie elephants hated and killed?

Ridiculous. Wankie is many miles away. But then, why did elephants so uncharacteristically come to a fire, pounding and trumpeting? Rhinos come to fires, the natives say, but not elephants. And why had they kept Gabriel Stoltz up that tree, in terror, until they heard our vehicle approaching?

We had been unable to track them then; they were headed for the boundary of tribal lands not far away, and the trackers said they were traveling too fast. If an elephant walks fast, a man must run.

This morning we had picked up the tracks crossing the same road, returning, and they were apparently the same three bulls, one much larger than the others. . . .

"Don't move!" commands Hallamore. "Slowly sit down below the grass."

From the corner of my eye I have already seen the giant gray mound move; incredible how something so mammoth can be so invisible until it moves—an elephant is so big it looks like the landscape.

Hallamore in one smooth movement is up a tree, climbing hand over hand to the top, then dropping lightly to the ground. He can be an incredible athlete when he is close to game and the hunting instinct lights his eyes.

"The other two are ahead," he whispers. "Can't make out which is the big one; they're facing away into the wind. We'll circle; stay bent over, watch every step, no camera clicks, no sneezes. We'll act as if we are just passing by the other way. They can't see well, but they can make out movement."

We crouch, crawl, stop to rest, and Chris opens the bolt of his battered .375, checking the chambered round. I do the same.

We sit with rifles across knees, inching forward on hands and butts to keep heads higher in the grass. We can see the vague, gray blobs. Finally, when they loom like gray mountains over us, we must slowly stand to judge the ivory. It is impossible to realize how big they really are until you are looking up at them, 11 feet tall at the shoulder, maybe 11,000 pounds. I can feel the sheer exhilaration of closeness to wild and dangerous creatures, but also other feelings entirely different from those I've had with less perilous game.

Cape buffaloes have been excitement and danger, cunning and willing to ambush and kill you until their last death bellow. But there has been no remorse for them.

The big cats have seemed so aloof, impersonal, uncaring for me or anything else, killing machines that play with victims and sometimes begin eating while the prey is still alive.

But this is different.

It is one thing to see the bones of a thousand elephants bleaching in the sun, to know the old crop-raiding bull would soon be dead anyway. It is something else entirely to realize you are about to be personally responsible for the end of a creature from another time, about your own age, with a degree of intelligence and loyalty to others of his clan that man cannot completely comprehend.

"Hold halfway between the ear and his eye," Hallamore is whispering, "Be absolutely sure. The instant you shoot, that young bull on the right probably will charge. I'm watching him; you must watch only the big bull. If you miss the brain, he'll get up; put another one instantly into the heart. Are you ready? I'm going to move to the right, so he will turn his head and give you a better angle and then we can see that other tusk better."

He takes two steps and suddenly the bull's trunk snakes up into the air like a huge rubbery antenna, scanning the sky, then pointing straight at us.

"Now!"

The trigger squeezes and the sound and jolt are distant, as if someone else has done this and time freezes into slow-motion frames as the bull slowly, ponderously sits down backwards, then rolls over. The ground jars and dust rises.

All hell breaks loose; both small bulls are coming, the one on the right fast with ears against his head, trunk coiled.

Kasare knows instantly he means business. The FN chatters in ear-splitting bursts, inches over the bull's head, and Chris has the .375 pointing upward at the huge, bulging forehead.

At 10 yards the young bull skids to a stop, trunk lashing and swinging, ears now flared forward in confused bluff. The bull on the left comes up beside him, growling like a huge dog.

Kasare cuts loose again over their heads, and perhaps it is a sound they remembered. They shuffle off, tails upraised and switching in anger, back to the dead bull. Defiantly they stand beside him like sentinels, refusing to let us come closer. Flies buzz, and the long grass rustles in the wind. Nobody speaks.

And then, as if by some signal, the two young bulls turn and melt into the brush.

I do not think I will ever kill another elephant.

—June, 1982

By David E. Petzal

The Children's CRUSADE

IF YOU GO TO AFRICA WITH YOUR EYES SEEING, YOUR EARS HEARING, AND YOUR WITS WORKING, YOU LEARN THAT THE HUNTING IS ONLY THE BEGINNING.

*I*N 1950, WHEN IT WAS still normal for kids to read, I got ahold of a book titled *Killers in Africa*, by a South African professional hunter named Alexander Lake. Three years later, I fell upon Robert Ruark's *Something of Value*, and what the first book started, the second book finished. Though the heavens might fall, I would go to Africa, and eventually I did, not once but several times.

Like many other people upon whom Africa has a hold, I discovered that the reason you go is not so much the hunting—although that is just as marvelous as you've heard—but the people and the country itself. This, then, is a sort-of hunting story about three weeks in Zimbabwe in June, 1992.

THE HUNTERS

DOUGLAS REYNOLDS MET me at the airport at Victoria Falls (photo on facing page). Douglas is 6 feet 1 inch tall, and 220 pounds of muscle. He looks like a middle linebacker, not only because of his size, but because

he is a linebacker's age—twenty-three. He was also sick, due to a week of furious carousing in between safaris. He had a wracking cough and a fever, which he blamed on riding a motorcycle at night without a jacket in the chilly night air of an African winter.

Douglas' stand-in for the first three days of the safari was Buzz (James) Charleton. He was the apprentice, or "appy." (It is the habit among Africans of European descent to apply the diminutive "py" in strange places. A soldier, for example, is called a "troopy," instead of a trooper.) When we met, Buzz had been in the bush for seventy-eight straight days, and had enough of hunting for the time being.

Buzz is small-framed, and seems to float when he walks. Later, I learned that he is an international-class squash player, and could probably have represented Zimbabwe in the 1992 Olympics, but chose hunting instead. He is a dedicated fly fisherman, and is intensely curious about the United States. Buzz had achieved the advanced age of nineteen.

THE CHILDREN'S CRUSADE

IN THE YEAR 1212, thousands of French and German children, caught in the outbreak of religious fervor that was sweeping Europe, embarked to the Middle East to free the Holy Land from the "infidels" who held it. The crusade was a catastrophe; almost to the last child they were drowned, murdered, or sold into slavery.

My first night in Zimbabwe, this gloomy bit of history was conjured up by the following train of thought: All of the PHs, or professional hunters, I had hunted with previously were in their mid-thirties, except for one who was pushing fifty. This was reassuring, since it meant that they had been skillful enough to survive at an exceedingly dangerous profession. Some of them were deeply crazy, but they were all very good at what they did, due at least in part to years of experience.

So I was not thrilled to be in the company of so much youth, although I kept this to myself. That night, I told the immense hairy spider on the wall of my hut: "I've joined the Children's Crusade." Unimpressed, the spider scuttled up into the thatch roof, bent on urgent arachnid matters.

As it turned out, I needn't have worried. Zimbabwe has the toughest licensing standards of any country in Africa which allows hunting. Most of the people who become PHs have already spent most of their lives in the bush, and become appys in their late teens. They are required to do two solid years of apprenticeship, at the end of which they take a series of lengthy written exams on everything pertaining to hunting. If they pass, they then go on a series of safaris with a member of the licensing board. In the course of these hunts, they are required to track and kill elephants and buffalo, and demonstrate their skill at everything from automobile repair to cooking to first-aid, marksmanship, running a camp, tracking, caping, etc. If they pass all this, they become licensed PHs, provided they've reached their twenty-first birthday.

And it's easy to get your license revoked. Enforcement of game laws is strict: Thou shalt not poach in another PH's concession. Thou shalt not suffer thy clients to be killed. And so on.

Youth manifests itself in odd ways. It was Doug Reynolds' ambition to build himself up to 270 pounds, and toward this end, he kept a set of barbells and a weight lifter's bench in camp. In the evening, after a full day of hunting, I sat by the fire watching the sun go down, trying to remember what it felt like to be twenty-three years old and bulletproof. While I did this, Douglas went behind the cookhouse and pumped iron.

If you combined the weight lifting noises with the cacophony of an African twilight, it sounded something like: screech…whoop, whoop, whoop…grunt, clank…aoooga… eeeeaaagh…grunt, clank…whuff…grunt, clank…waugh, waugh, waugh…grunt, clank. I envied him the energy, and pointed out that he would have to take huge doses of steroids regularly, just like American football players and Eastern European women shot-putters, if he wanted to put on 50 pounds of solid muscle. He looked at me strangely.

Later, we switched to a camp quite close to Victoria Falls. Douglas, who was of a romantic nature, would leave me in camp after dinner and spend the night in town reciting poetry underneath the balconies of young women. He'd return in the small hours of the morning, grab a couple of hours' sleep, and then hunt all day. One night he took me to dinner in Vic Falls, and I met a Doberman pinscher who fell desperately in love with me. That was as close as I came to romance. And it was a boy dog, too.

THE BUFFALO

IF YOU GREW up reading Robert Ruark, as I did, you are well aware that the Cape buffalo is an engine of destruction whose sole delight in life is dancing on the poor oafs who try to shoot him. I haven't hunted all the buffalo there are, but I've hunted a fair number, and I can tell you this:

Buffalo, like most other wild animals, want nothing more than to stay away from man at all costs. In areas where they are hunted and/or poached, it can be difficult just to get close to them. If they have not been pressured by humans, they will stand and look curiously at you while you approach.

When shot, however, buffalo take it very poorly. Since they are possessed of enormous vitality, they can be almost impossible to kill.

If a buffalo gets ahold of you, you are unlikely to survive. Old *nyati* is not content to stick a horn through you; he will gore you, then toss you, and when you land, he will stomp you.

There were five of us hunting buffalo: Douglas; Buzz; myself; Fineas, a Shona tracker; and Moyo, a Ndebele tracker. The way you hunt buffalo is simple enough: drive the roads until you see a fresh track, then follow it on foot. And that is what we did.

We cut the track at 9 in the morning and followed it into the trees and high grass where visibility was limited to perhaps 50 yards. It was a herd of 150 animals, buffalo that had had plenty of experience with men and their rifles, and would spook if they got a whiff of us.

We followed the trail until the herd bedded down to graze and chew its collective cud. It was now 10 A.M. The buffalo would stay in this semi-open stuff until noon, and then would head for the *gusu*—thick scrub in which visibility is virtually nil and which buffalo love because they are safe there until evening when they graze again.

Douglas, who was in the lead, motioned for us to get down and crooked his finger for Fineas. He and the tracker inched their way in front of us until they were 20 yards away. They saw something.

We waited. Around us, we heard grunts and moos and the occasional click of horns. Every minute or so, Moyo squeezed a plastic bottle filled with talcum powder and sent a small white puff into the air. It hung there, and drifted back to earth. If a breeze came up, the talcum would show it, and we would have to make our play right away, before the herd caught our scent and galloped off.

Twenty minutes passed. Finally, Douglas and Fineas crawled back. Douglas hissed: "There's a group of six bulls 50 meters ahead. The one under the tree is a good one. Get up slowly, stand by that tree over there and get ready. I'll yell and get them up. Then you shoot."

I did as he said and Douglas gave out with a Zimbabwean cattle-frightening call: *"Huh. . . huh. . .huh."* Except that it did not frighten these animals. He yelled again, and they lurched uncertainly to their feet. I saw the big bull, who walked in front of me, looking for the source of the noise. I shot him in the ribs and he went down.

He staggered up, feet spread, head down. I shot him again in the chest. He stumbled for 10 yards and fell.

This was a drama-less hunt. It was as coldly and skillfully executed as a chess match. Douglas Reynolds, twenty-three years old, was slow and careful and patient—above all, patient. And he reminded me that patience, when applied liberally, is as deadly as any rifle.

SERPENTS

LET ME PUT it plainly: Snakes scare me spitless. And Zimbabwe is copiously endowed with a variety of the worst that you can find. There is the Egyptian cobra, the *ringhals,* or spitting cobra, the puff adder, the boomslang, the black mamba, the green mamba, and the gaboon viper. On a day off from hunting, we drove into Victoria Falls to visit this merry crew at the snake exhibit.

Cape buffalo, an engine of destruction.

The two most frightening were the gaboon viper and the black mamba. The gaboon viper has the longest fangs (2 inches) of any venomous snake. They are set in a wedge-shaped head that's as wide as a big man's hand. The neck is slender, but the body is massive; as thick as an adult human's thigh, and 4 feet long.

The gaboon viper is a massive snake that is nearly invisible in its habitat.

The gaboon viper on display was in a glass cage set at eye level. It was sleeping on a bed of leaves, as it would be in the wild. Its scales formed brilliant mottles of tan, gray, powder blue, and brown, and the scariest thing about it was, *I knew it was there, right in front of me, not 3 feet away, but I couldn't see it.* I stared for 5 minutes, and finally I could make out its massive head. Then the rest of it came in focus.

Although the puff adder probably kills more humans than any other, the black mamba is generally acknowledged as the deadliest and most feared snake in Africa. (The puff adder is common, whereas the mamba is comparatively scarce. The puff adder is fond of lying in the dust of footpaths, taking in the morning and evening sun. It is phlegmatic, and will not move for man nor beast. Therefore, when you step on it, it will bite you fatally and go right back to its nap, all without a change of position.)

Black mambas are large (8 to 12 feet), intelligent, territorial, aggressive, and equipped with a huge dose of highly potent venom. They have the unnerving habit of traveling with most of their body in the air. The Zulus call the mamba "the snake that walks on its tail." Because of this, most black mamba bites are in the head, neck, or upper chest.

The other snakes in the exhibit were motionless. Their day did not offer them a lot of excitement. But the black mamba—an 8-footer that was trapped in a garage in Victoria Falls— ceaselessly prowled its cage, looking for a way out, never resting, tongue flicking, unblinking black eyes watchful for any opening. You've heard the expression "… made my blood run cold." If you set eyes on a black mamba, in the wild or in a cage, you will learn what that feels like.

THE MAGICAL SAFARI CAT

THERE ARE HUNTS where you break your back trying, expend all your skill, persevere to the end, and come up with an unpunched license. There are hunts where you will do exactly the same and succeed beyond any reasonable expectation. That's why you'll become superstitious if you hunt enough.

The buffalo I took was a very big one— much bigger than anything I'd gotten previously, much bigger than I had any right to expect in this part of Africa. The dawn of the morning I killed him, a cat wandered over to the fire where Douglas and I were drinking coffee and eating toast. Being a sucker for cats, I gave the creature a saucer of milk and a piece of buttered toast. It guzzled both, and asked for more, which it got.

Thereafter, it became our guest at all three meals, and became the best-fed cat in that part of Zimbabwe. I addressed it formally as "Your Highness, the Exalted, Magical Safari Cat." My good luck held for the entire trip.

The safari that followed mine was for elephants, and did not pay the Safari Cat the homage to which it was accustomed. Buzz wrote and said that Doug and his client walked themselves nearly to death for three solid weeks and never even saw an elephant. Cats have powers we cannot guess at.

LUCIAN AND THE ZAMBESI RIVER BOAT CLUB

MOST PHs ARE outgoing and extroverted. You'd pick them out of a crowd as men who do something unusual for a living. That is why, when I met Lucian Ward (not his real name), I assumed that he was some kind of misfit. Lucian was thirty-one. He spoke in a near whisper, smiled shyly, and was so mild-mannered and reticent that I doubted his ability as a PH, if not his actual manhood.

Douglas put me straight. On the shore of the Zambesi River, a few kilometers before it turns into Victoria Falls, is a small building called the Zambesi River Boat Club. No member owns a boat. It is a place where the young set from Vic Falls goes to listen to music, drink, pick each other up, and fight.

The fighting is taken seriously, and it is considered good form for the women to join in. Lucian, Doug told me, was probably the most unpredictable and ferocious brawler in the Z.R.B.C., the owner of a savage left hook that would come out of nowhere and usher you into what Mohammad Ali described as "the room where the snakes scream and the alligators play trombone." A few years before I met him, Lucian got in an argument with a trio of British troopies and annihilated all three. They dragged themselves off, came back with reinforcements, and beat him so badly that he spent a week in an intensive-care unit.

Lucian has been a professional hunter since 1984, and before that, was a game-control officer. That innocuous-sounding title means that he was one of the men charged with trimming Zimbabwe's thriving herds of big game to the level where the land could support them. In that capacity, he had taken, by official record, 5,000 elephants, 500 buffalo, and 300 hippos. Looks can be deceiving.

LIFE ON THE EDGE

VICTORIA FALLS WAS named by the explorer David Livingstone, who first saw it in 1855. The local tribes called it *Mosi oa tunya*, "the smoke that thunders." The Falls are nearly a mile long, and the gorge into which their waters plummet is 355 feet deep.

It is one of the natural wonders of the world, but what I found most interesting was the fact that you can walk right up to the edge of the chasm. In the United States, the Land of Litigation, there would be a chain-link fence, razor ribbon, and warning signs to keep you back from the precipice, since the rocks are wet and slippery, and if you take a header into the maelstrom below, you may consider your existence terminated.

I walked right up to the edge, looked down, swallowed hard, decided I had proved whatever I had set out to prove, and retreated. Douglas told me that every once in a while someone slips, and their body floats in the whirlpools and eddies below until the police shoot it. Then the body sinks and the current takes it downstream where it can be recovered. I didn't know at the time if he was pulling my leg or not. And I still don't.

—July, 1993

By Robert C. Ruark

SUICIDE
Made Easy

IT TAKES A FOOL TO
MESS AROUND WITH
MBOGO, THE MONSTER
BUFFALO THAT REFUSES
TO DIE WHEN HE'S DEAD.
BUT ONCE YOU HAVE
THE FEVER, EVERYTHING
ELSE IS JUST TOO TAME.

SOME PEOPLE ARE afraid of the dark. Other people fear airplanes, ghosts, their wives, death, illness, bosses, snakes or bugs. Each man has some private demon of fear that dwells within him. Sometimes he may spend a life without discovering that he is hagridden by fright— the kind that makes the hands sweat and the stomach writhe in real sickness. This fear numbs the brain and has a definite odor, easily detectable by dog and man alike. The odor of fear is the odor of the charnel house, and it cannot be hidden.

I love the dark. I am fond of airplanes. I have had a ghost for a friend. I am not henpecked by my wife. I was through a war and never fretted about getting killed. I pay small attention to illness, and have never feared an employer. I like

snakes, and bugs don't bother me. But I have a fear, a constant, steady fear that still crowds into my dreams, a fear that makes me sweat and smell bad in my sleep. I am afraid of Mbogo, the big, black Cape buffalo. Mbogo, or Nyati, as he is sometimes called, is the oversized ancestor of the Spanish fighting bull. I have killed Mbogo, and to date he has never got a horn into me, but the fear of him has never lessened with familiarity. He is just so damned big, and ugly, and ornery, and vicious, and surly, and cruel, and crafty. Especially when he's mad. And when he's hurt, he's always mad. And when he's mad, he wants to kill you. He is not satisfied with less. But such is his fascination that, once you've hunted him, you are dissatisfied with other game, up to and including elephants.

＋—◆—＋

THE SWAHILI LANGUAGE, which is the lingua franca of East Africa, is remarkably expressive in its naming of animals. No better word than *simba* for lion was ever constructed,

From a standpoint of senses, the African buffalo has no weak spot. He sees as well as he smells, and he hears as well as he sees, and he charges with his head up and his eyes unblinking. He is as fast as an express train, and he can haul short and turn himself on a shilling. He has a tongue like a wood rasp and feet as big as knife-edged flat-irons. His skull is armor-plated and his horns are either razor-sharp or splintered into horrid javelins. The boss of horn that covers his

not even by Edgar Rice Burroughs, Tarzan's daddy. You cannot beat *tembo* for elephant, nor can you improve on *chui* for leopard, *nugu* for baboon, *fisi* for hyena or *punda* for zebra. *Faro* is apt for rhinoceros, too, but none of the easy Swahili nomenclature packs the same descriptive punch as *mbogo* for a beast that will weigh over a ton, will take an 8.8 millimeter shell in his bread-basket and still toddle off, and that combines crafty guile with incredible speed, and vindictive anger with wide-eyed, skilled courage.

brain can induce hemorrhage by a butt. His horns are ideally adapted for hooking, and one hook can unzip a man from crotch to throat. He delights to dance upon the prone carcass of a victim, and the man who provides the platform is generally collected with a trowel, for the buffalo's death-dance leaves little but shreds and bloody tatters.

But mostly Mbogo flatly refuses to die. He will soak up enough lead to sink a carrier and still keep coming. Leave him alone, and he is cattle and will mostly gallop off at a loud "Shoo!" Kill him dead with the first shot through the nose and up into the brain, or get his heart and break his shoulder, and he dies. But wound him, even mortally, and he engenders a certain glandular juice that makes him almost impossible to kill. I would not know the record for lead absorption by a buffalo; I do know of one that took sixteen .470 solids in the chest and still kept a-coming. I know another that took a couple through the heart and went more than two miles. Don't ask me how. He just did.

I expect I have looked at several thousand buffalo at close range. I have stalked several hundred. I have been mixed up in a stampede in high reeds. I have stalked into the precise middle of a herd of two hundred or more, and stayed there quietly while the herd milled and fed around me. I have crawled after them, and dashed into their midst with a whoop and a holler, and looked at them from trees, and followed wounded bulls into the bush, and have killed a couple. But the terror never quit. The sweat never dried. The stench of abject fear never left me. And the fascination for him never left me. Toward the end of my first safari I was crawling more miles after Mbogo than I was walking after anything else—still scared stiff, but unable to quit. Most of the time I felt like a cowardly bullfighter with a hangover, but Mbogo beckoned me on like the sirens that seduced ships to founder on the rocks.

⊷⊰◈⊱⊶

FOR THIS I blame my friend Harry Selby, a young professional buffalo—I mean hunter—who will never marry unless he can talk a comely cow Mbogo into sharing his life. Selby is wedded to buffalo, and when he cheats he cheats only with elephants. Four times, at last count, his true loves have come within a whisker of killing him, but he keeps up the courtship. It has been said of Selby that he is uninterested in anything that can't kill him right back. What is worse, he has succeeded in infecting most of his innocent charges with the same madness.

Selby claims that the buffalo is only a big, innocent kind of he-cow, with all the attributes of bossy, and has repeatedly demonstrated how a madman can stalk into the midst of a browsing herd and commune with several hundred

black tank cars equipped with radar and heavy artillery on their heads without coming to harm. His chief delight is the stalk that leads him into this idyllic communion. If there are not at least three mountains, one river, a trackless swamp and a cane-field between him and the quarry, he is sad for days. Harry does not believe that buffalo should be cheaply achieved.

Actually, if you just want to go out and shoot a buffalo, regardless of horn size, it is easy enough to get just any shot at close range. The only difficulty is in shooting straight enough, and/or often enough, to kill the animal swiftly, before it gets its second wind and runs off into the bush, there to become an almost impregnable killer. In Kenya and Tanganyika, in buffalo country, you may almost certainly run onto a sizable herd on any given day. I suppose by working at it I might have slain a couple of hundred in six weeks, game laws and inclination being equal.

As it was, I shot two—the second better than the first, and only for that reason. Before the first, and in between the first and the second, we must have crawled up to several hundred for close-hand inspection. The answer is that a 42- or 43-inch bull today, while no candidate for Rowland Ward's records, is still a mighty scarce critter, and anything over 45 inches is one hell of a good bull. A fellow I know stalked some sixty lone bulls and herd bulls in the Masai country recently, and never topped his 43-incher.

But whether or not you shoot, the thrill of the stalk never lessens. With your glasses you will spot the long, low black shape of Mbogo on a hillside or working out of a forest into a swamp. At long distances he looks exactly like a great black worm on the hill. He grazes slowly, head down, and your job is simply—simply!— to come up on him, spot the good bull, if there is one in the herd, and then get close enough to shoot him dead. Anything over thirty yards is not a good safe range, because a heavy double—a .450 No. 2 or a .470—is not too accurate at more than one hundred yards. Stalking the herd is easier than stalking the old and wary lone bull, which has been expelled from the flock by the young bloods, or stalking an old bull with an askari—a young bull that serves as stooge and bodyguard to the oldster. The young punk is usually well alerted while his hero feeds, and you cannot close the range satisfactorily without spooking the watchman.

⊹⊱⊰⊹

IT IS NEARLY impossible to describe the tension of a buffalo stalk. For one thing, you are nearly always out of breath. For another, you never know whether you will be shooting until you are literally in the middle of the herd or within a hundred yards or so of the single-o's or the small band. Buffalo have an annoying habit of always feeding with their heads behind another buffalo's rump, or of lying down in the mud and hiding their horns, or of straying off into eight-foot sword-grass or cane in which all you can see are the egrets that roost on their backs. A proper buffalo stalk is incomplete unless you wriggle on your belly through thorn-bushes, shoving your gun ahead of you, or stagger crazily through marsh in water up to your rear end, sloshing and slipping and falling full length into the muck. Or scrambling up the sides of mountains, or squeezing through forests so thick that you part the trees ahead with your gun barrel.

There is no danger to the stalk itself. Not really. Of course, an old cow with a new calf may charge you and kill you. Or the buffs that can't see you or smell you, if you come upwind in high cover or thick bush, might accidentally stampede and mash you into the muck, only because they don't know you're there. Two or three hundred animals averaging 1,800 pounds apiece make a tidy stampede when they are running rump to rump and withers to withers. I was in one stampede that stopped short only because the grass thinned out, and in another that thoughtfully swerved a few feet and passed close aboard us. If the stampede doesn't swerve and doesn't stop, there is always an out. I asked Mr. Selby what the out was.

"Well," he replied, "the best thing to do is to shoot the nearest buffalo to you, and hope you kill it dead so that you can scramble up on top of it. The shots may split the stampede, and once they see you perched atop the dead buffalo they will sheer off and run around you."

⊹⊱⊰⊹

I MUST CONFESS I was thoroughly spooked on buffalo before I ever got to shoot one. I had heard a sufficiency of tall tales about the durability and viciousness of the beasts—tall tales, but all quite true. I had been indoctrinated in the buffalo hunter's fatalistic creed: Once you've wounded him, you must go after him. Once you're in the bush with him, he will wait and charge you. Once he's made his move, you cannot run, or hide, or climb a tree fast enough to get way from a red-eyed rampaging monster with death in his heart and on his mind. You must stand and shoot it out with Mbogo, and unless you get him through the nose and into the brain, or in the eye and into the brain, or break his neck and smash his shoulder and rupture his heart as he comes, Mbogo will get you. Most charging buffaloes are shot at a range of from fifteen to three feet, and generally through the eye.

Also, we had stalked up to a lot of Mbogo before I ever found one good enough to shoot. We had broken in by stalking a herd that was feeding back into the forest in a marsh. Another herd, which had already fed into the bush and which we had not seen, had busted loose with an awful series of snorts and grunts and had passed within a few feet, making noises like a runaway regiment of heavy tanks. This spooked the herd we had in mind, and they took off in another direction, almost running us down. A mud-scabby buffalo at a few feet is a horrifying thing to see, I can assure you.

The next buff we stalked were a couple of old and wary loners, and we were practically riding them before we were able to discern that their horns were worn down and splintered from age and use and were worthless as trophies. This was the first time I stood up at a range of twenty-five yards and said "Shoo!" in a quavery voice. I didn't like the way either old boy looked at me before they shooed.

The next we stalked showed nothing worth shooting, and the next we stalked turned out to be two half-grown rhino in high grass. I was getting to the point where I hated to hear one of the gun-bearers say, "Mbogo, Bwana," and point a knobby, lean finger at some flat black beetles on a mountainside nine miles away. I knew that Selby would say, "We'd best go and take a look-see," which meant three solid hours of fearful ducking behind bushes, crawling, cursing, sweating, stumbling, falling, getting up and staggering on to something I didn't want to play with in the first place. Or in the second place, or any place.

But one day we got a clear look at a couple of bulls—one big, heavily horned, prime old stud and a smaller askari, feeding on the lip of a thick thorn forest. They were feeding in the clear for a change, and they were nicely surrounded by high cane and a few scrub trees, which meant that we could make a fair crouching stalk by walking like question marks and dodging behind the odd bush. The going was miserable underfoot, with our legs sinking to the knees in ooze and our feet catching and tripping on the intertwined grasses, but the buff were only a few thousand yards away and the wind was right; so we kept plugging ahead.

"Let's go and collect him," said Mr Selby, the mad gleam of the fanatic buff hunter coming into his mild brown eyes. "He looks like a nice one."

Off we zigged and zagged and blundered. My breath, from overexertion and sheer fright, was a sharp pain in my chest, and I was wheezing like an overextended pipe-organ when we finally reached the rim of the high grass. We ducked low and snaked over behind the last bush between us and Mbogo. I panted. My belly was tied in small, tight knots, and a family of rats seemed to inhabit my clothes. I couldn't see either buffalo, but I heard a gusty snort and a rustle.

Selby turned his head and whispered: "We're too far, but the askari is suspicious. He's trying to lead the old boy away. You'd best get up and wallop him, because we aren't going to get any closer. Take him in the chest."

I lurched up and looked at Mbogo, and Mbogo looked at me. He was 50 to 60 yards off, his head low, his eyes staring right down

"I never saw such malevolence in the eyes of any animal or human being, before or since. So I shot him."

my soul. He looked at me as if he hated my guts. He looked as if I had despoiled his fianceé, murdered his mother, and burned down his house. He looked at me as if I owed him money. I never saw such malevolence in the eyes of any animal or human being, before or since. So I shot him.

I was using a big double, a Westley-Richards .470. The gun went off. The buffalo went down. So did I.

I had managed to loose off both barrels of this elephant gun, and the resulting concussion was roughly comparable to shooting a three-inch anti-aircraft gun off your shoulder. I was knocked as silly as a man can be knocked and still be semiconscious. I got up and stood there stupidly, with an empty gun in my hands, shaking my head. Somewhere away in Uganda I heard a gun go off, and Mr. Selby's clear Oxonion tones came faintly.

"I do hope you don't mind," said he. "You knocked him over, but he got up again and took off for the bush. I thought I'd best break his back, although I'm certain you got his heart. It's just that it's dreadfully thick in there, and we'd no way of examining the wound to see whether you'd killed him. He's down, over there at the edge of the wood."

Mbogo was down, all right, his ugly head stretched out and twisting. Blood seeped from his nostrils, and from his throat came the most awful moaning, like the bellowing you hear in the knacker's room of the stockyards. He was lying sideways, a huge, mountainous hulk of muddy, tick-crawling, scabby-hided monster. He was down, dying, bellowing, and there was a small hole just abaft his forequarters, about three inches from the top of his back—Mr. Selby's spine shot.

"You got him through the heart, all right," said Mr. Selby cheerfully. "Spine shot don't kill 'em, and they don't bellow unless they're dying. Load that cannon and pop him behind the boss in the back of his head. Knew a dead buffalo once that got up and killed the hunter."

I sighted on his neck and fired, and the

great head dropped into the mud. I looked at him and shuddered. If anything, he looked meaner and bigger and tougher dead than alive.

"Not too bad a buff," Selby said. "Go forty-three, forty-four. Not apt to see a bigger one unless we're very lucky. Buff been picked over too much. See now 'twasn't any use my shooting him. He'd have been dead twenty yards inside the bush, but we didn't know that, did we? I'll bet he's a mess inside. Kidogo! Adam! Taka head-skin!" he shouted to the gun-bearers and sat down on the buffalo to light a cigarette. I was still shaking.

The boys made the correct cuts to strip off the cape and the head-skin, sliced through the vast neck and took a panga to the neck vertebrae, and dragged Mbogo's scalp to one side. Three of them, husky Africans, could barely lift it. Then with knife and panga they performed an autopsy.

As I said, I was shooting a double-barreled Express rifle that fires a bullet as big as a banana. It is a 500-grain bullet powered by 75 grains of cordite. It has a striking force of 5,000 foot-pounds of energy. It had taken Mbogo in the chest. Its impact knocked him flat—2,500 pounds of muscle. It had cut his windpipe. It severed his jugular. It smashed the top of his heart, and completely destroyed the main arteries. It had continued on to wreck the lungs. There were no lungs—only a gallon or so of blackened blood. Yet Mbogo had not known he was dead. He had gotten up and had romped off as blithely as if I had fired an air-gun at his hawser-network of muscles, at his inch-thick hide that the natives use to make shields. What had stopped him was not the fatal shot at all but Harry's backbreaker.

"Fantastic beast," Selby murmured. "Stone-dead and didn't know it."

We stalked innumerable buffalo after that. I did not really snap out of the buffalo-fog until we got back in Nairobi, to find that a friend, a professional hunter, had been badly gored twice and almost killed by a "dead" buffalo that soaked up a dozen slugs and then got up to catch another handful and still boil on to make a messy hash out of poor old Tony.

I am going back to Africa soon. I do not intend to shoot much. Certainly I will never kill another lion, nor do I intend to duplicate most of the trophies I acquired on the last one. But I will hunt Mbogo. In fear and trembling I will hunt Mbogo every time I see him, and I won't shoot him unless he is a mile bigger than the ones I've got. I will hate myself while I crawl and shake and tremble and sweat, but I will hunt him. Once you've got the buffalo fever, the rest of the stuff seems mighty small and awful tame. This is why the wife of my bosom considers her spouse to be a complete and utter damned fool, and she may very well be right.

—January, 1954